IMAGES
of America

COLUMBIA

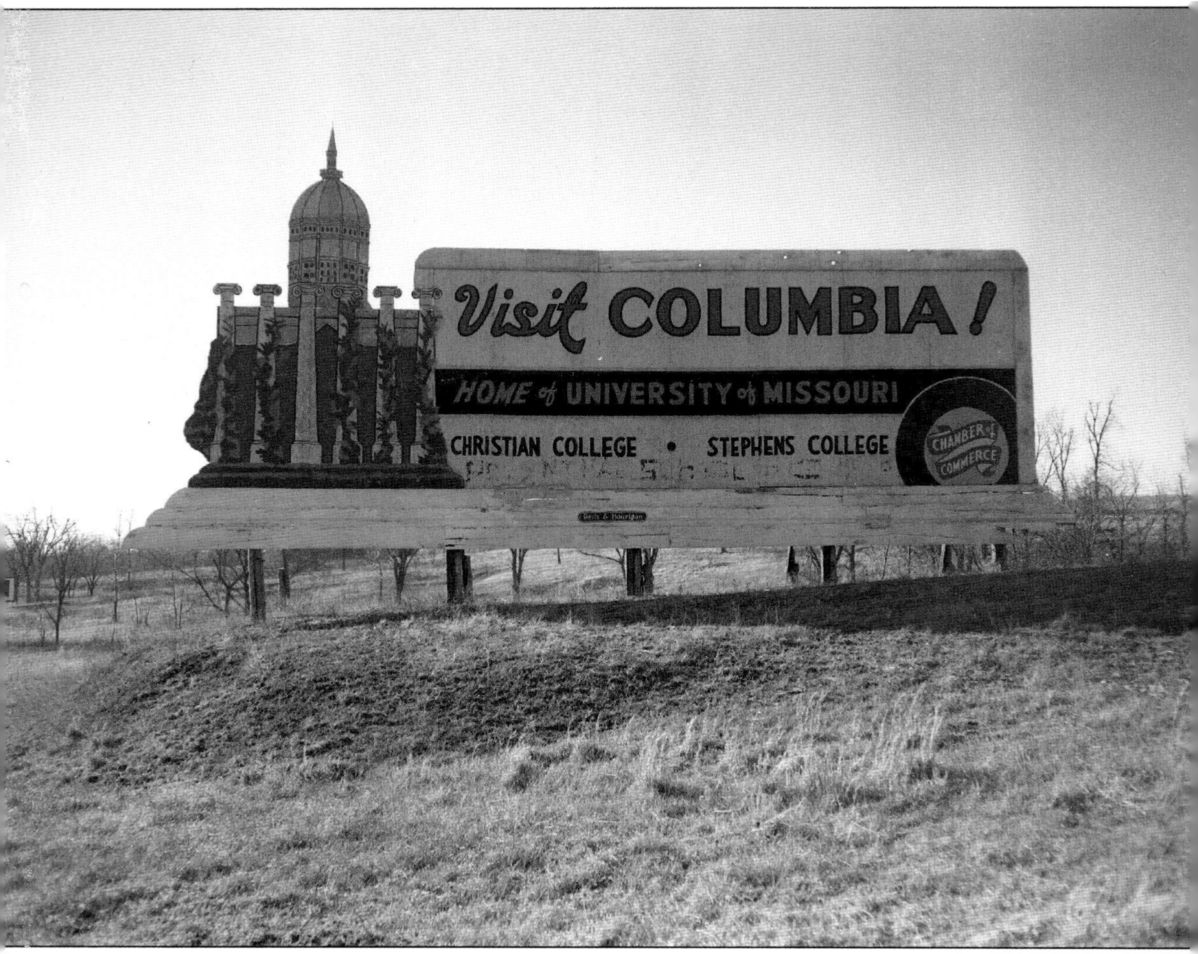

Columbia is home to three historic education institutions: The University of Missouri, first land grant university west of the Mississippi River; Stephens College; and Columbia College, formerly Christian College, the first women's college west of the Mississippi chartered by a state legislature. The Columbia Chamber of Commerce promoted the city's reputation for educational excellence on this early highway billboard, which features the University of Missouri's six Ionic columns. (The State Historical Society of Missouri.)

On the Cover: Generations of students at Christian College and Stephens College rode horses when not attending classes or studying. Posing here in 1929 are nine members of Christian College's Carolyn Drew riding club. They wear matching jackets, trousers, neckties, and hats—no dresses and side saddles for these modern girls. (The State Historical Society of Missouri.)

IMAGES
of America

COLUMBIA

Valerie Battle Kienzle
with The State Historical Society of Missouri

ARCADIA
PUBLISHING

ISBN 978-1-4671-1300-7

Published by Arcadia Publishing
Charleston, South Carolina

Printed in the United States of America

Library of Congress Control Number: 2014944521

For all general information, please contact Arcadia Publishing:
Telephone 843-853-2070
Fax 843-853-0044
E-mail sales@arcadiapublishing.com
For customer service and orders:
Toll-Free 1-888-313-2665

Visit us on the Internet at www.arcadiapublishing.com

*Dedicated to those who called Columbia home—
whether for a few semesters or a lifetime. They helped
it earn the nickname College Town, USA.*

Contents

ACKNOWLEDGMENTS

The author wishes to thank The State Historical Society of Missouri, particularly executive director Gary R. Kremer and manuscript specialist, photographs, Anne E. Cox. I am grateful to the countless people who through the years have chronicled and preserved Missouri's history in publications and journals. The gifts they left for future generations enable us to see the state's changes, growth, and progress. And I am especially grateful to the amateur photographers and visual historians whose images of daily life in and around Columbia allow us to take a peek at the past and to reflect on a way of life that no longer exists.

The State Historical Society of Missouri is the source and repository for all images included in this book.

Introduction

Columbia is located in the center of Missouri, connected to St. Louis on the east and Kansas City on the west by a major highway artery, Interstate 70. With a population of less than 120,000, it has the amenities and cultural assets of a large city, yet maintains a small-town feel.

Columbia is home to three historic education institutions: The University of Missouri, the first land grant university west of the Mississippi River; Stephens College; and Columbia College, the first women's college west of the Mississippi chartered by a state legislature. The city's reputation for educational excellence has earned it two nicknames: "College Town, USA" and "The Athens of Missouri." But Columbia is not tied only to education. The city's story begins with the great westward migration of the early 1800s.

Thomas Jefferson was president when the 1803 Louisiana Purchase doubled the size of the United States. In 1804, he ordered William Clark and Meriwether Lewis to travel the Missouri River to find a water connection to the Pacific Ocean. Their two-year expedition provided valuable information in planning and developing the country's western expansion. Soon, pioneers were moving west in an effort to escape crowded East Coast settlements.

Frontiersman Daniel Boone and his family were among those who moved west. They left Kentucky in the 1790s and settled south of St. Charles, Missouri. St. Charles was the first permanent settlement on the Missouri River and, later, the first state capital. Boone's son Daniel M. Boone discovered a mineral deposit area, or salt lick, on property west of their homes. The consumption of the minerals found there was important to the growth and development of a variety of animals. Daniel M. and his brother Nathan worked at the salt lick. The path they created to reach the lick became a popular travel route, and people began referring to the path leading across Missouri as Boone's Lick Trace (later, Trail).

President Jefferson believed the construction of a national road was important to unify the vast land that was now part of the United States. In 1806, Congress and the president authorized the construction of such a road. Westward migration increased after the War of 1812, with many travelers using the National Road. St. Charles was a supply stop for overland travelers headed west. Hundreds of wagons and carts passed through St. Charles each month. The path the travelers followed west from St. Charles and across Missouri included part of Boone's Lick Trail.

Boone's Lick Trail passed through Central Missouri, just north of what today is Columbia. It continued west toward what became Independence and Kansas City. There, it connected to other well-traveled paths that, in the 1820s, became known as the Santa Fe and Oregon Trails. These trails were part of the National Road or Old Trails Route.

Enterprising businessmen, seeing westward migration as an opportunity for financial gain, formed land-speculation firms. The Smithton Land Company had 35 shareholders. In 1818, it bought 2,720 acres of land in Central Missouri with the idea of establishing a town. A reliable water source was necessary, so the settlers began building log cabins for the town of Smithton just west of the Flat Branch in what became Boone County.

Unfortunately, the location did not have an adequate water supply. Several unsuccessful attempts were made to dig wells. Finally, tired of hauling water, the settlers decided to abandon the site and relocate a short distance east along the Flat Branch and near other tributaries. The settlers, most from the South, began clearing land. Timber and stones were plentiful, and home construction began. Some of Smithton's existing homes and buildings were taken down and reassembled at the new site.

Before he died in St. Charles County in September 1820, Daniel Boone traveled as far west as Independence, Missouri, and later Fort Leavenworth, Kansas. He was greatly admired in Central Missouri. Within two months of his death, the territorial legislature enacted, and the governor approved, dividing what was at that time Howard County to create Boone County.

The new town of Columbia was platted in 1821. The Smithton Land Company donated parcels of land to the town, including a public square, where the courthouse still stands, and a market square. In addition, 10 acres were set aside with the idea of someday establishing a state university. It was decided to make the main east-west thoroughfare, today's Broadway, 100 feet wide.

Since its beginning, the settlement area has remained the center of Columbia's commercial and civic life. The flow of settlers migrating west led to growth as stores and businesses were established. Realizing the potential to make even more money, Columbia's founding fathers in 1822 rerouted the Boone's Lick Trail five miles south so that it came through Columbia along Broadway.

Columbia became the county seat on April 7, 1821, and the town was incorporated on November 7, 1826. By 1828, a courthouse had been built.

During the 1830s, Columbia had a dozen general merchandise stores. Most storekeepers accepted items in trade. In 1834, the editor of the *Missouri Intelligencer* said: "Never within our recollection, has there been such an influx of emigrants as are now, and have for some weeks, been passing through this place to the more western part of the state. There appears to be an almost unbroken line of wagons, carts, carriages, cattle, etc."

Many Missourians thought the proposed state university should be located near the Missouri River in Jefferson City, the state's capital, or in other parts of the state, including Howard, Callaway, Saline, Cole, and Cooper Counties. The pledge of private land and money by approximately 900 Columbia and Boone County residents, including five widows, persuaded decision makers to select Columbia. Missouri State University, as it was called at the time, became the first public university west of the Mississippi River when it opened in 1839, and the first university in Louisiana Purchase territory. A direct route between Columbia's courthouse and the site of the university resulted in commercial growth in and around that area.

Initially, the state university was open only to men. And because Columbia did not have regular passenger railroad service, travel to attend school sometimes was a challenge. Many students traveled by steamboat to the Missouri River town of Rocheport. From there, they took a mostly daily commercial hack service over a toll road between Rocheport and Columbia.

Columbia was already home to a local school for girls when the university opened. In 1833, a Columbia father and 14 others who valued educational opportunities for their daughters united to form Columbia Female Academy. For the first session, 25 women enrolled. The academy closed in 1855. In 1856, Columbia Baptist Female College was founded. When James L. Stephens, a local farmer and entrepreneur, endowed the school in the 1860s, it became Stephens College.

Continued concern about their daughters' education led another group of influential Columbians to seek a legislative charter of a second girls' school. When the Missouri legislature chartered Christian Female College (today Columbia College) in January 1851, it became the first women's college west of the Mississippi River chartered by a state legislature. Both Columbia girls' schools were located near the public square, and continue to occupy those sites today.

The California Gold Rush impacted Columbia as even more travelers passed through town on the Boone's Lick Trail. On March 8, 1850, the *Columbia Missouri Statesman* listed the names of 353 local residents who had traveled to California in search of gold. The city's main thoroughfare was crowded with people and wagons headed west. So sure were the newspaper's editors that the publication could be mailed and received in the Sacramento or San Joaquin areas, they even suggested newspaper gift subscriptions to help those far away keep up with the news in Columbia.

Columbia had approximately 700 residents by 1843. Its early homes and buildings were made of locally hewn logs. Brick and frame buildings lined both sides of Broadway by the mid-1800s. An 1849 visitor described Columbia as "one of the neatest and handsomest little towns that I have seen in my life." By 1860, over 100 companies and professionals were located in the city, including banks, blacksmiths, mercantile operators, taverns, and newspapers. The population was more than 1,400.

The university was closed from spring until fall in 1862. Although no Civil War battles or skirmishes were fought in or near Columbia, residents most likely were affected by the war. The Columbia Tigers Company was organized to protect the city, university, and two colleges from guerilla attacks. The name was selected to reflect the fierce nature of its members and their ability to scare encroachers. The cupolas of the university's administration building and the courthouse were used as lookout posts. The ringing of the courthouse bell signaled approaching soldiers. Later, the Tigers name was adopted by the university's athletic teams.

In 1871, women were admitted to Missouri State University's academic programs. The city limits expanded as farmland around the center of town became residential property. By 1900, the population was 5,600. Within the next 10 years, the population doubled.

The extension of two railroad branches or spurs—one in 1867 with what became the Wabash Railroad, and the other in 1899 with the Missouri-Kansas-Texas (MKT) Railroad—simplified personal travel and freight shipping to and from Columbia. Before the spurs opened, freight was shipped on the Missouri River and then hauled overland on wooden-planked and rutted roads.

The 20th century brought new developments, including running water, electricity, automobiles, and telephone service. Several hundred businesses called Columbia home. The banking, insurance, and medical industries were well represented, as were lodging establishments and entertainment venues. Soon, a new courthouse was needed.

Some early-20th-century Columbians referred to themselves as "Pioneer Heroes of Higher Education." In 1907, Christian College promoted itself as a school "for the higher education of young ladies—affiliated with Missouri State University, Wellesley College and other Eastern schools."

The state university, now known as the University of Missouri, had expanded to include the Colleges of Arts and Science, Agriculture, Education, and Engineering, and the Schools of Medicine, Law, and Journalism. Intercollegiate athletic teams were organized and developed a loyal following of students, faculty, and alumni.

The years of the Great Depression were not as difficult in Columbia as they were in some areas. Officials made use of federal and local funds to construct municipal buildings, including a new city hall, a police and fire building, and a new post office. The city benefited from the buildings, and the projects provided jobs for area residents. In addition, the university and colleges provided a ready market for goods and services offered by local retailers and businesspeople.

By the 1940s, Columbia's population was approximately 20,000, greater than that of the state's capital, Jefferson City. The 1950s brought a secondary commercial area near State Highway 40, the predecessor to Interstate 70 that stretched across Missouri and connected St. Louis to Columbia and Kansas City. More rural farmland was replaced with residential developments. The university and the colleges continued to expand, and the downtown area remained the hub of business activity.

Forward-thinking residents and community leaders have worked through the years to ensure that educational, cultural, and recreational opportunities abound. In recent years, Columbia was named a top place in the United States to retire due to its varied amenities and available activities. *Forbes* magazine also named it one of the best small places for business and careers.

Today, Columbia residents, students, and visitors enjoy the conveniences of life in the 21st century while being surrounded by buildings of historical and educational significance. The university's 2012 athletic affiliation with the Southeastern Conference is bringing a new segment of visitors to Columbia and the Midwest. The faces of the thousands of individuals who have lived and worked here are forever changing, yet Columbia retains its small-town atmosphere. This book's images are a reminder of the city's growth and development from the early years.

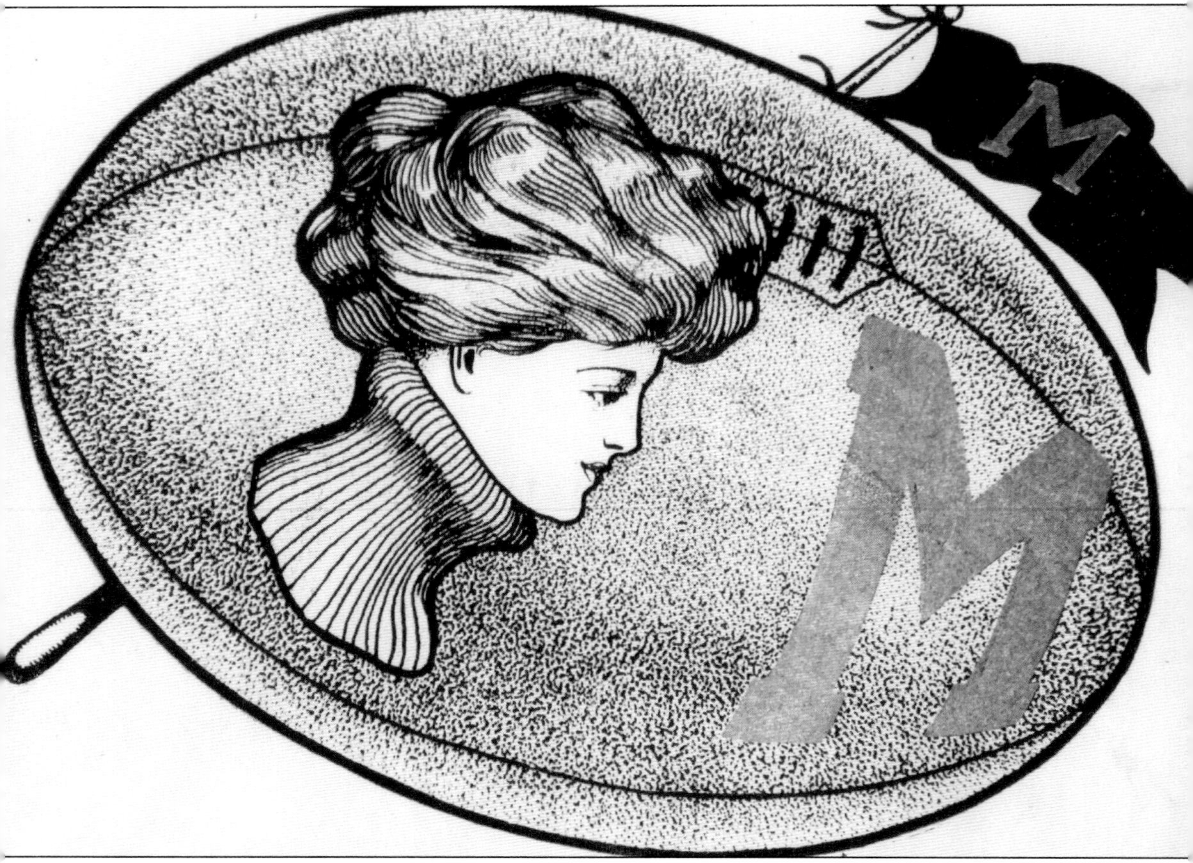

The University of Missouri and Kansas University had the oldest football rivalry west of the Mississippi River, dating to 1891. Their annual game was held in neutral territory (Kansas City) until NCAA rules changed, requiring that games be played on college fields. In 1911, university athletic director Chester Brewer invited alumni to "come home" for the game and festivities. After a spirit rally, 9,000 people watched the game. A new tradition—homecoming—was born.

One

From Frontier Town to Education Hub

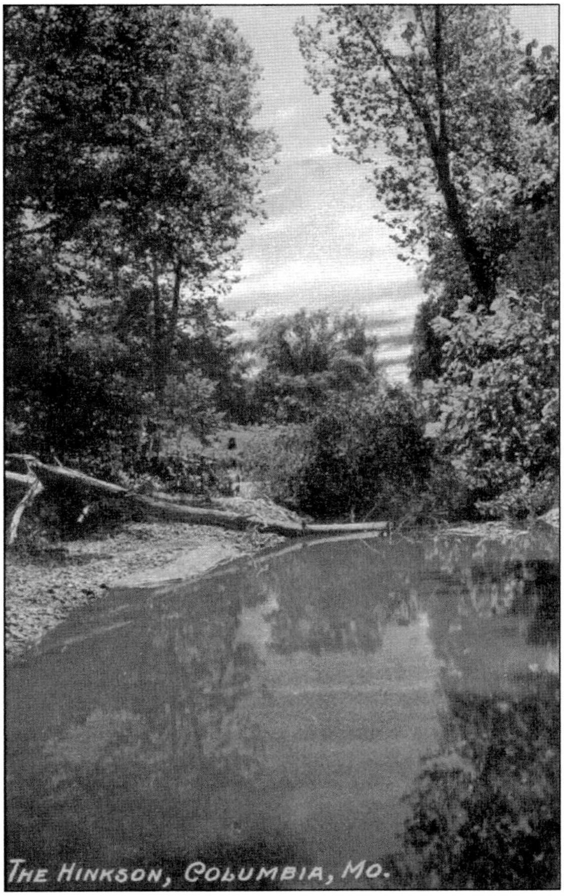

Most of the 35 members of the Smithton Land Company came from Kentucky and other Southern locales. They journeyed west across the Mississippi and Missouri Rivers into territory that was part of the Louisiana Purchase. Adequate water supplies were essential for the success of new settlements. They decided on land near two sources of water in what today is Columbia. The waterways were Flat Branch and Hinkson Creeks.

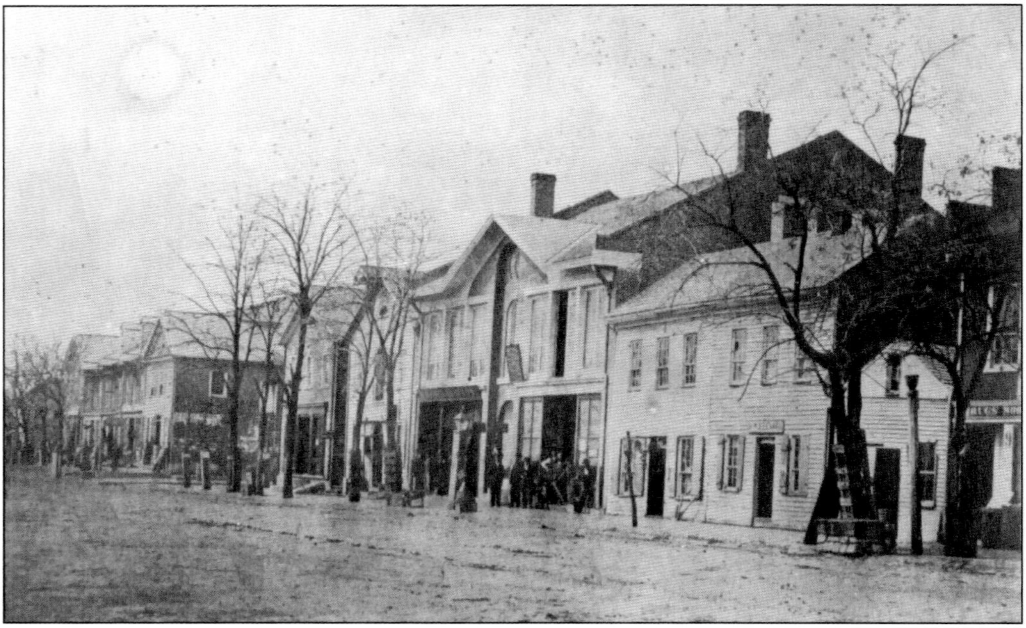

The original plat for Columbia included a wide thoroughfare through the center of town. This path became Broadway, shown here in 1863. The Civil War was in progress, but no battles were fought in Columbia. The occupants of these Broadway buildings suggest that Columbia was a progressive city. Several banks and stores, a tailor, a barbershop, a doctor's office, and a drugstore were situated along this northern section of the street.

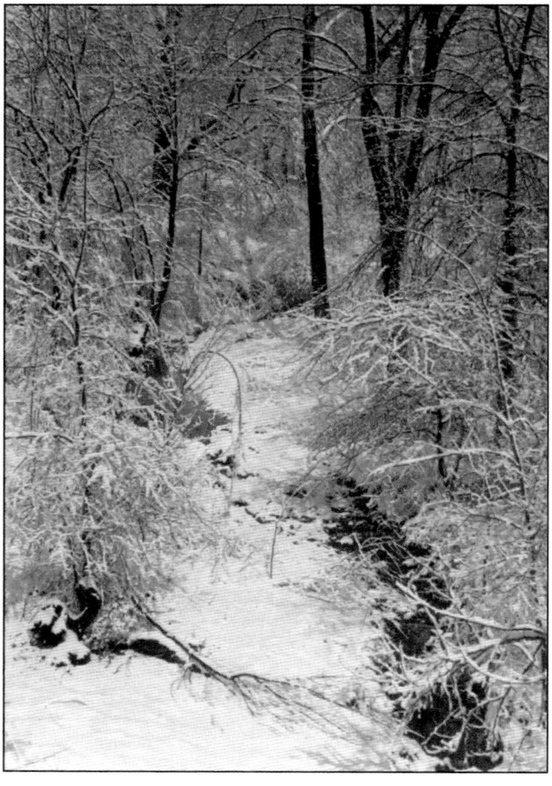

Early settlers in the area found a landscape that looked much like this. After an initial failed attempt at creating a settlement, they relocated to an area nearby where water from Flat Branch was more easily accessible. The wilderness was cleared, and cabins were built. The new town was platted near what today is the corner of Broadway and Fifth Street.

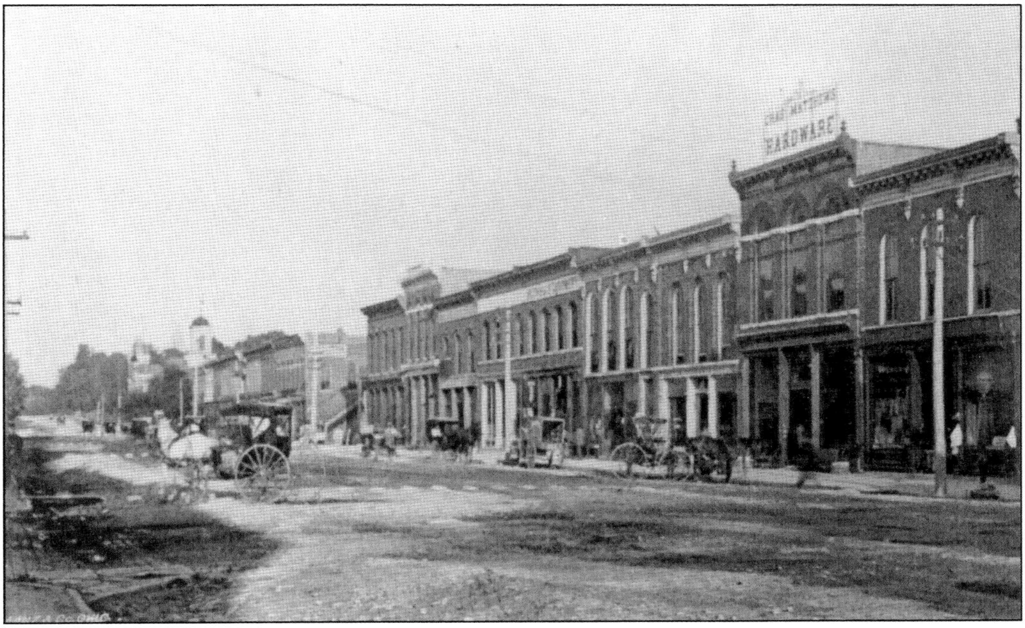

Broadway was still paved with dirt and macadamized rocks when this photograph was taken from Eighth Street looking east. Horses and buggies were the modes of transportation. Charles Matthews advertised his hardware store with a large sign. Many of these buildings feature cornices and ornamentation that were popular on commercial buildings throughout America. Such enhancements could be ordered and attached to existing buildings.

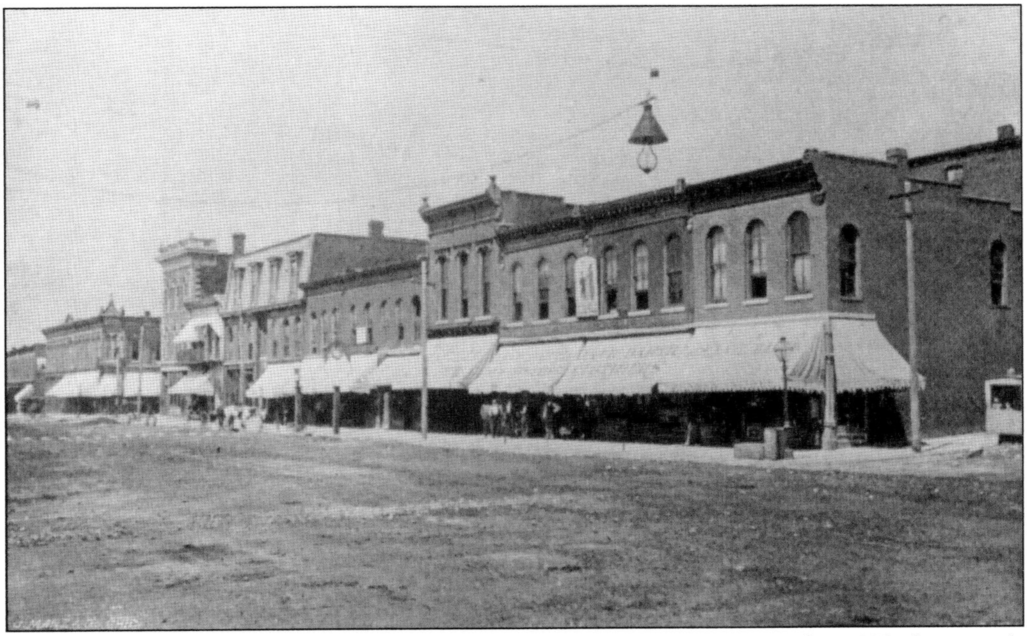

Canvas awnings were popular additions to Broadway buildings, as seen in this 1893 photograph looking west. They provided shoppers with protection from the elements and welcome shade during the humid summer months. Columbia was a progressive city. Overhead wires indicate that the downtown area had electricity. Many changes had taken place in the decades since the area was first settled.

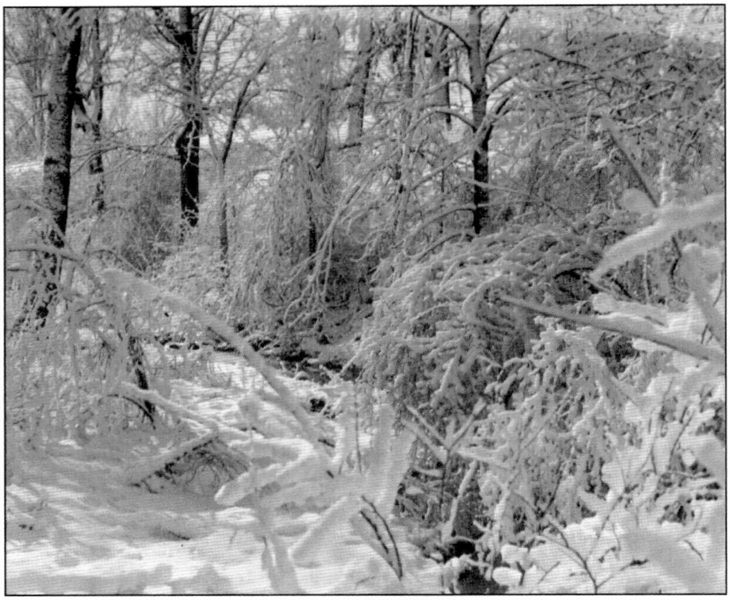

Early settlers found plenty of timber and plant life in mid-Missouri, including oak, pine, black walnut, pecan, and hickory. Native flowering trees included dogwood, red bud, and hawthorn. Edible berries included blackberries, gooseberries, and elderberries. The winter months often brought thick blankets of snow to the area. By 1900, Boone County contained approximately 3,500 farms.

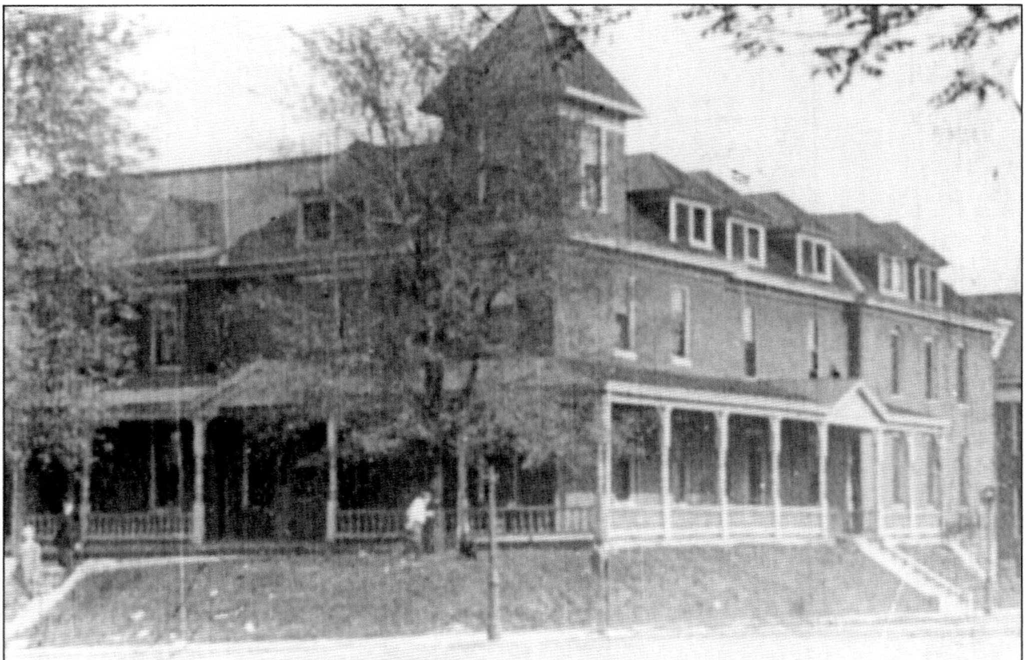

Parts of the Niedermeyer Apartments, at Tenth and Cherry Streets, date to 1837, making it Columbia's oldest building. Richard Gentry, seeking quality education for his five daughters, opened a female academy. The school remained until the 1850s, when Baptist College (later Stephens College) began. The building was sold, becoming a residence and then the Cottage Hotel. F.W. Niedermeyer operated it as the Gordon Hotel. It housed the university's Department of Domestic Science and finally became apartments in 1921.

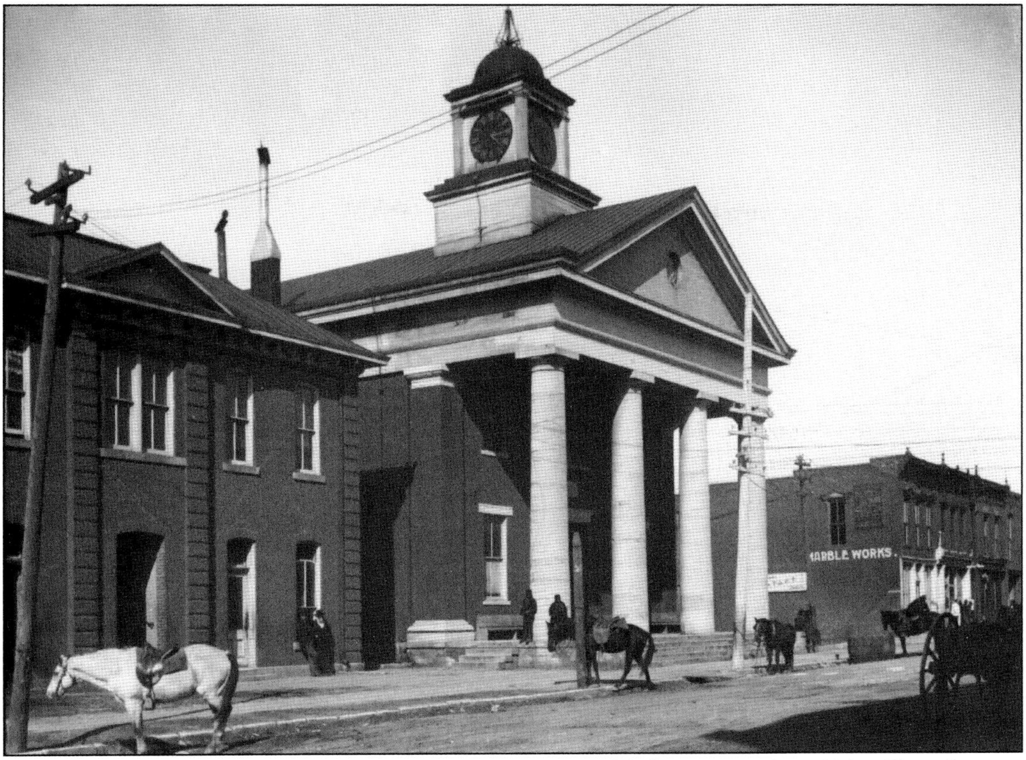

Boone County has had three courthouses since its establishment in the 1820s. Show here is the second courthouse, which was used from 1847 until 1909. Columbians disagreed about the removal of the columns from the university's quadrangle after Academic Hall burned down in 1892. They also disagreed about the removal of this building's columns.

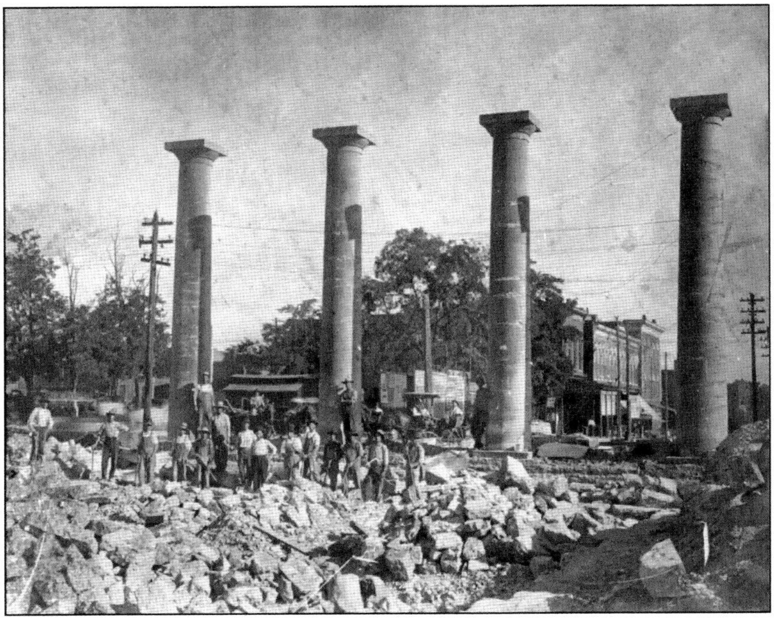

The decision was made to keep the courthouse columns and tear down the remainder of the courthouse. The wrecking crew and interested observers in buggies are shown here. The two sets of columns sit in perfect alignment. Lights were later added to the top of each of the four courthouse columns.

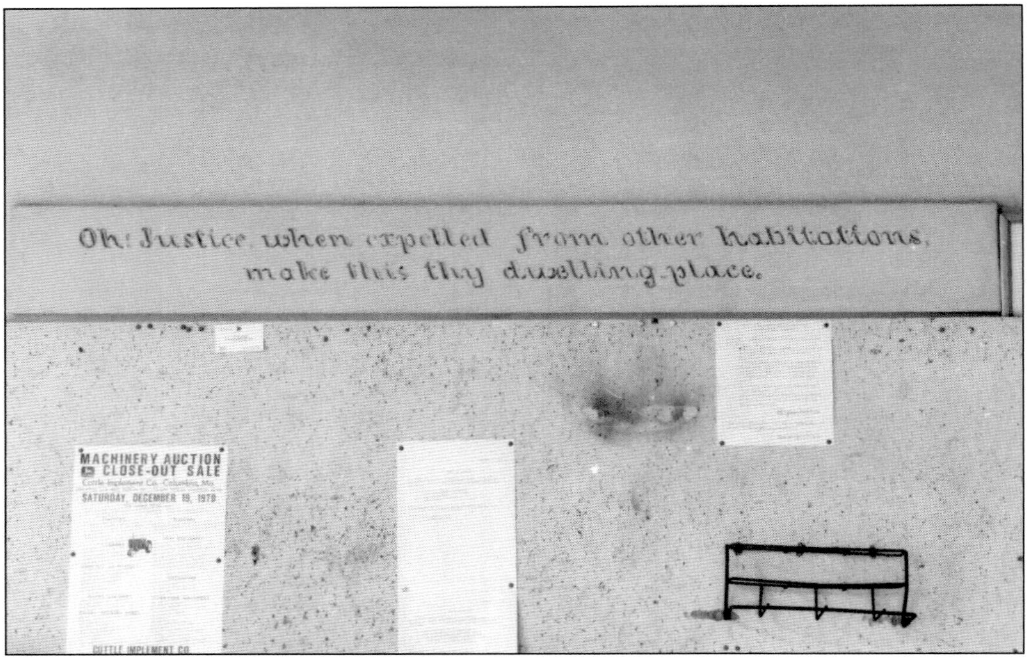

Also saved before the destruction of Columbia's 1847 courthouse was a rectangular section of engraved stone. It was salvaged and incorporated into the current courthouse. The inscription says, "Oh Justice, when expelled from other habitations, make this thy dwelling place."

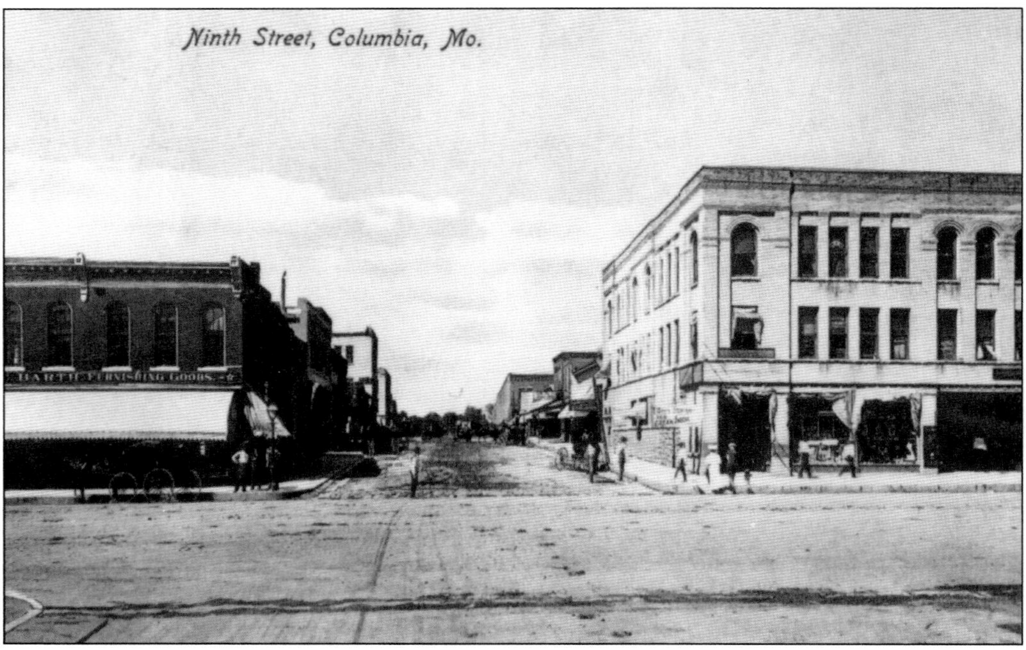

Joe L. Douglass was a popular Columbia photographer who specialized in portraits. One day in 1907, he stopped while walking along Broadway, aimed his camera north, and took this photograph. Barth Furnishing Goods Store can be seen on the left. Tilley's Pharmacy and a tailor are on the right. It was a busy day downtown with horses, buggies, and pedestrians.

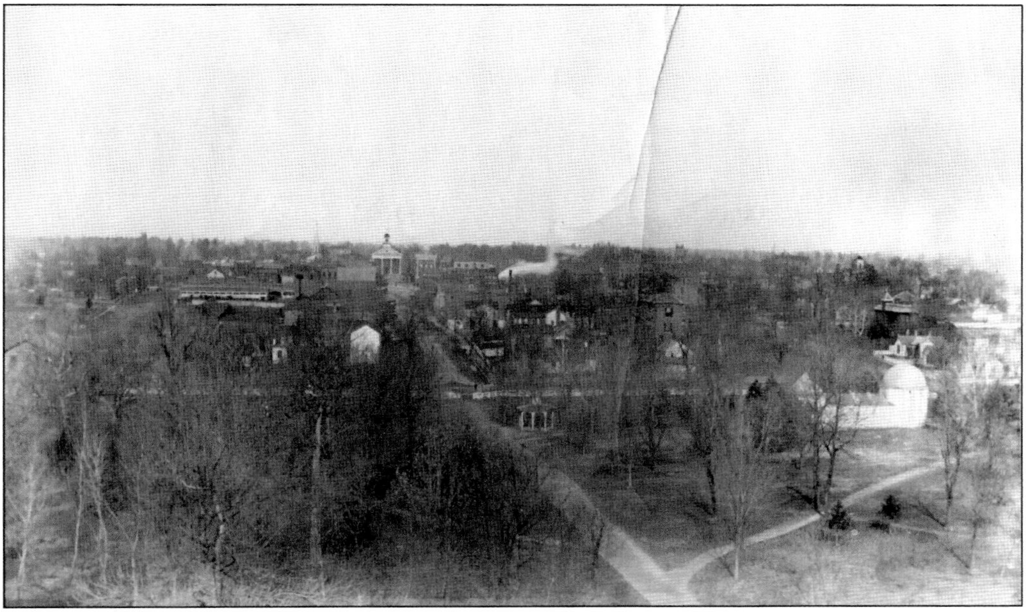

Columbia was an established city when this photograph was taken in 1885 from the university's Academic Hall. Its columns are symmetric with the columns of Boone County's second courthouse, seen in the distance. The gazebo near Chalybeate Spring and the university's Laws Observatory can be seen on the site now occupied by the buildings of the School of Journalism.

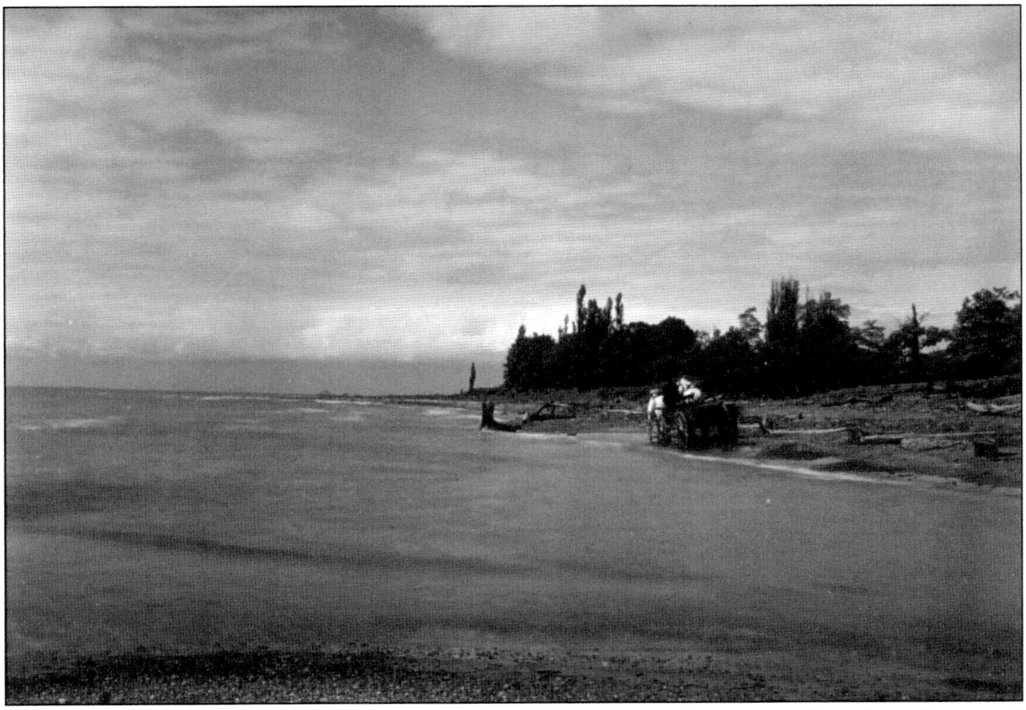

Columbia is not located on the Missouri River, but flooding sometimes affected residents and students. Until train service arrived in Columbia, freight and passengers often traveled on the river to Rocheport. Drivers with horses and hacks picked them up and made their way along the bumpy and rutted roads to Columbia. The addition of railroad spurs was an asset to the community.

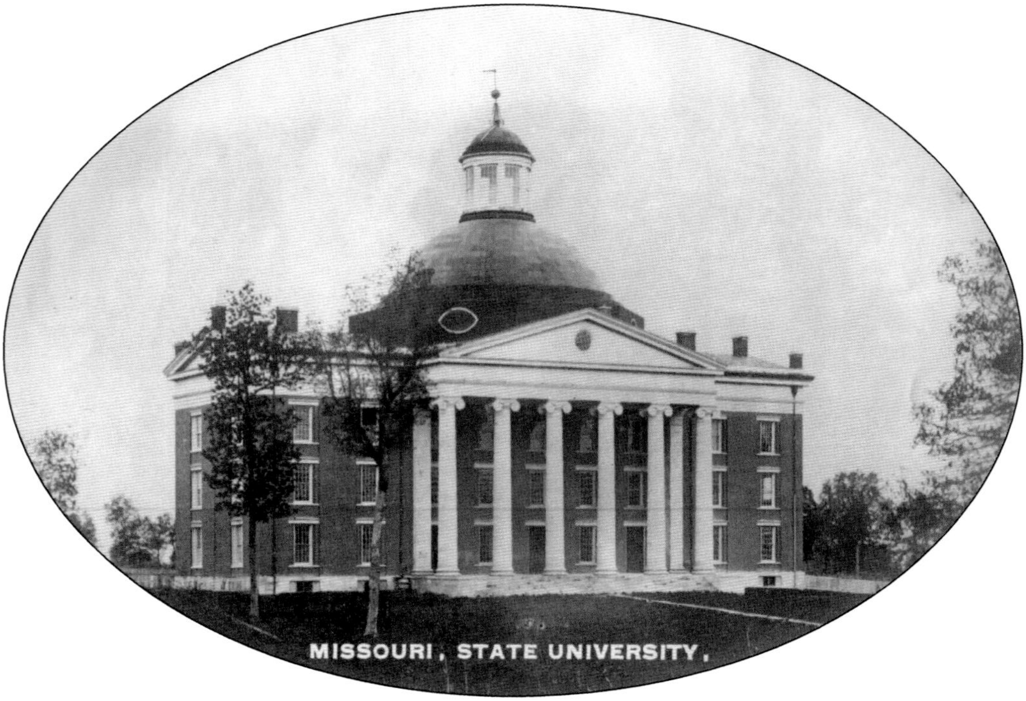

The university at Columbia was for years referred to as Missouri State University. Academic Hall, shown here prior to its destruction by fire in January 1892, was the university's main building. It housed administrative offices as well as classrooms. When it burned down, student records were destroyed. Thanks to quick-thinking administrators, classes previously held in Academic Hall were relocated. No classes were cancelled due to the fire.

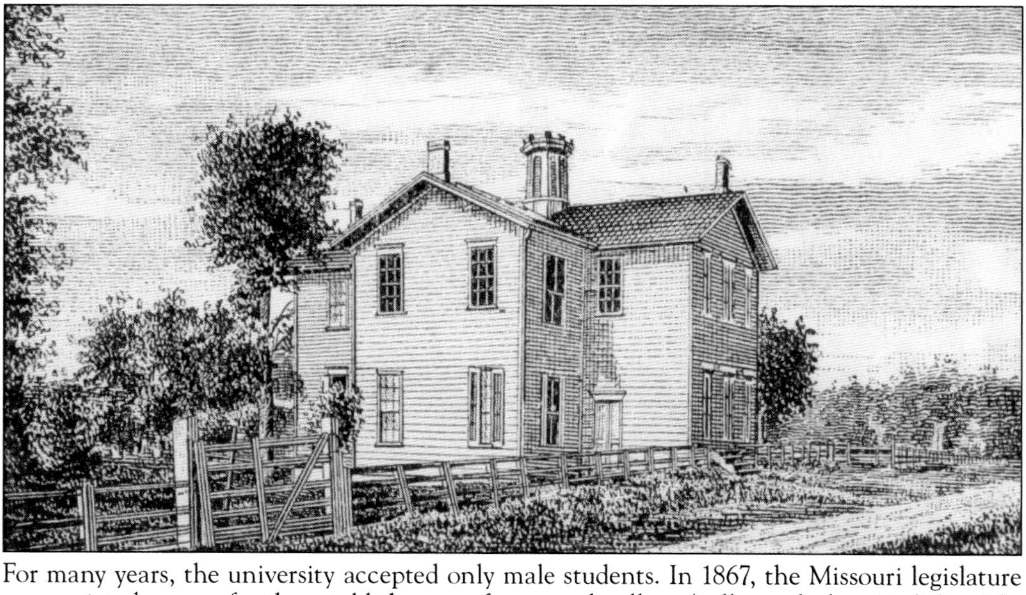

For many years, the university accepted only male students. In 1867, the Missouri legislature appropriated money for the establishment of a normal college (college of education) for girls. The first girls were admitted in 1868. Women were admitted to all university programs beginning in 1871. The English and art school was part of the program that became the College of Arts and Sciences.

Two

College Town, USA

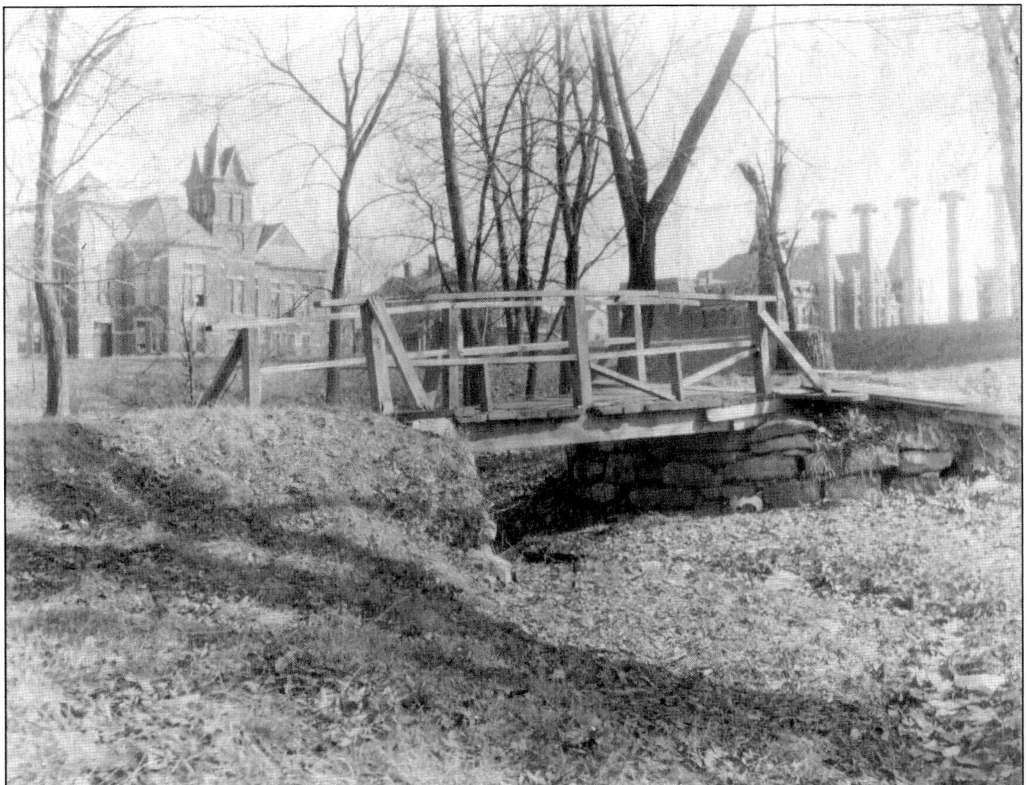

Chalybeate Spring, a natural spring, flowed through the University of Missouri's quadrangle of original buildings. A small bridge allowed passage across the spring to a wooded area near today's Neff Hall and the School of Journalism buildings. This early 1900s photograph looks southwest toward Pickard Hall (left) and the columns. Enrollment at that time included students from Russia, Poland, Japan, Germany, England, Egypt, and the Argentine Republic.

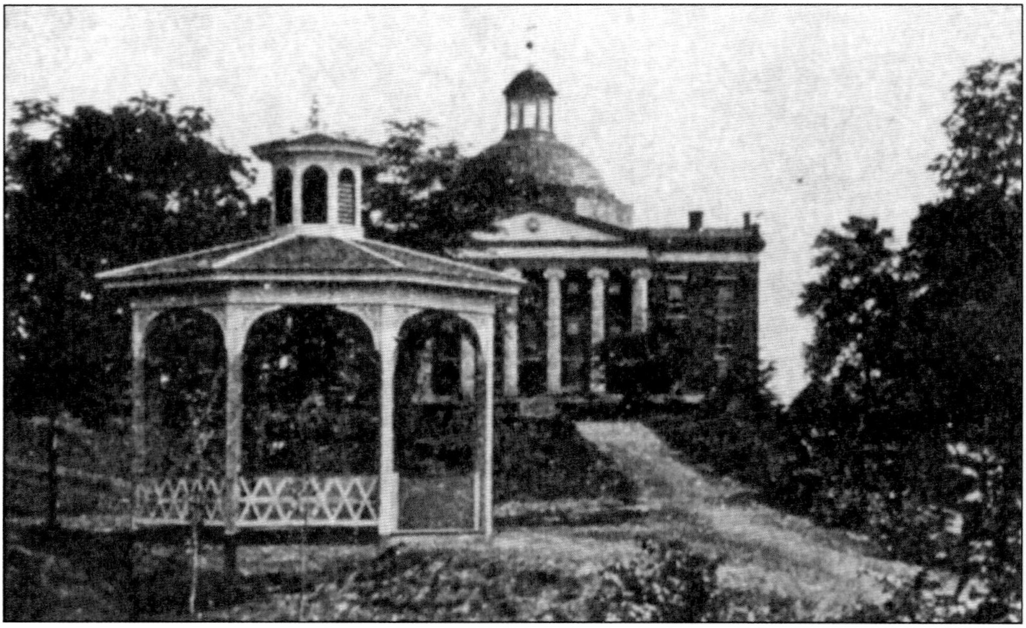

In the late 1800s, a gazebo was built in the wooded area near Chalybeate Spring on the university's quadrangle. It provided a pleasant view of the main building, Academic Hall. The fire that destroyed the building in 1892 left only the six Ionic columns. Some townspeople wanted them torn down. Since then, the columns have served as a symbol of the University of Missouri at Columbia.

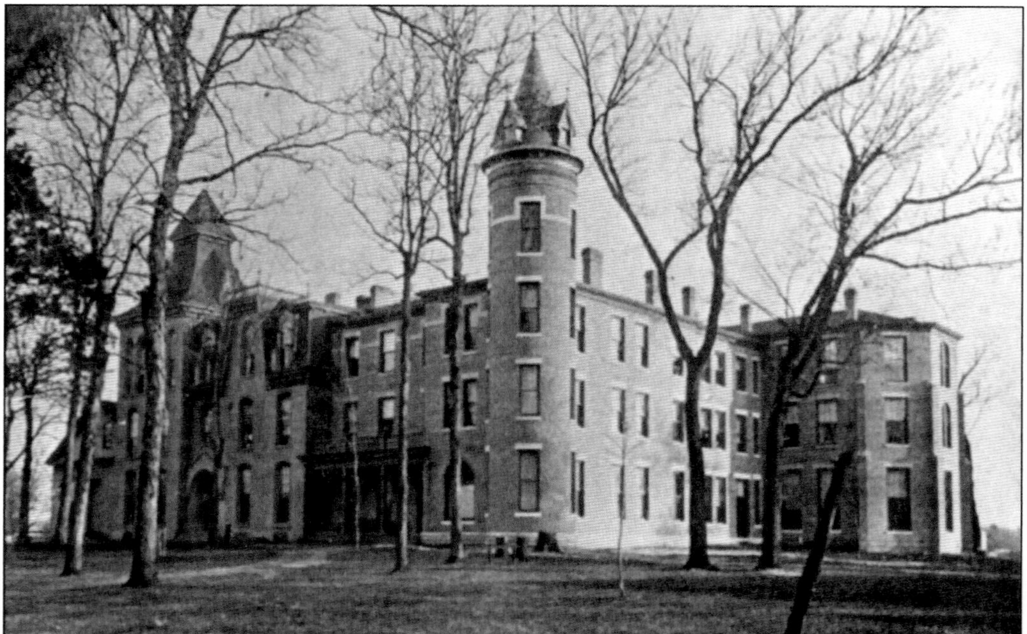

A Columbian's concern about his daughters' education led to the establishment of Columbia Female Academy. The school began in 1833 when Col. Richard Gentry gathered other citizens who also valued women's education. The first 25 students attended classes in a church. The academy closed in 1855. In 1856, Columbia Baptist Female College was founded. When entrepreneur James L. Stephens endowed the school in the 1860s, it became Stephens College.

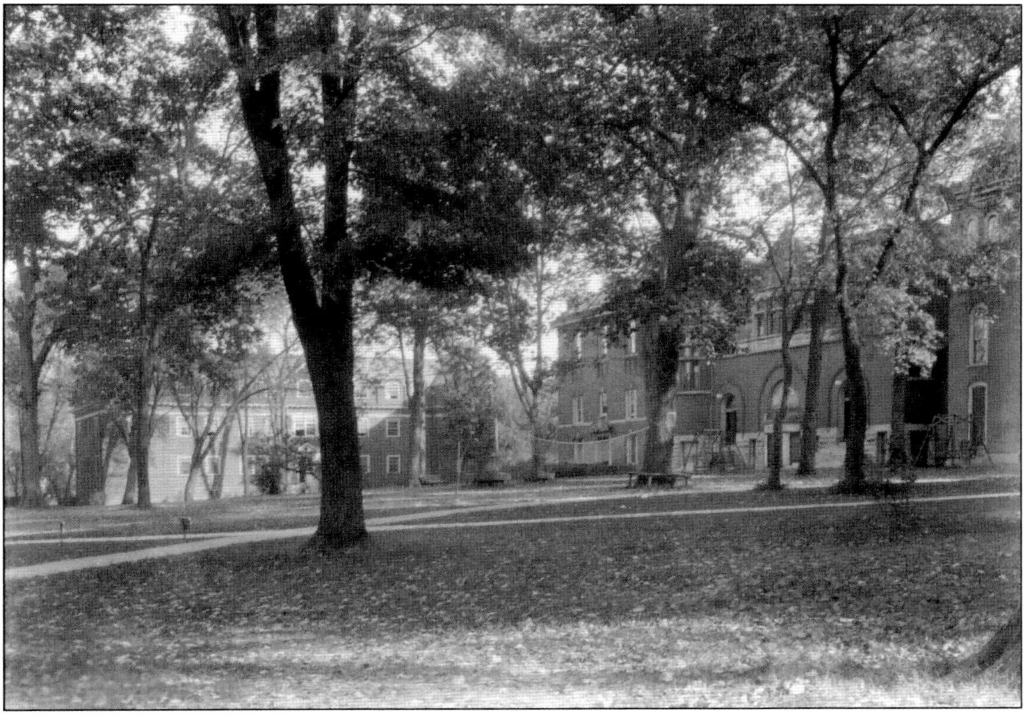

Stephens College's campus occupies 86 acres adjacent to downtown Columbia. In this 1927 photograph, Columbia Hall, Wood Hall, and Sappington Memorial Chapel stand among mature trees and lush surroundings. Swings, benches, and a badminton net invite students to linger outside after classes. Stephens is the second-oldest women's college in the United States. In 1875, the college offered a rigorous academic schedule plus electives including waxwork, vocal music, and embroidery.

Academic Hall was built in the early 1840s and dedicated in 1843. It was the center of university activities until it was destroyed by fire in January 1892. The remains were removed, and the limestone columns, measuring 40-plus feet high, were retained. Additional buildings were constructed around a central quadrangle theme. By 1895, a new Academic Hall had been built. It was renamed Jesse Hall in 1922.

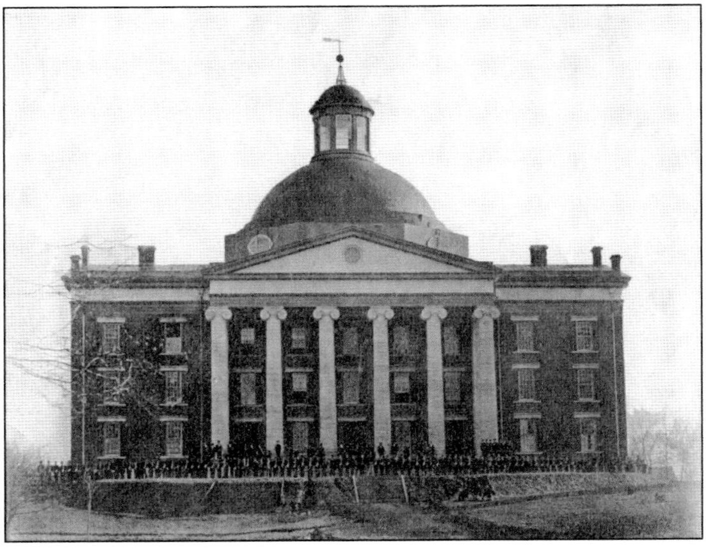

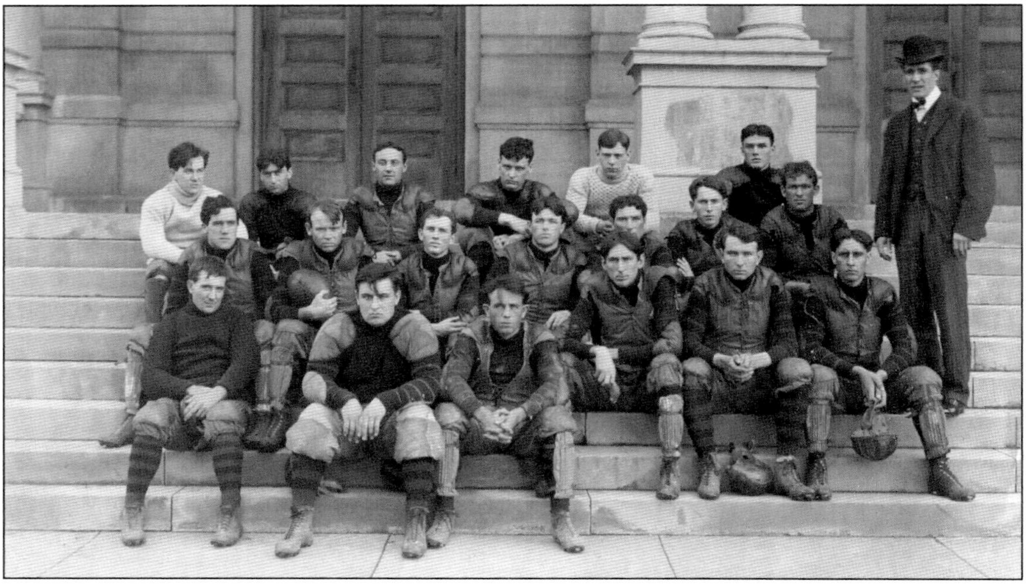

Much has changed since 1905, when 19 members of the University of Missouri's football team and one coach posed for this photograph outside the university's new Academic Hall. Helmets, shoes, and padding seem primitive compared to today's uniforms and equipment. Then, as now, football was serious business. There are no smiles on these players' faces. All-male "yell leaders" were introduced at games in 1909.

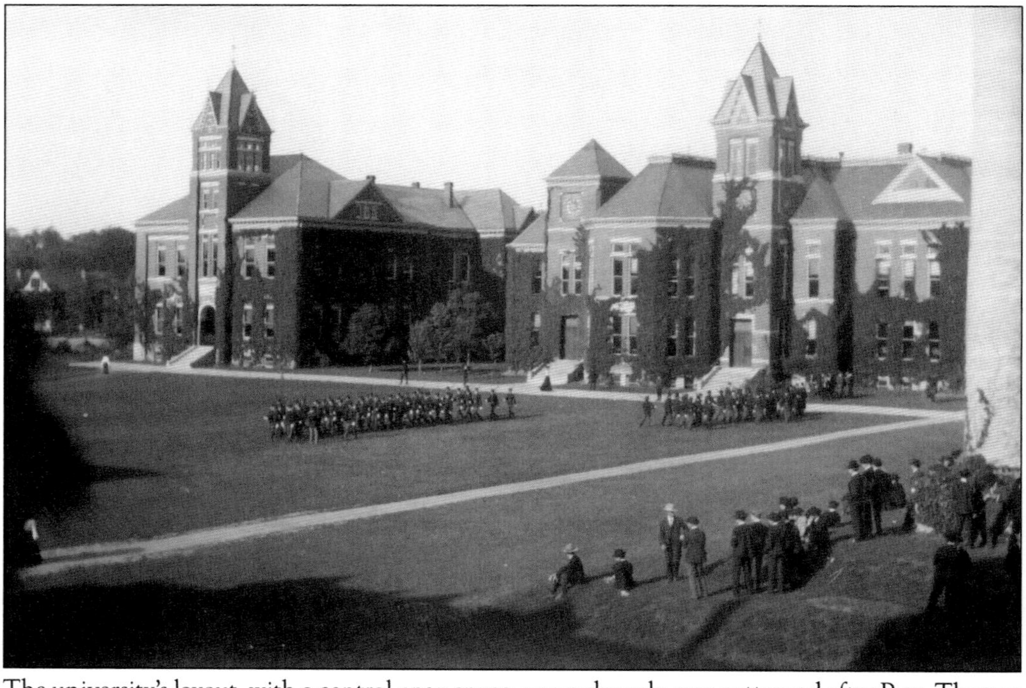

The university's layout, with a central open space, or quadrangle, was patterned after Pres. Thomas Jefferson's academical village design at the University of Virginia. Through the years, the quad has been the scene of pageants, graduations, parades, and public demonstrations. In this early 1900s photograph, uniformed Reserve Officers' Training Corps (ROTC) cadets march in formation as other students look on. Cannons once stood near old Academic Hall's columns.

Switzler Hall is located on the university's Francis Quadrangle. Built in 1871, it is the oldest existing classroom building on campus. During its history, it has been known as Scientific Hall and the Agricultural Building. In 1910, it provided classroom space for the newly formed School of Journalism. Today, it houses the communications department. The building's 1882 bell rang each hour that classes were in session until 1936.

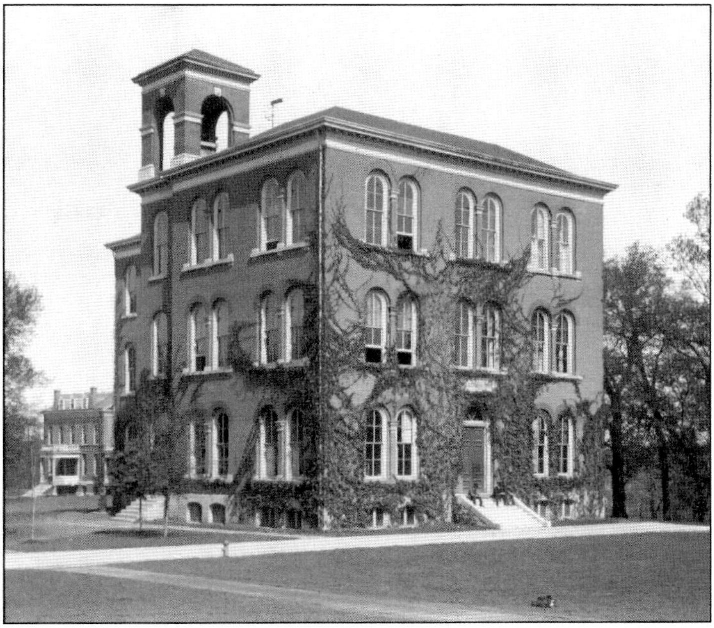

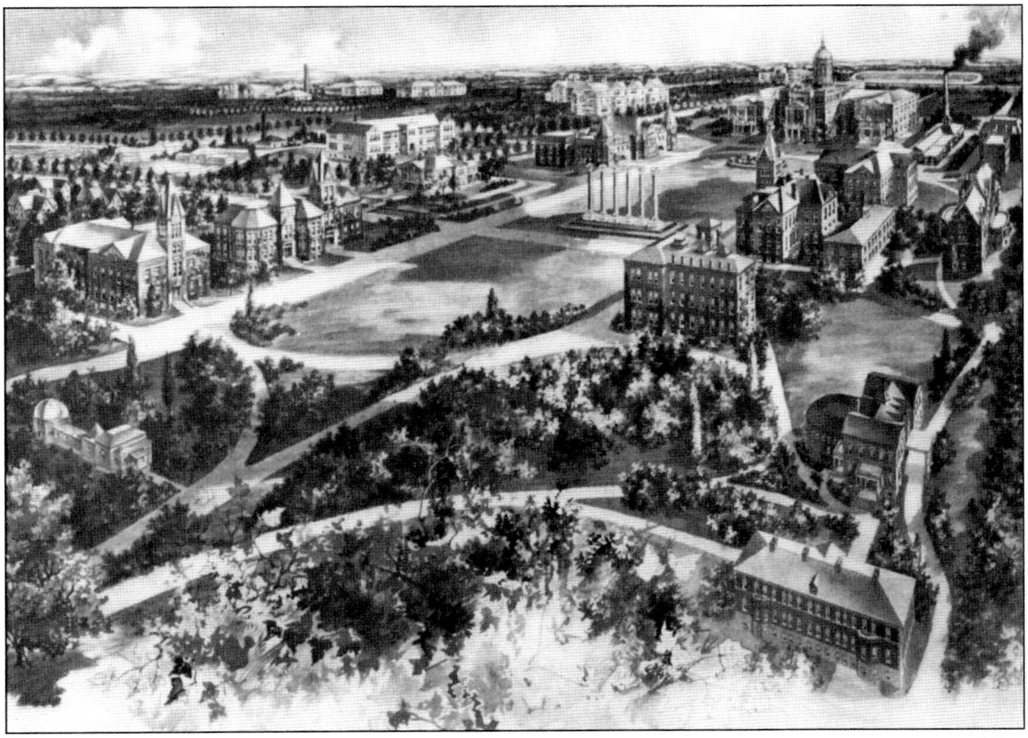

This 1906 view of the university's quadrangle shows a large and prosperous campus. Most of the buildings shown here remain today. The columns and Jesse Hall are easy to spot, but the land where Memorial Union and the white campus are located was undeveloped. In the days before Memorial Stadium was built, home football games were held at Rollins Field, visible near the top right.

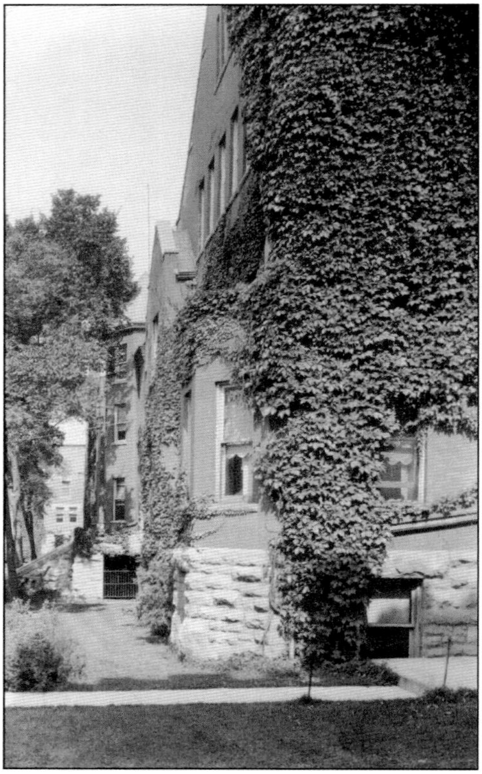

When the Missouri legislature granted a charter to Christian Female College in 1851, it became the first women's college west of the Mississippi River chartered by a state legislature. At that time, the University of Missouri did not admit female students. In 1970, the school became a four-year coeducational institution and its name changed to Columbia College.

Generations of students have put on boots and layers of clothing to trudge through snow to classes. A winter woodland scene is shown here in the early 1900s. Today, the multi-building School of Journalism complex is located here. A section of the area remains undeveloped and is known as Peace Park. The university's seal, seen throughout campus, contains the Latin phrase *salus populi*, "the welfare of the people."

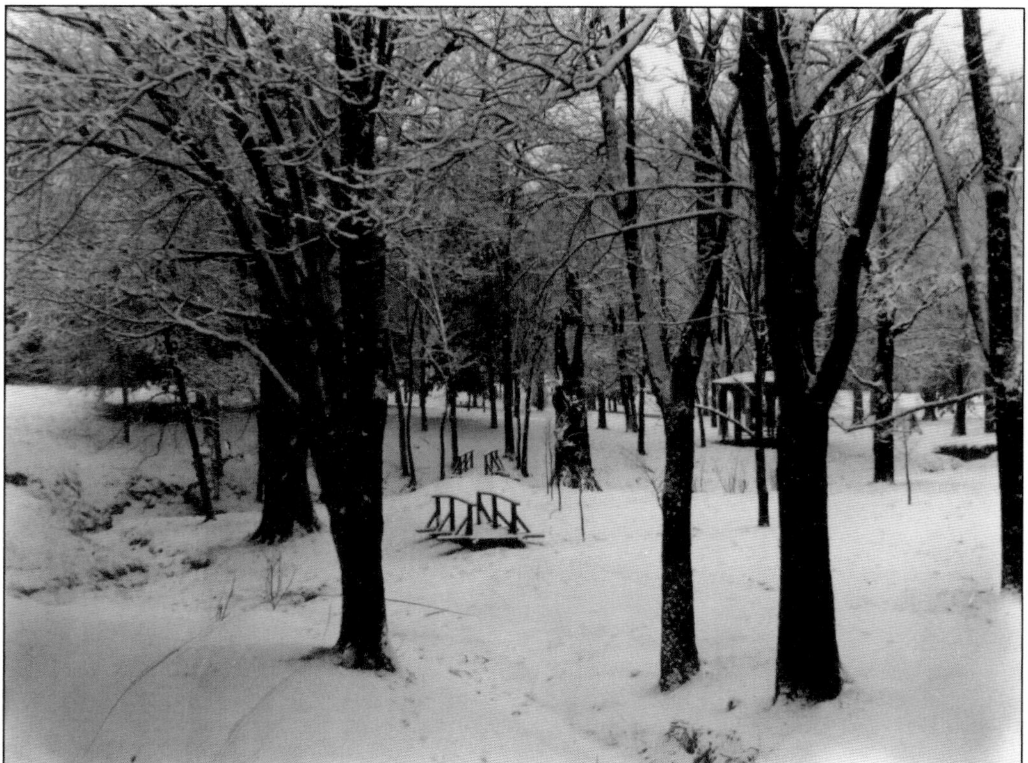

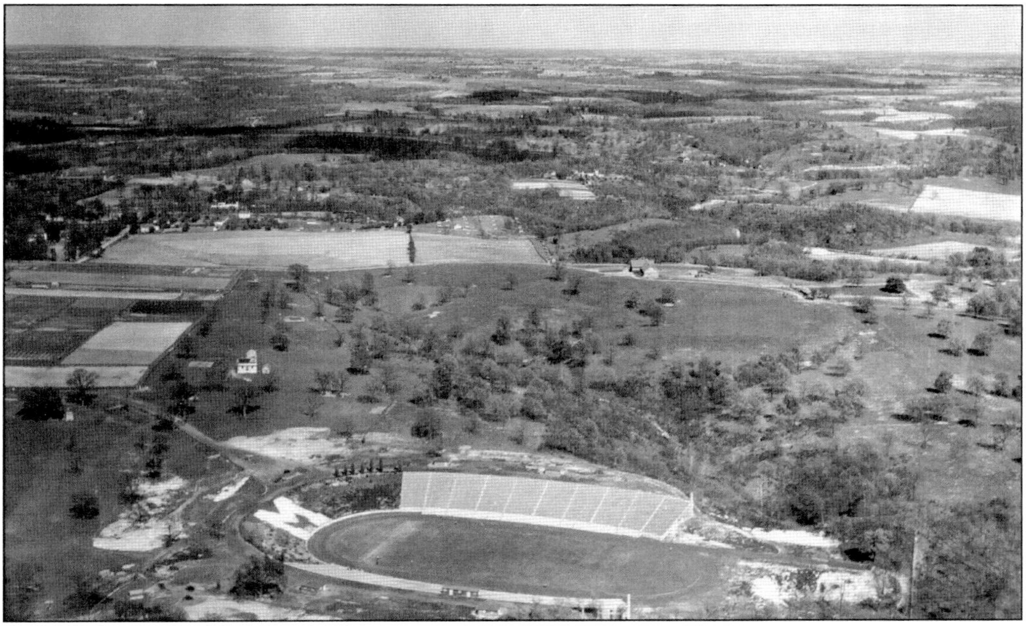

In 1940, the University of Missouri's Memorial Stadium and signature white-rock M had been frequently photographed—from the ground. Enterprising photographers discovered a market for aerial shots of notable landmarks. This photograph was taken from west of the stadium, looking east. Much of the land surrounding the stadium remained undeveloped. Today, the area is filled with university buildings, dormitories, multi-lane streets, and parking lots.

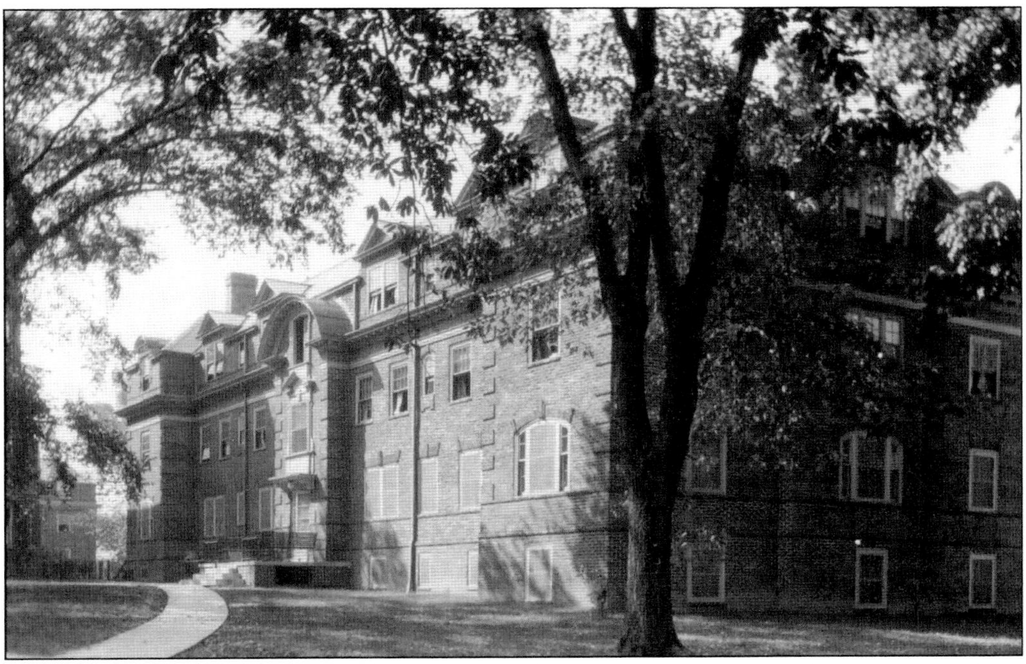

Columbia Hall, shown here in 1927, was built in 1919 on the southern part of the Stephens College campus. The brick-and-limestone building served as a residence hall and was expanded in 1937. It was renovated in 2008 to provide suite-style student housing. It is included in the Stephens College South Campus Historic District.

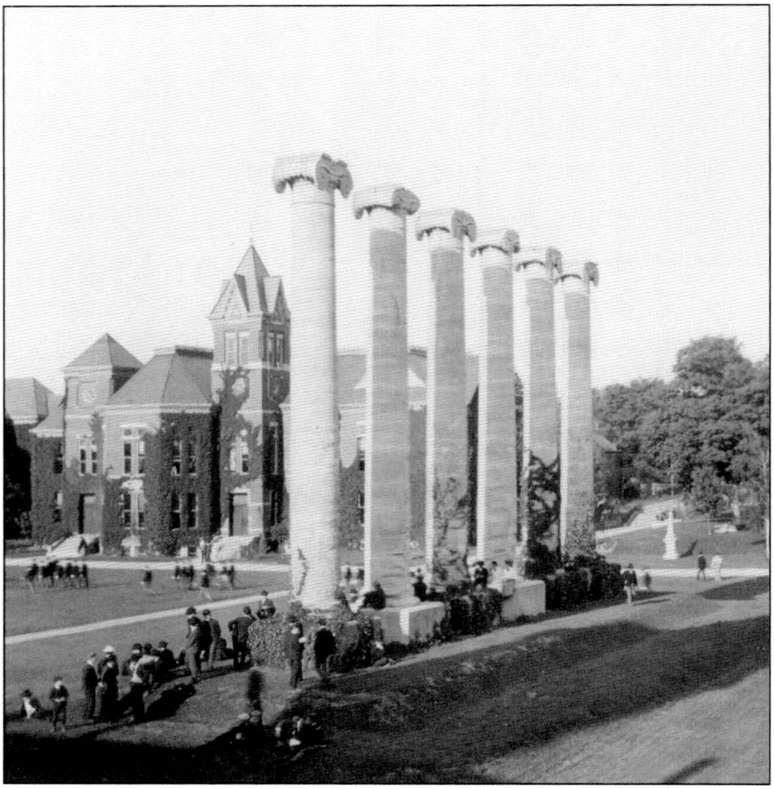

The University's Francis Quadrangle was named for influential Missourian David R. Francis. He was St. Louis mayor from 1885 to 1889 and then Missouri's governor. He was instrumental in the rebuilding of the university after the 1892 fire destroyed Academic Hall. Francis was president of the 1904 Louisiana Purchase Exposition (World's Fair) in St. Louis and is credited with asking the Olympic committee to hold the 1904 games there.

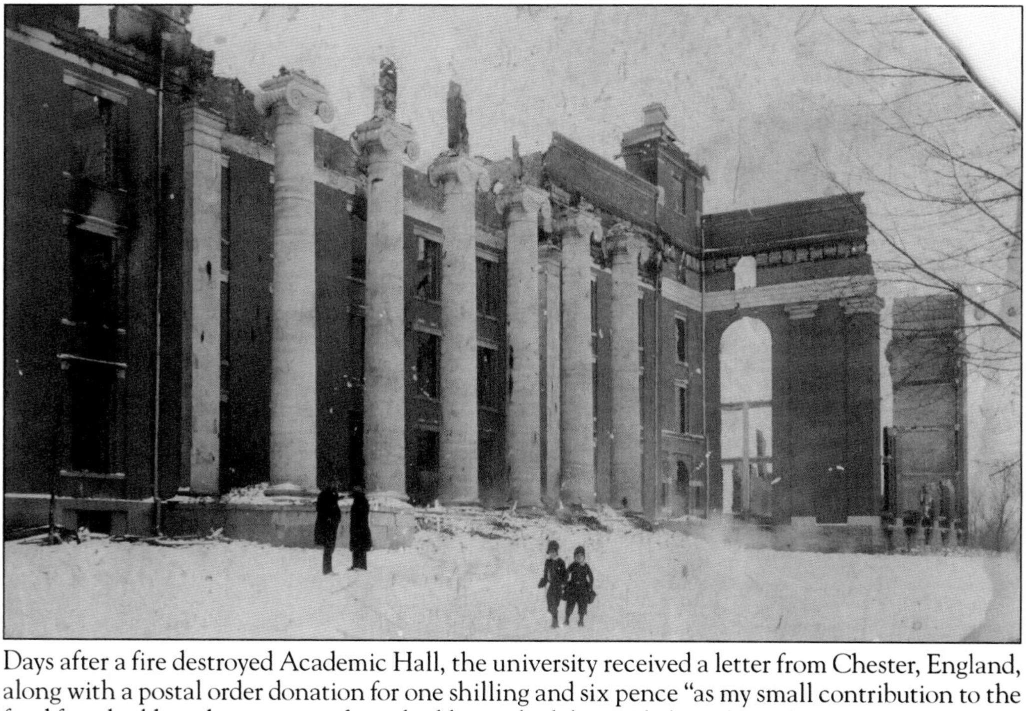

Days after a fire destroyed Academic Hall, the university received a letter from Chester, England, along with a postal order donation for one shilling and six pence "as my small contribution to the fund for rebuilding the portions of your buildings which have, I believe, been destroyed by fire." Plans for the construction of a new Academic Hall (later called Jesse Hall) were soon under way.

The University of Missouri offered men a variety of athletic opportunities during the 1899–1900 school year. Sports included football, handball, tennis, track and field, Indian clubs, gymnastics, and baseball. The practice clothing worn by these freshman football players bears little resemblance to today's uniforms. The university's first "foot ball" game was held on Thanksgiving Day 1890 against Washington University. The Missouri team lost.

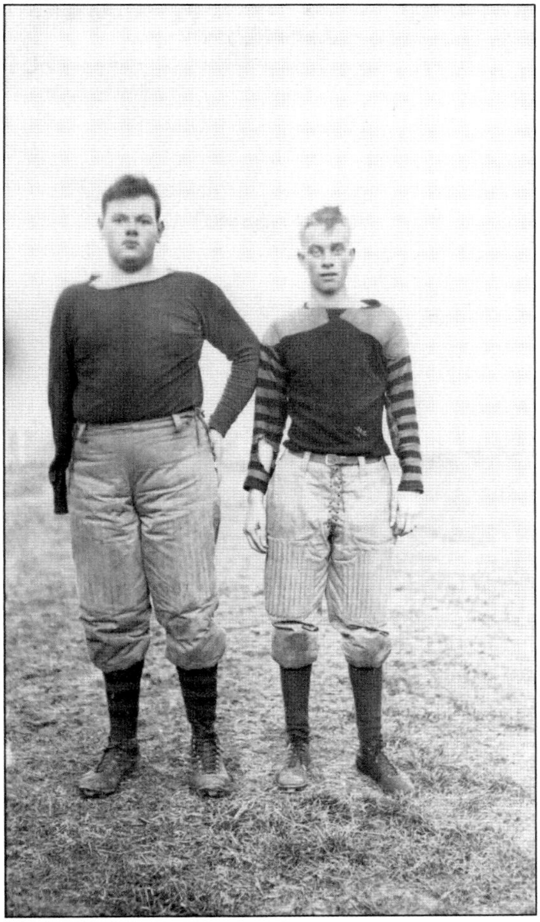

Fans of the University of Missouri football team have faithfully attended games and cheered for their team since 1890. Game day has been and continues to be an event for enthusiastic celebration. This group of students piled onto an early automobile for a postgame celebration—the original tailgate party. The first game in Memorial Stadium was held in 1926.

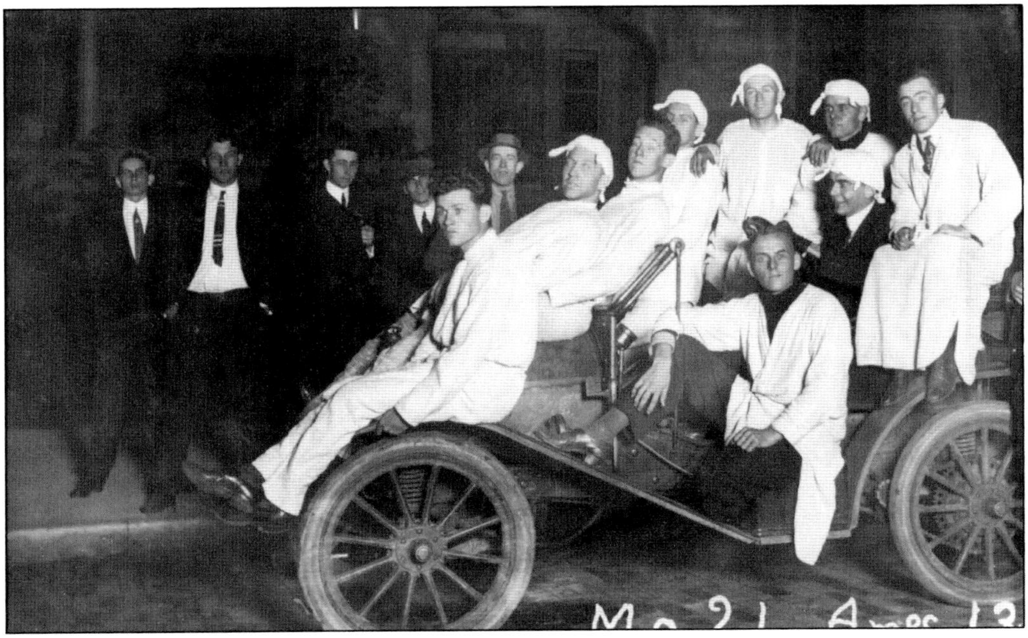

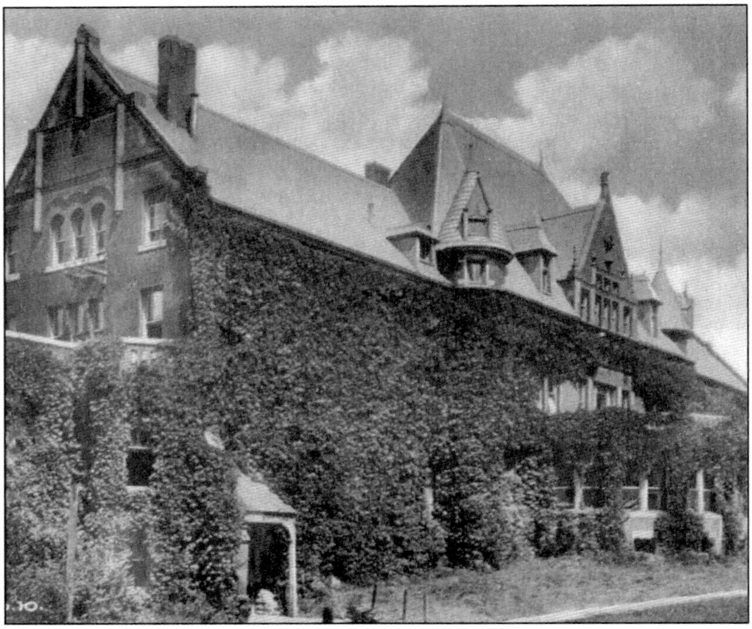

The first Lathrop Hall, shown here in 1905, was built west of Jesse Hall in 1899. It housed the university's fine arts and music departments, a student dining facility, and dormitory rooms. John Hiram Lathrop was the university's first president. His son, Gardiner Lathrop, member of the board of curators, pleaded with the curators to preserve the six columns following the 1892 Academic Hall fire.

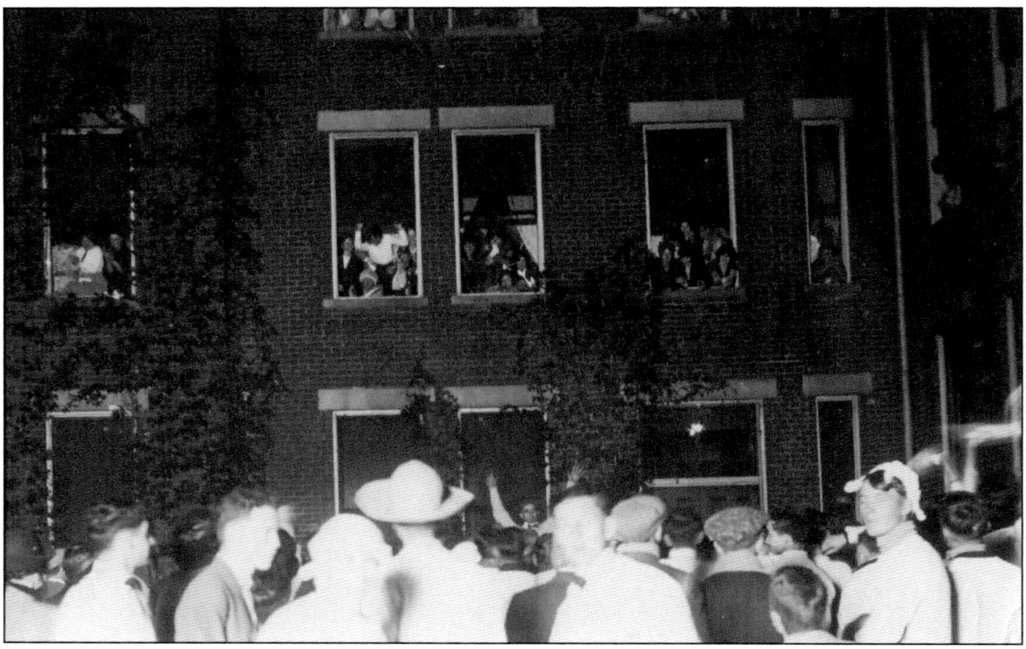

In May 1952, Columbia's colleges soon would be dismissed for the summer. Under the cover of darkness, male university students descended on Christian College, Stephens College, and the university's girls' dormitories. The panty-raid craze sweeping the nation at major universities had arrived. Damage included broken windows and screens and damaged landscaping. Some Christian College students pummeled the men with hot-water bottles and soft-drink bottles.

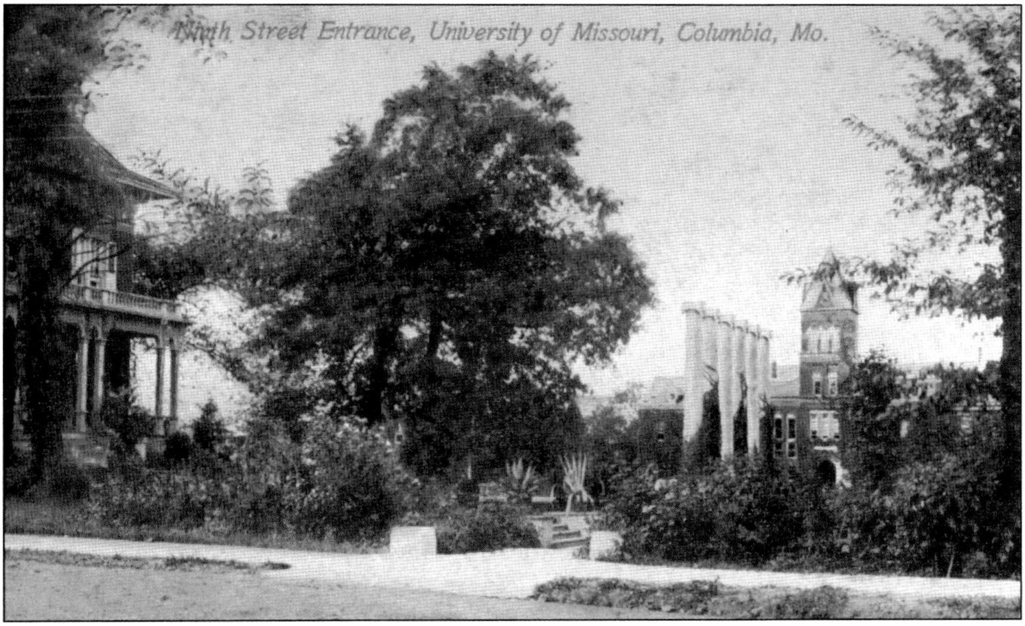

This early-20th-century view shows the university's Francis Quadrangle as approached from Ninth Street. The University of Missouri for decades maintained a single campus in Columbia. Today, it is the flagship of the University of Missouri system, which maintains campuses in Rolla, Kansas City, and St. Louis. Various buildings constructed on the Columbia campus in the 1930s were part of the Public Works Administration program.

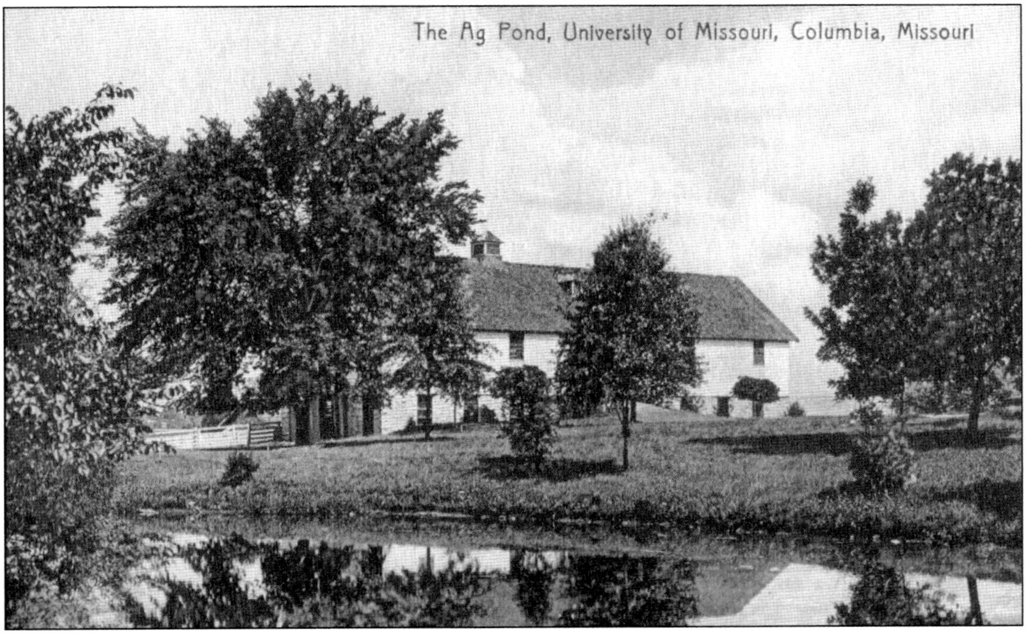

The 1862 Morrill Act granted states thousands of acres of land for "the endowment, support, and maintenance of at least one college . . . related to agriculture." Locating the new College of Agriculture at the university seemed logical, but not everyone agreed. Many Missouri cities wanted the college. The Missouri Board of Agriculture did not want it affiliated with the university. Columbians argued for eight years before the college finally opened there in 1870.

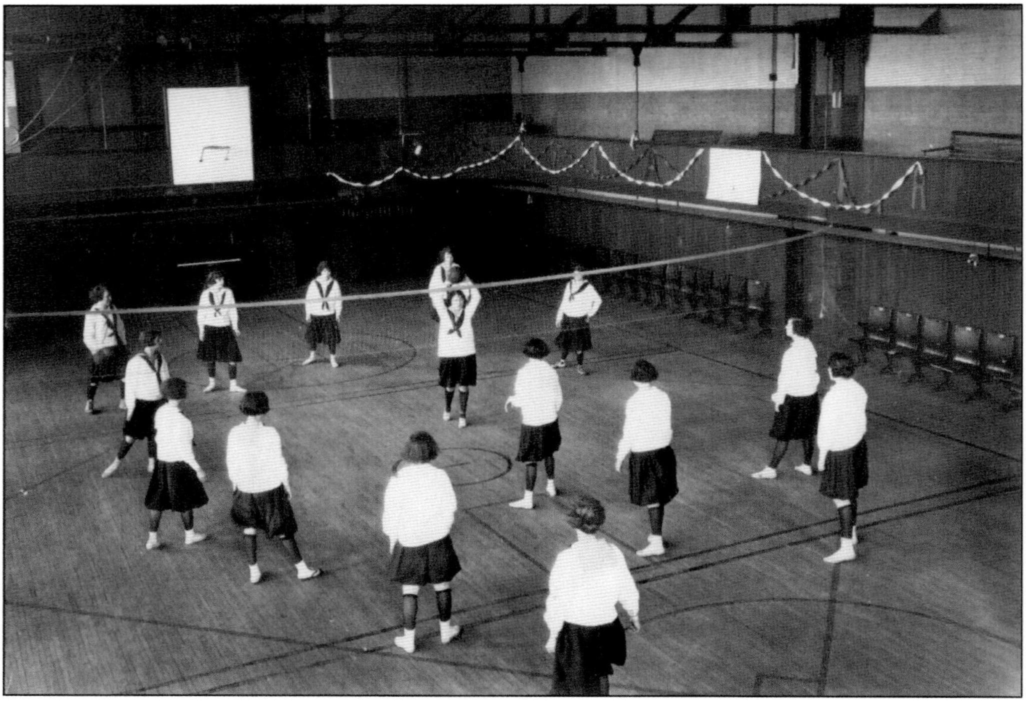

The founders of Christian College wanted it to be more than just a girls' finishing school. The university did not yet admit women, and school founders wanted the college to be a place where women could get a four-year education. The college remained open during the Civil War. From the beginning, exercise of the body as well as of the mind was emphasized. This 1924 photograph shows students playing volleyball.

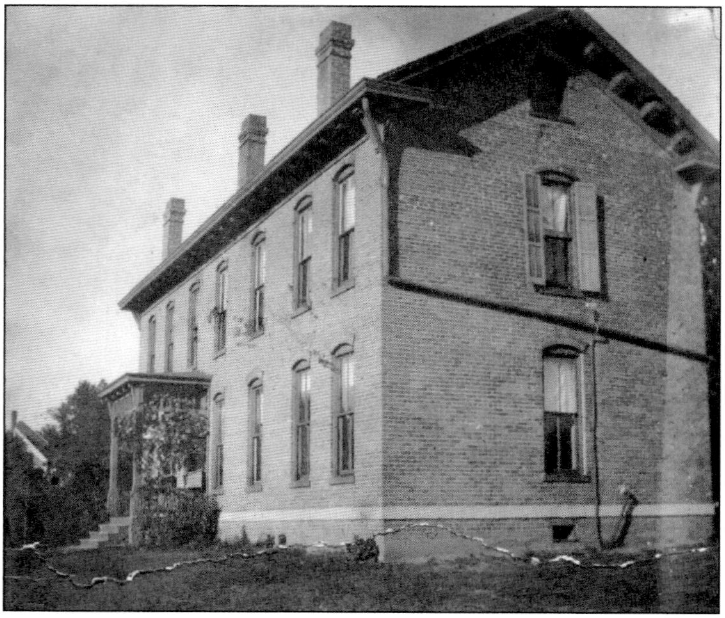

The study of horticulture began at the university in 1870 with the establishment of the College of Agriculture. An early horticulture building is seen here in 1900. In 1902, work was completed on Whitten Hall, one of several buildings constructed of Missouri white limestone to house agriculture classrooms and activities. It is part of the university's white campus. The study of horticulture is now called plant science.

This c. 1950 aerial photograph of the university looks southeast, from the northwest section of campus. Ellis Library, completed in 1915, stands left of Jesse Hall. In the center and to the left of Ellis Library is Memorial Tower, prior to construction of its additions. Agriculture fields lie beyond Memorial Tower.

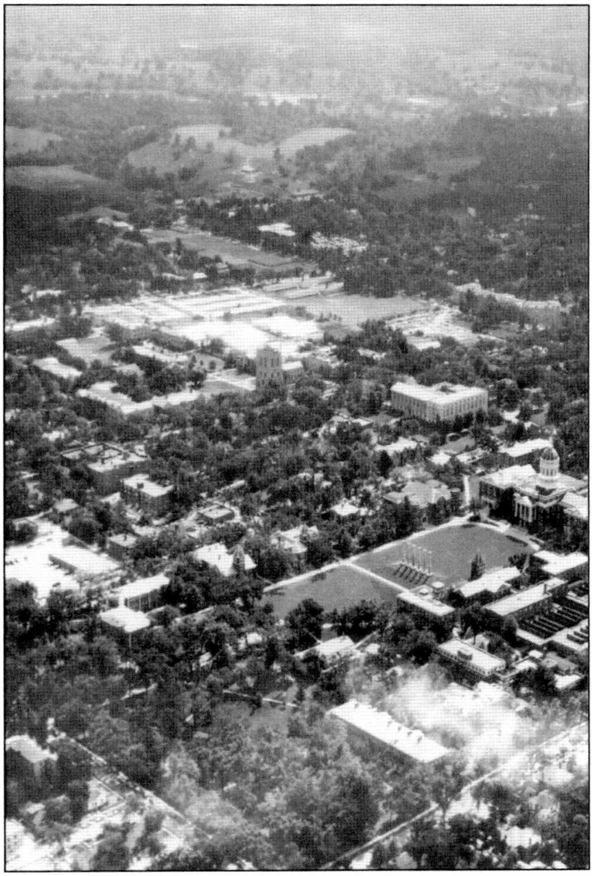

Education was and continues to be an important and serious matter to Stephens College students. While these girls from 100 years ago wore similar uniform-like clothing, each added a bit of personal ornamentation to reflect her own style, including a pin, a watch, an ascot, a special way of tying a scarf, and large satin hair bows.

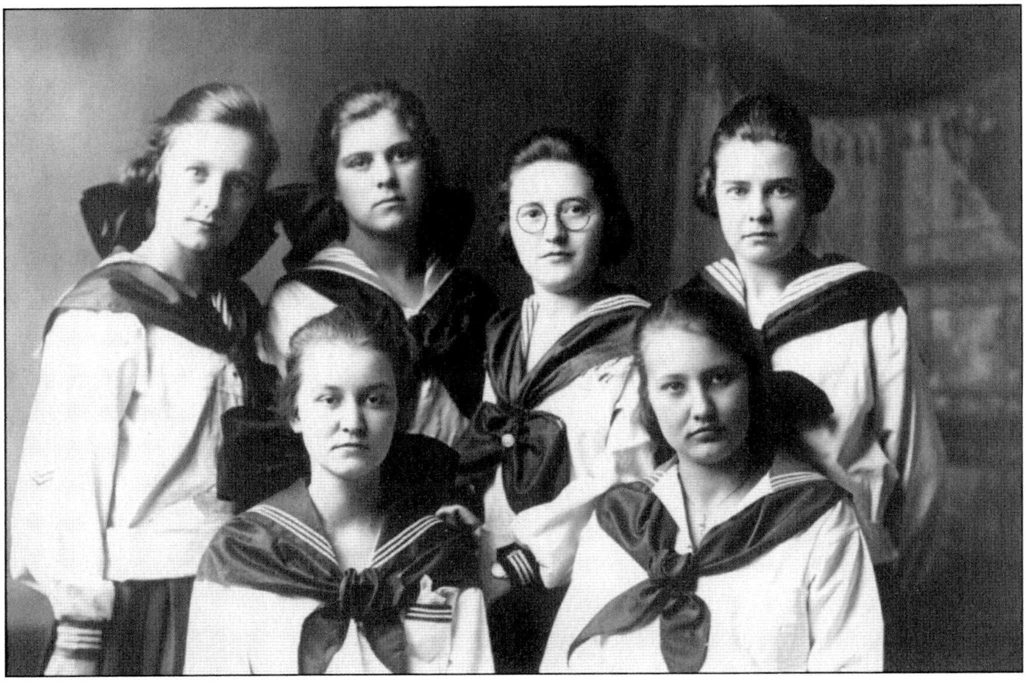

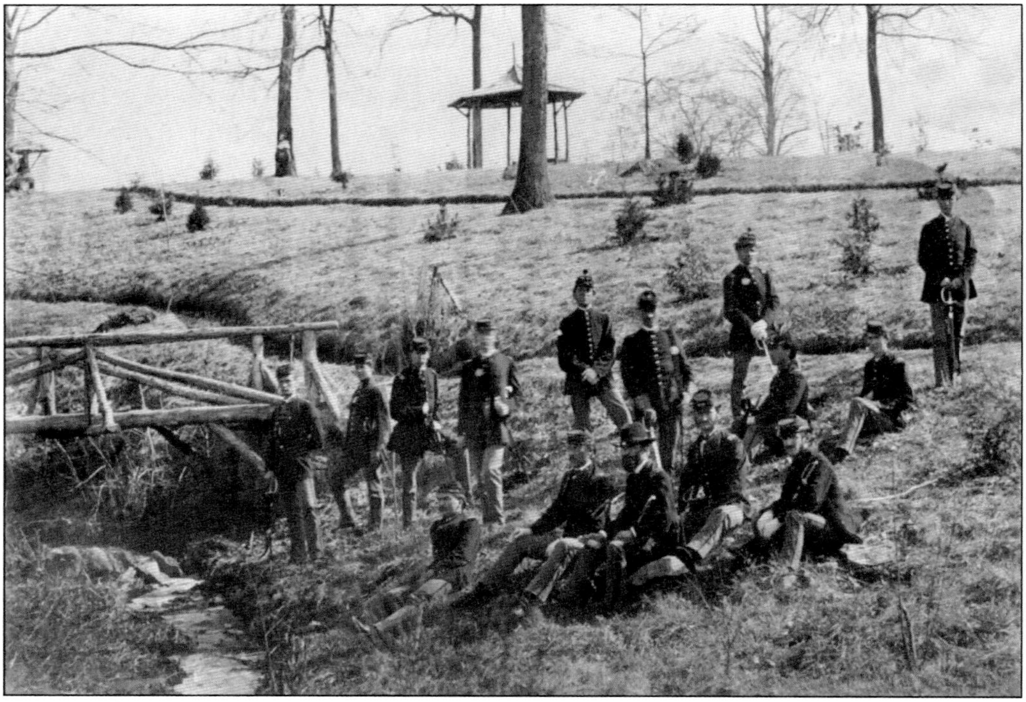

In 1868, the university became one of the first 20 colleges to include military science in its curriculum, as required by provisions of the Morrill Act of 1862. Cadets frequently marched on campus. Shown here around 1872, cadets take a break near Chalybeate Spring and the gazebo, the site today of Neff Hall and the School of Journalism buildings.

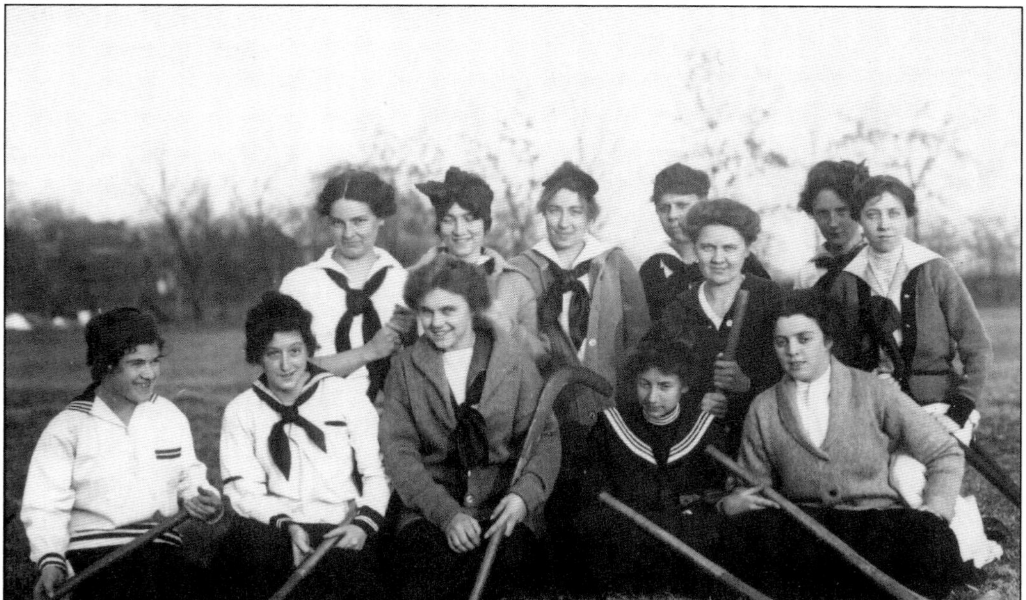

In 1889, the university's board of curators decided that female students needed one semester of physical exercise in order to graduate. Until 1923, a top-floor room in Jesse Hall and a small dressing shack were the only athletic facilities for women. The Women's Athletic Association was formed in 1910, the same year the women's field hockey team posed for this photograph.

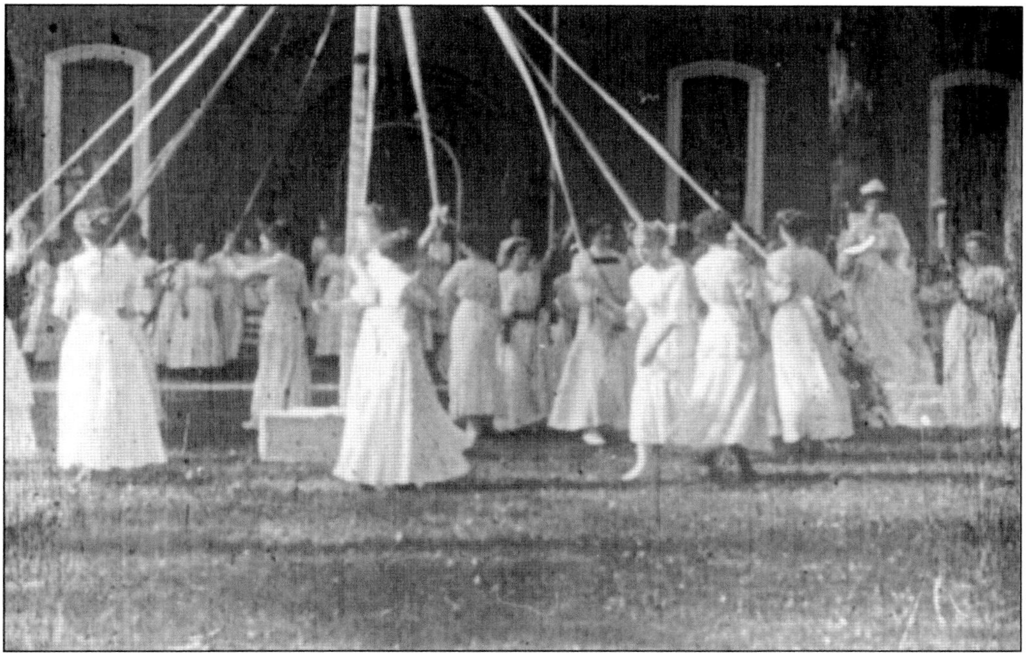

Spring was traditionally a time of celebration on the Stephens College campus. In this 1907 photograph, Stephens students are shown in white dresses, doing a dance and braiding ribbons on a May pole. The May Day queen wears a crown and is seated on a raised platform to the right of the May pole.

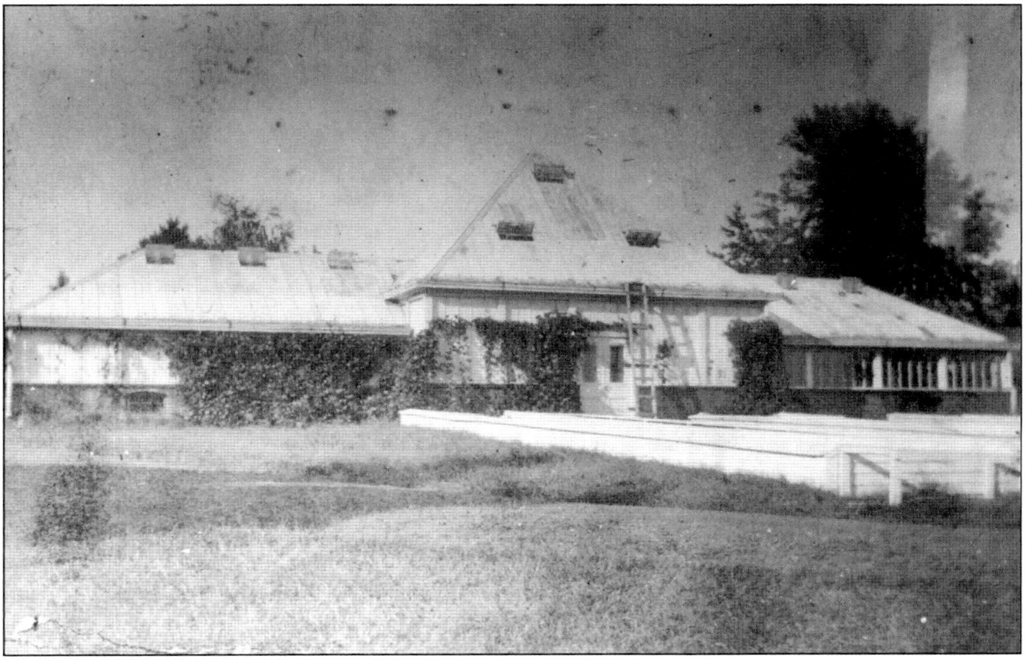

This c. 1900 photograph shows the university's ivy-trimmed greenhouse. The manually operated openings in the roof allowed air to circulate. The studies of plant science and biology have grown in the last 100-plus years, as have the resources devoted to them. The result today is state-of-the-art buildings and programs.

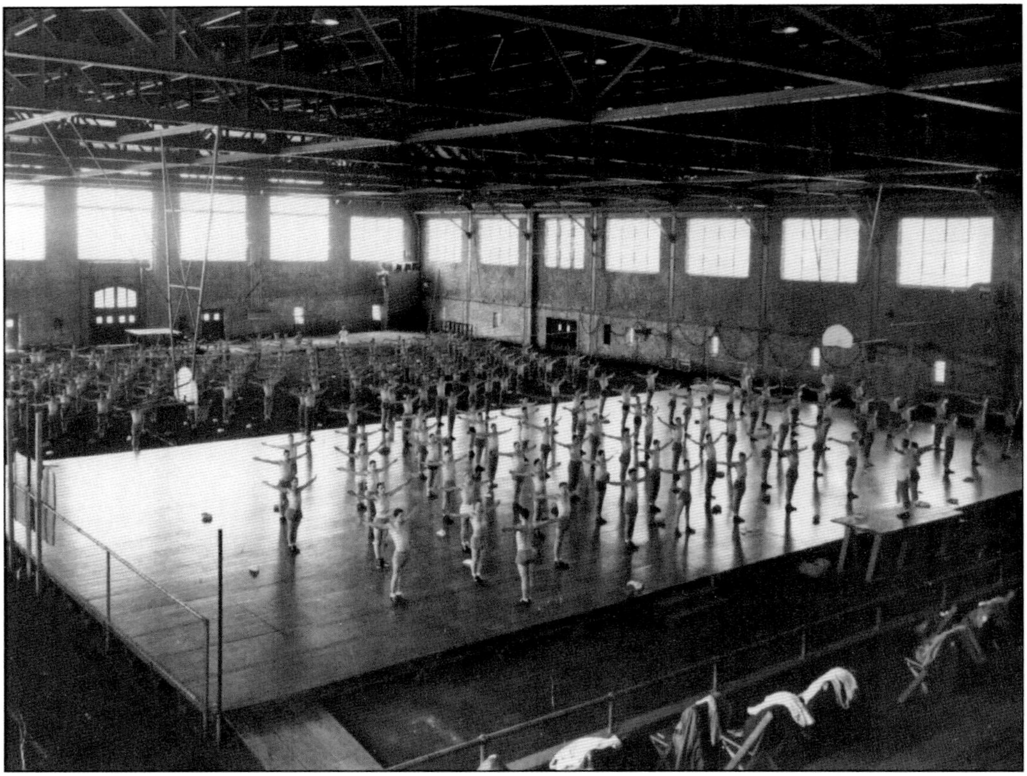

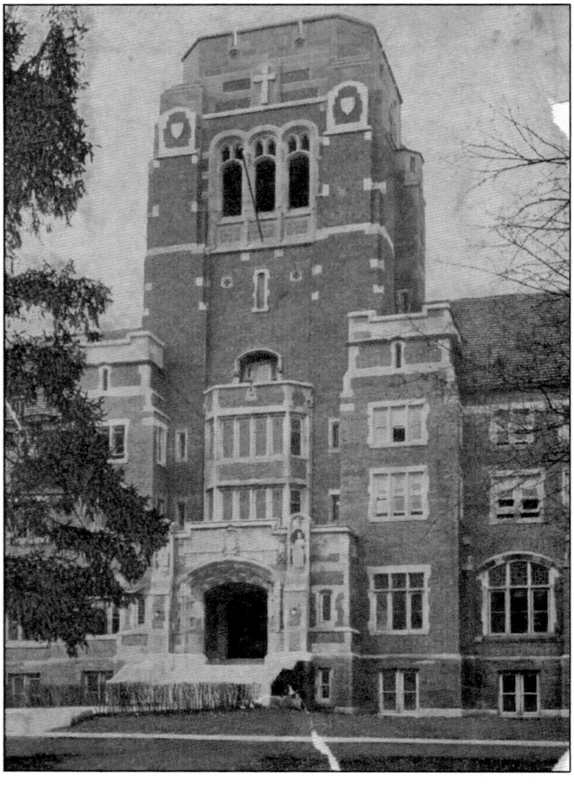

This c. 1940 photograph of men doing calisthenics was taken inside the university's Rothwell Gymnasium. The gym was one of the university's first intercollegiate sports facilities. The building was named for Gideon Rothwell, a state congressman who was chairman of the university's board of curators in 1892 when fire destroyed Academic Hall. He worked to save the building's six iconic columns.

At more than 100 years old, Tower Hall has witnessed generations of the coming and going of Stephens College students. It is located on the college's historic quadrangle and is listed in the National Register of Historic Place's Stephens College South Campus Historic District. It remains in use today as a residence hall.

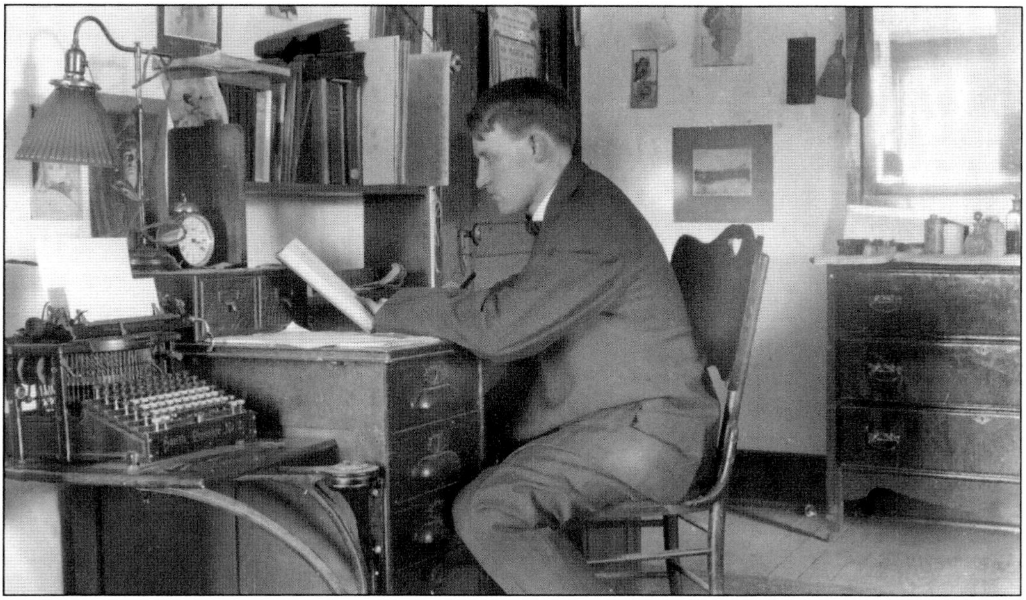

The clothing and furnishings may have changed since 1909, but the goal of university students is the same: to study and to learn. Today's students still need a desk and chair, shelves, an alarm clock, and a lamp. Computers may have replaced this Smith Premier No. 2 typewriter, but writing papers remains a requirement in many classes.

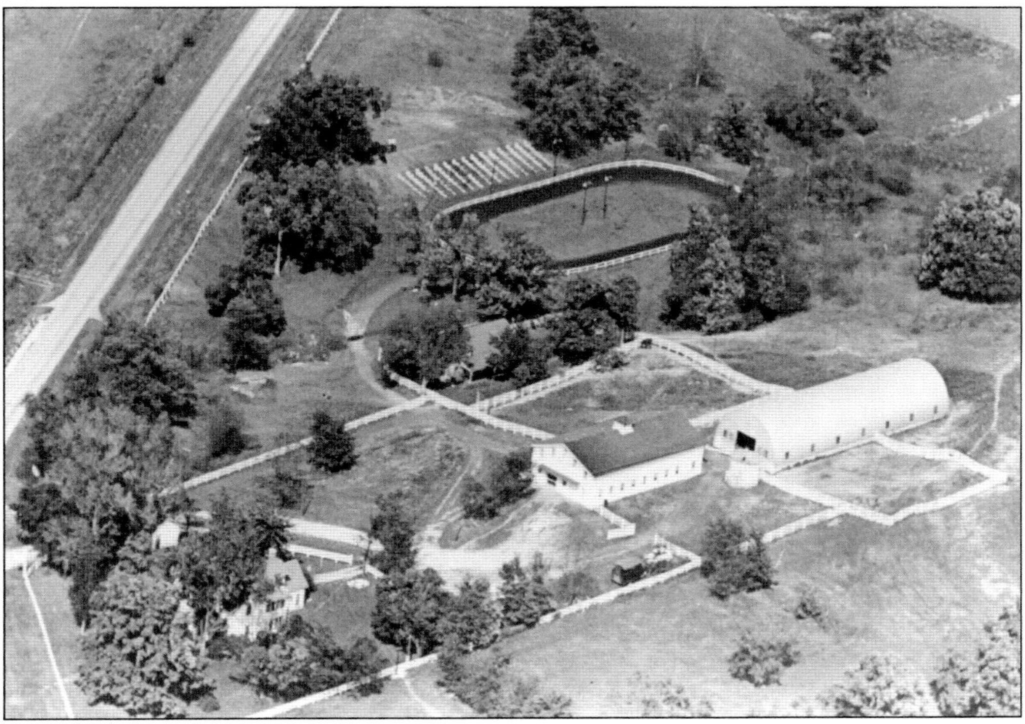

Carolyn Drew (Reed) taught horsemanship classes at Christian College beginning in 1927. She remained at the college for more than 35 years. Eagle Rock Farm, located on Highway 63, was purchased in 1945 and called the Christian College Riding Farm. Interest in the horsemanship program had declined by the 1960s. The program was discontinued and the farm sold in 1964.

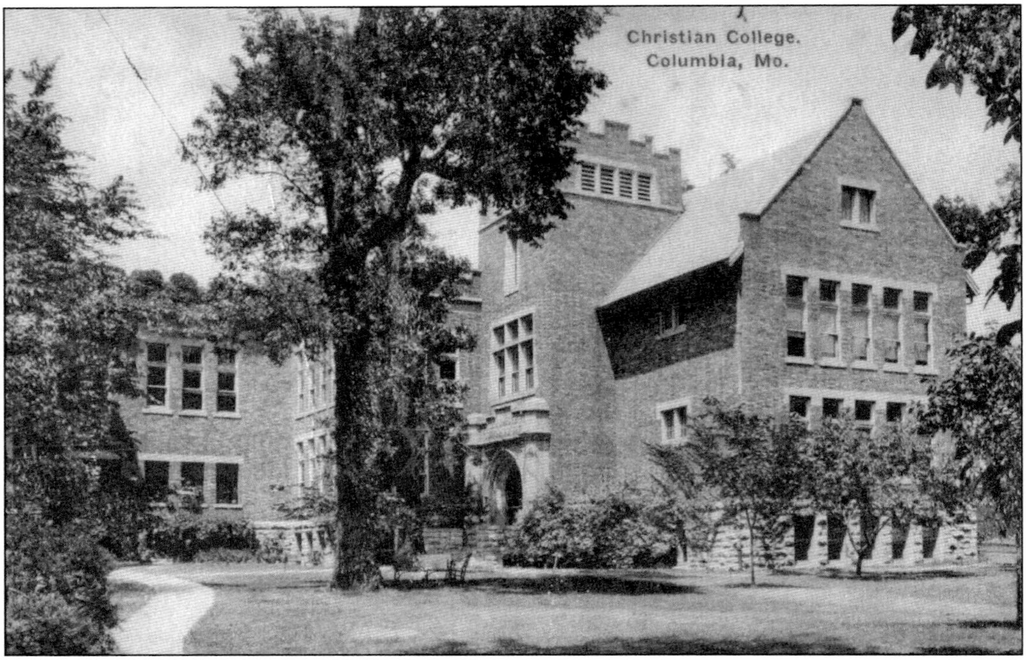

Christian Female College was chartered on January 18, 1851, by the Missouri General Assembly. The name was shortened to Christian College in 1929 and changed again in 1970 to Columbia College. From 1884 until 1923, each student was required to sign a pledge "to obey all rules and regulations." Dorsey Hall, built in 1911, houses classrooms, a chapel, and a studio named for alumnus Jane Froman.

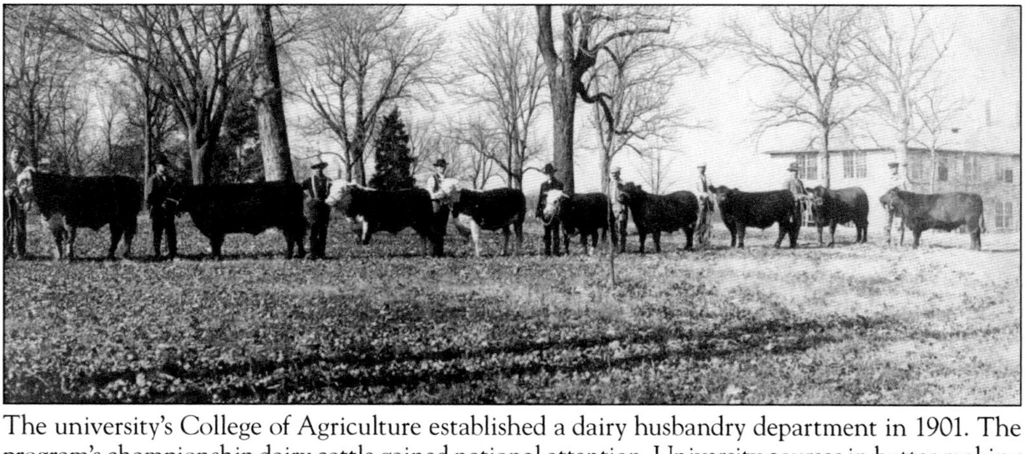

The university's College of Agriculture established a dairy husbandry department in 1901. The program's championship dairy cattle gained national attention. University courses in butter-making and ice cream production were available in the 1920s. Today, the Division of Animal Sciences is one of the most diverse programs in the country.

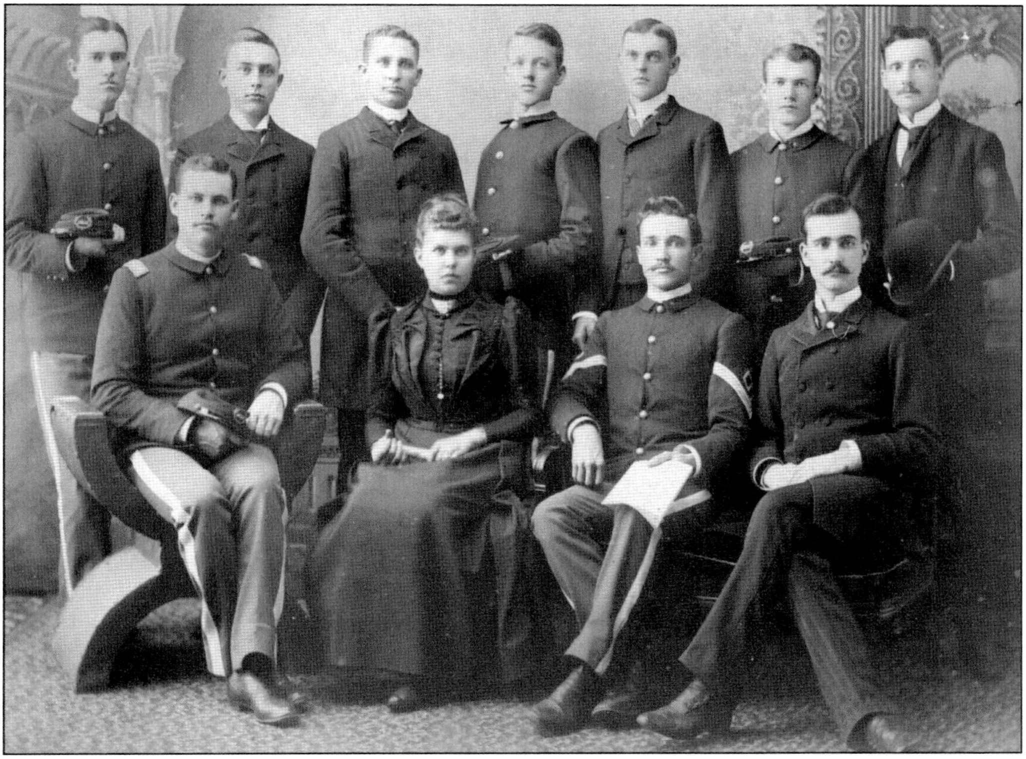

The University Argus was a monthly magazine published by The Athenian and The Union, the university's literary societies, from 1888 until 1896. It featured campus stories, editorials, and a women's section. The *Argus* staff is shown here in 1890.

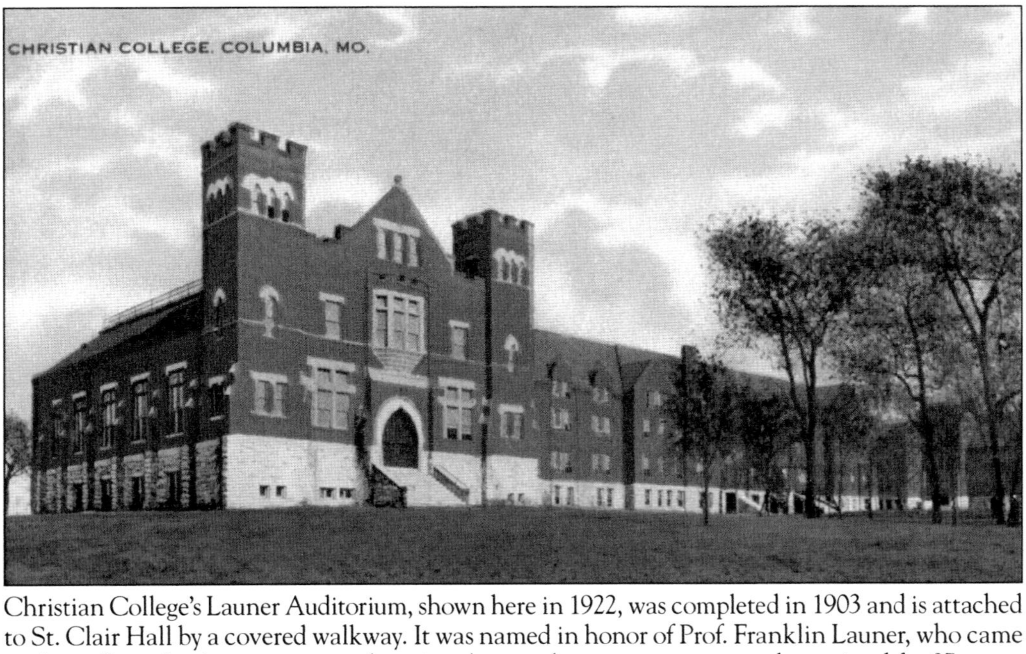

Christian College's Launer Auditorium, shown here in 1922, was completed in 1903 and is attached to St. Clair Hall by a covered walkway. It was named in honor of Prof. Franklin Launer, who came to the college thinking it was coeducational, agreed to stay one year, and remained for 37 years. With seating for more than 500, the facility hosts convocations and campus performances.

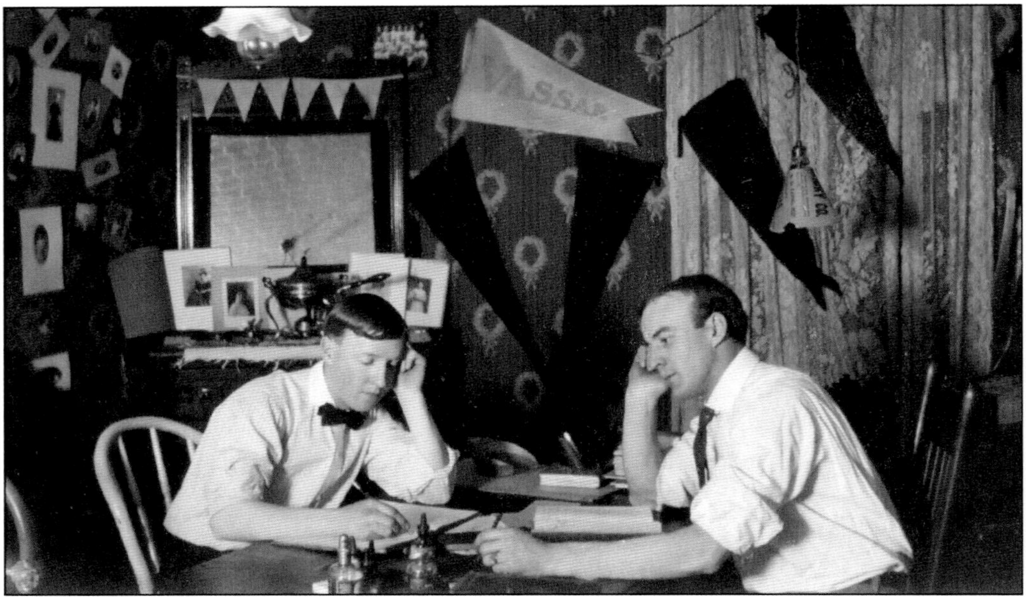

This turn-of-the-20th-century photograph features university students studying in their room. Each holds the latest in essential student equipment: the fountain pen. Wool pennants and images of women adorn their walls. At that time, everyday attire for male students included dress shirts and neckties. The university had approximately 2,000 students enrolled, and Columbia's population was 6,000.

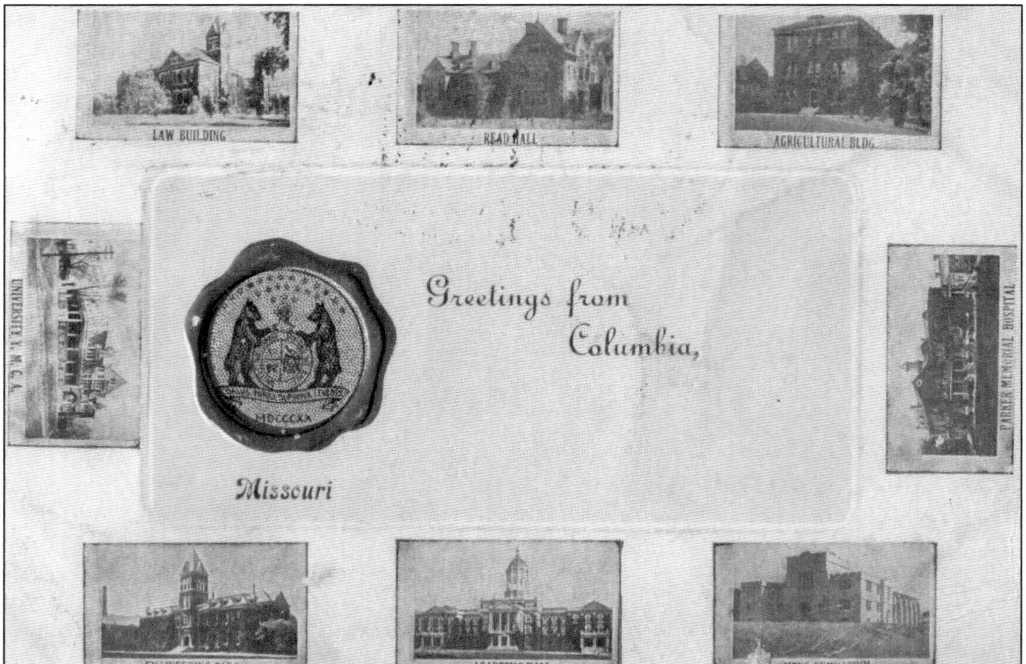

In the early 1900s, before chambers of commerce, public relations firms, and mass-mailing advertisements, companies and organizations created collages and printed them on the popular penny postcard. This card features eight structures: seven university buildings and Columbia's YMCA. Although some buildings have been repurposed and renamed, all but the YMCA remain in use.

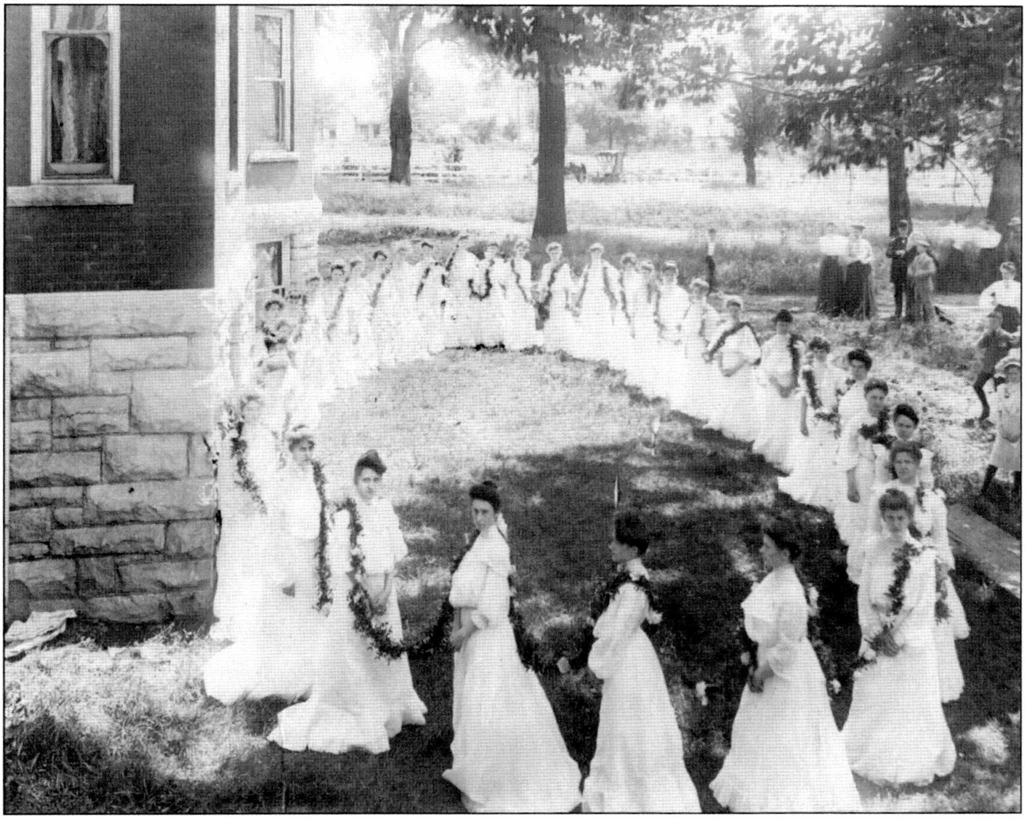

The Ivy Chain Ceremony at Christian College, first held in 1900, is believed to be one of the oldest commencement traditions in the country. Graduating students form a circle, with a long ivy chain connecting them. This is said to represent their unity as students of the college. The ivy is then cut between each student, symbolizing their entry into a new phase of life.

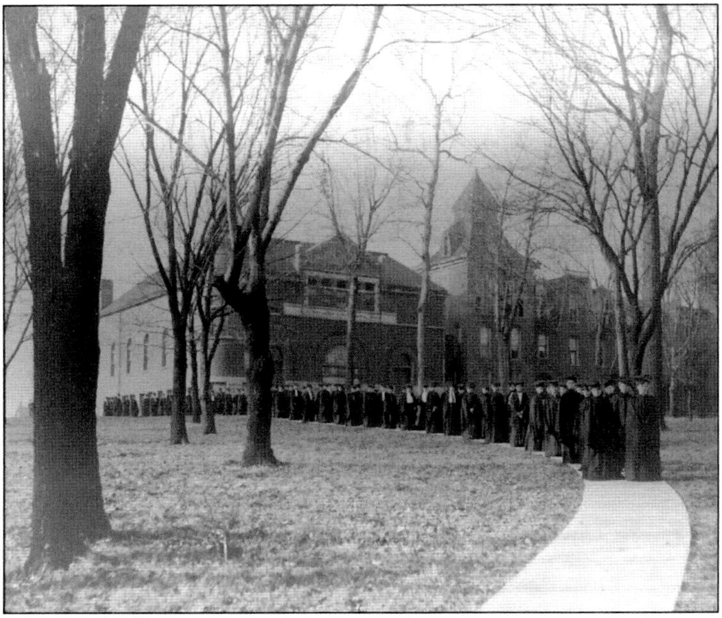

In this 1903 photograph, candidates for graduation line up outside the R.E. Sappington and Wife Memorial Chapel on the Stephens College campus. The chapel was built in 1897 with funds raised in Columbia and nearby communities. When completed, the chapel seated 860 people. It was razed in 2004 when it was deemed a structural safety risk not worth restoring.

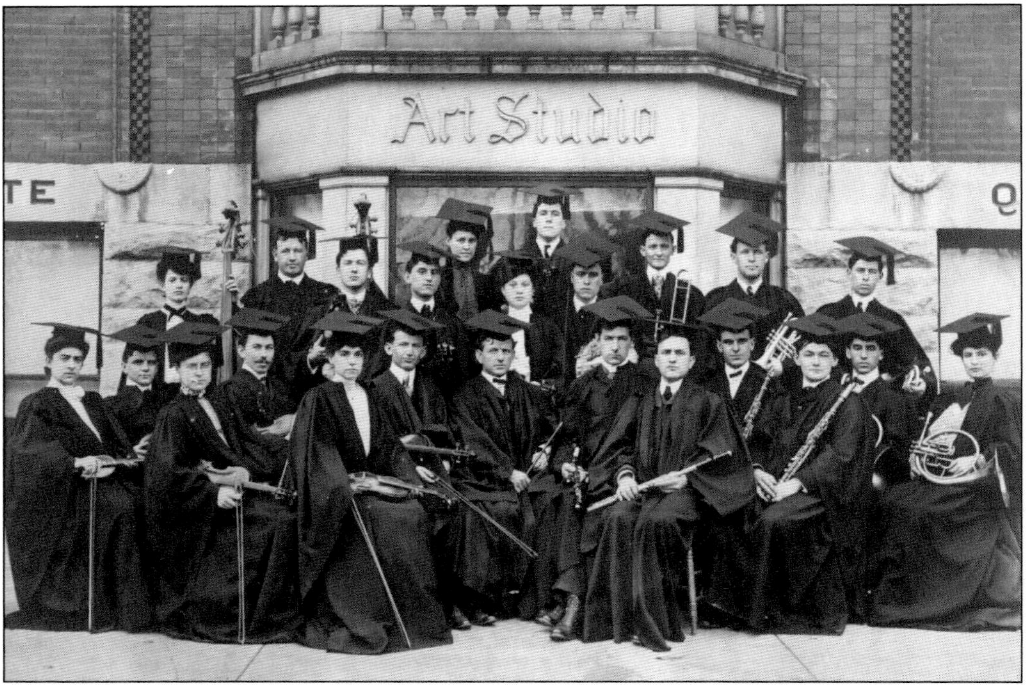

Stephens College is located on 86 acres in the heart of Columbia. It was founded as Columbia Baptist Female College under the leadership of the Baptist Church. The Stephens College orchestra of 1902–1903 is seated in front of the R.E. Sappington and Wife Memorial Chapel during graduation ceremonies. The faculty at Stephens was predominantly male, except for teachers of domestic subjects.

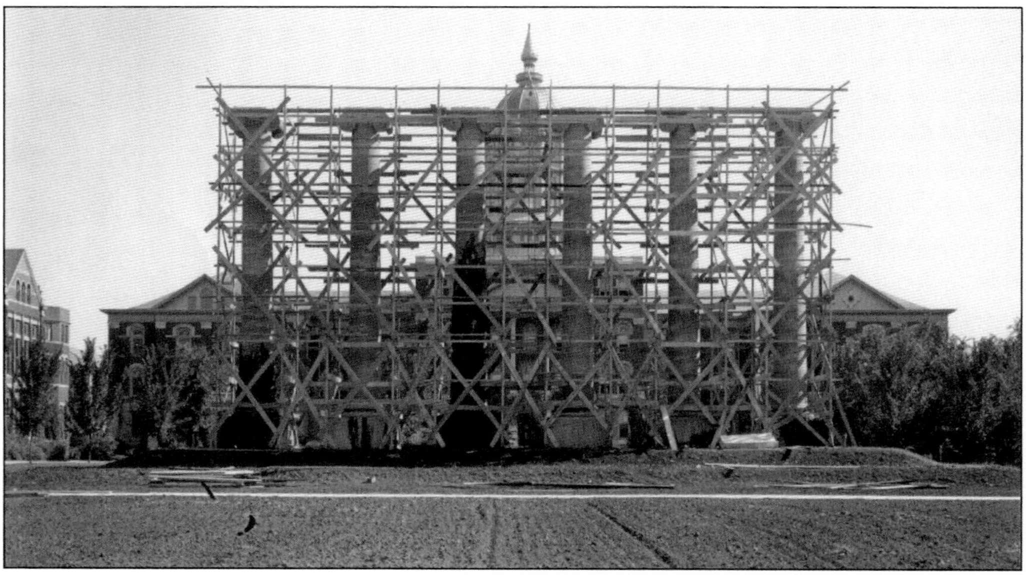

Six Ionic columns are all that remain of the university's Academic Hall, which burned down in 1892. The columns have been a symbol of tradition and pride for generations of students. Routine maintenance and restoration are necessary to preserve the columns. Scaffolding surrounds them in this 1937 photograph. At one time, ivy grew on five of the columns. The quadrangle and red campus buildings are National Register properties.

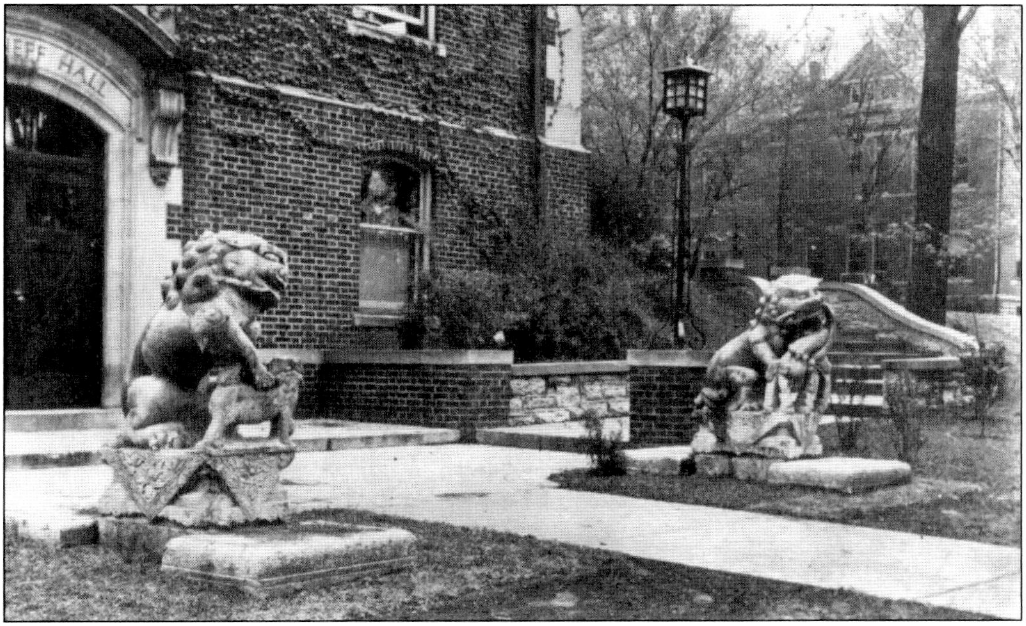

A pair of stone lion statues once guarded the entrance to the School of Journalism's Neff Hall on the university's quadrangle. Prior to their relocation to Columbia, they spent several hundred years guarding a Confucian temple in China. The Chinese government donated them as an act of goodwill during 1931's Journalism Week. Today, they guard the School of Journalism archway. The school had two Chinese students enrolled when it opened in 1908.

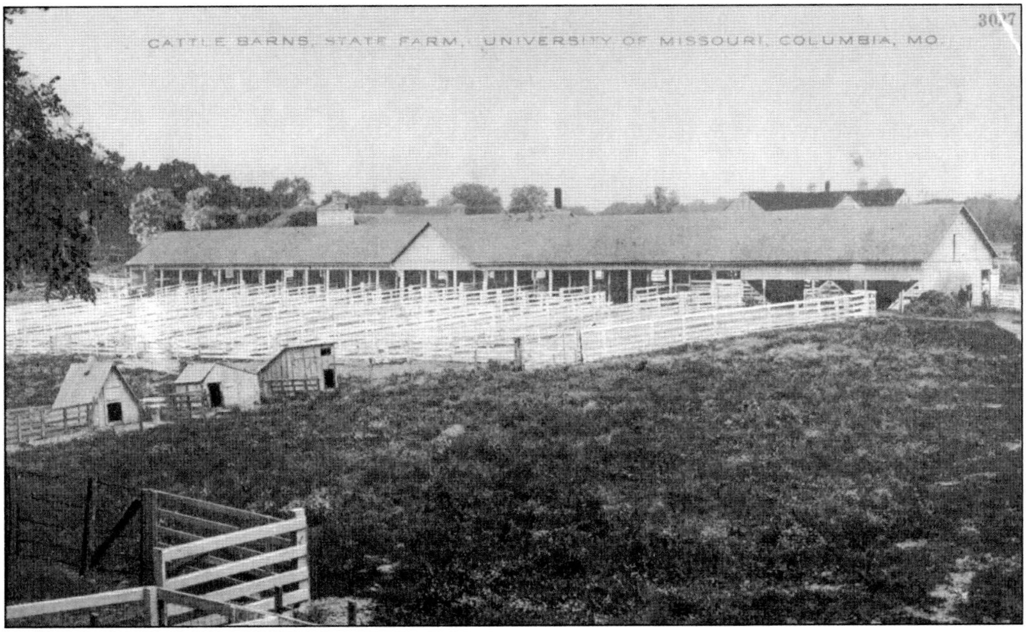

The university's College of Agriculture established a dairy husbandry department in 1901. The animal husbandry department was established in 1904, and the poultry husbandry department began in 1911. Here, numerous cattle barns and pens are seen on property near the main campus in 1913. The college's first dean was George Clinton Swallow. He was also the first professor of geology, chemistry, and agriculture, and the first state geologist.

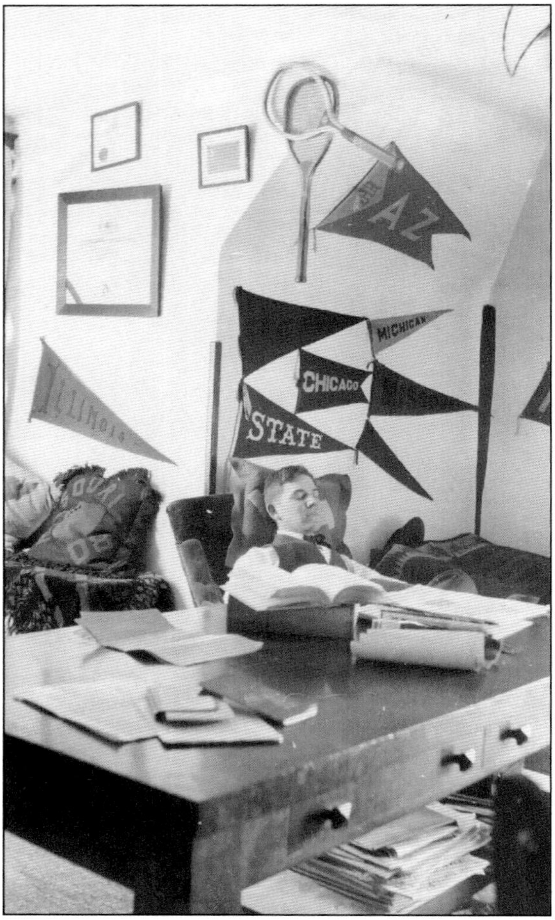

This postgraduate university student, surrounded by textbooks and papers, catches a quick nap while studying in his room. On his bed is a pillow promoting the 1908 Missouri football team. The Missouri Store in Jesse Hall sold student supplies and school-spirit items. Various wall pennants suggest he is a fan of multiple Midwestern universities. Christian College students were not allowed to attend university football games until 1908.

Joseph K. Rogers was Christian College's third president, serving from 1858 until 1877. The J.K. Rogers stone gate was built in 1912 as the main entrance to Christian College. It serves as a symbol to students of their entry to and exit from college life. In 1900, when female architects were rare, Columbia architect Mary Louise Hale designed St. Clair Hall, which remains in use as the administration building.

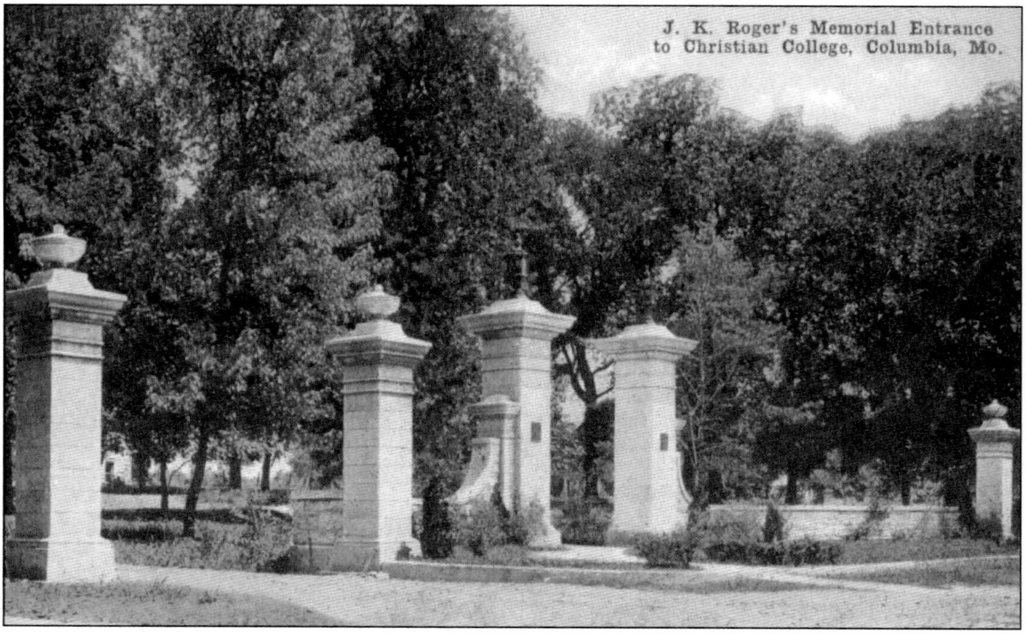

Three

Trails, Rails, and Highways

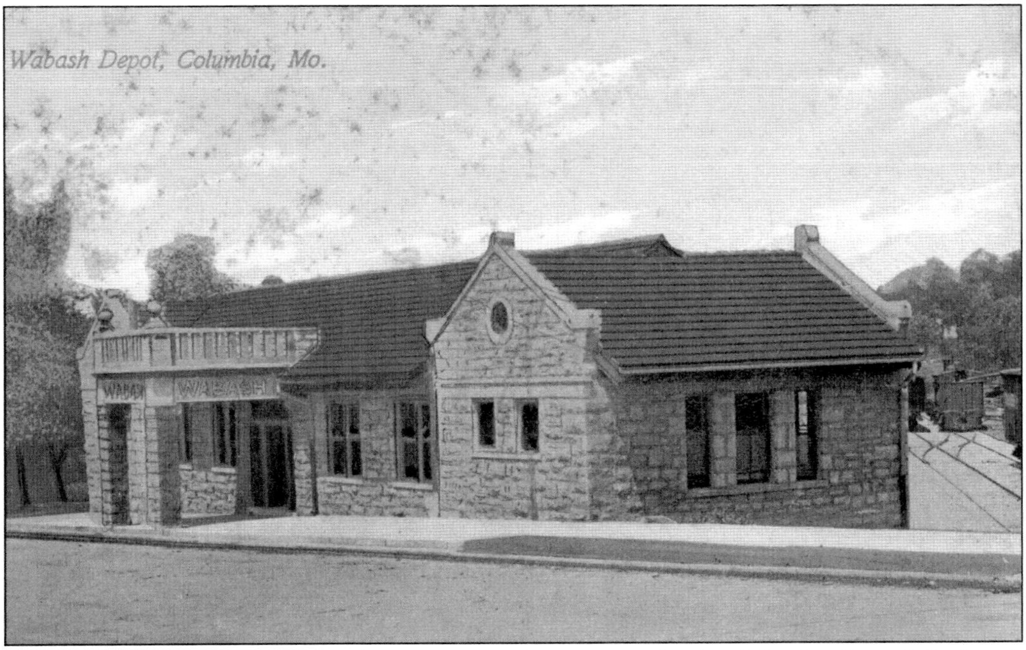

For decades, the Wabash Station depot served as the terminus for the Columbia Branch Railroad, a 21.7-mile short-line railroad connecting Centralia to Columbia. As home to the university, two colleges, and a growing population, Columbia needed a means to transport passengers to and from major railroad hubs. The Wabash depot opened in 1910 and saw multiple passenger trains arrive and leave each day, including the coach named *City of Columbia*.

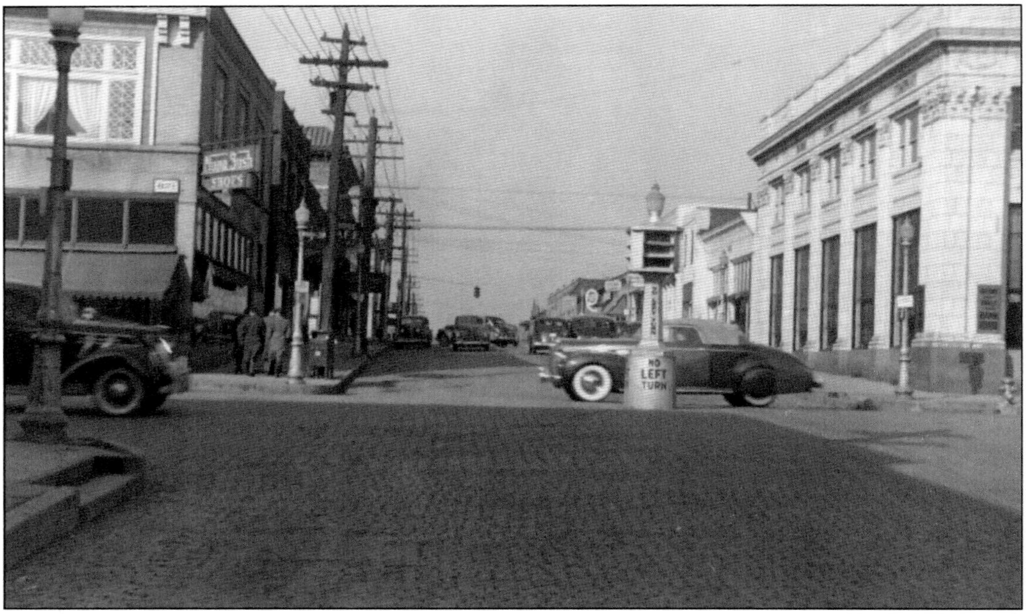

The intersection of Ninth Street and Broadway, in the heart of downtown Columbia, has been a busy intersection since the days of 19th-century westward migration. In 1911, the speed limit for downtown was eight miles per hour. This 1941 photograph shows a traffic signal in the middle of the intersection. The Boone County National Bank building is on the right.

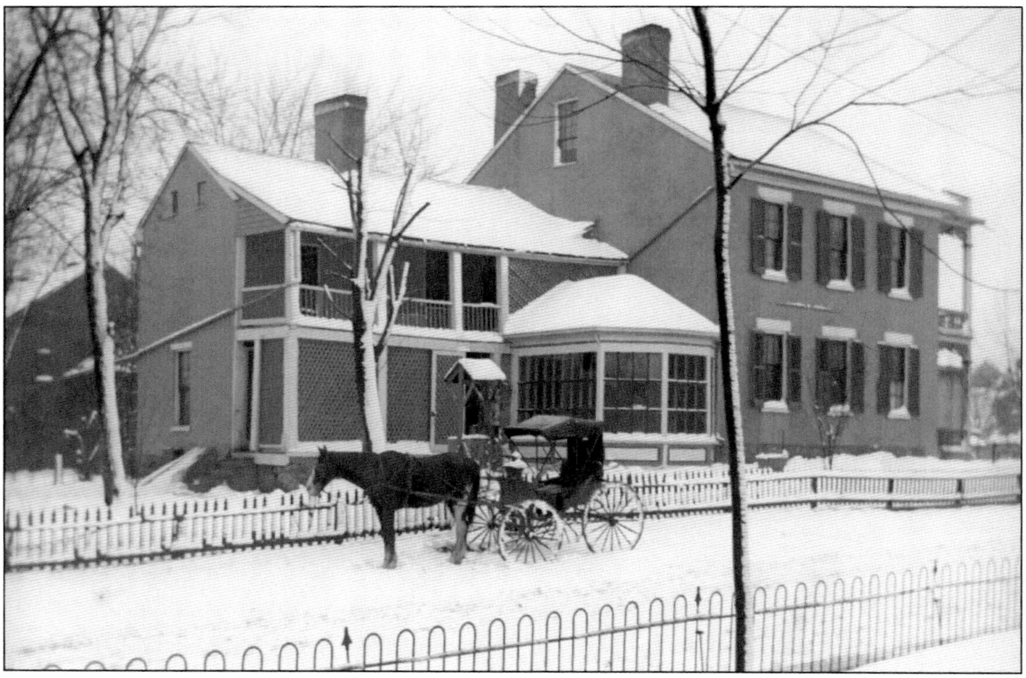

Columbia's streets were not always filled with motorized vehicles. Until 1909, horses, buggies, and wagons were the means of transportation. Here, a horse and buggy sit in front of the Pines House, at the southwest corner of Hitt and Cherry Streets. An overcast, snowy day and an open carriage made for a chilly ride. Carriage riders often covered themselves with thick lap blankets and placed heated bricks on the carriage floor.

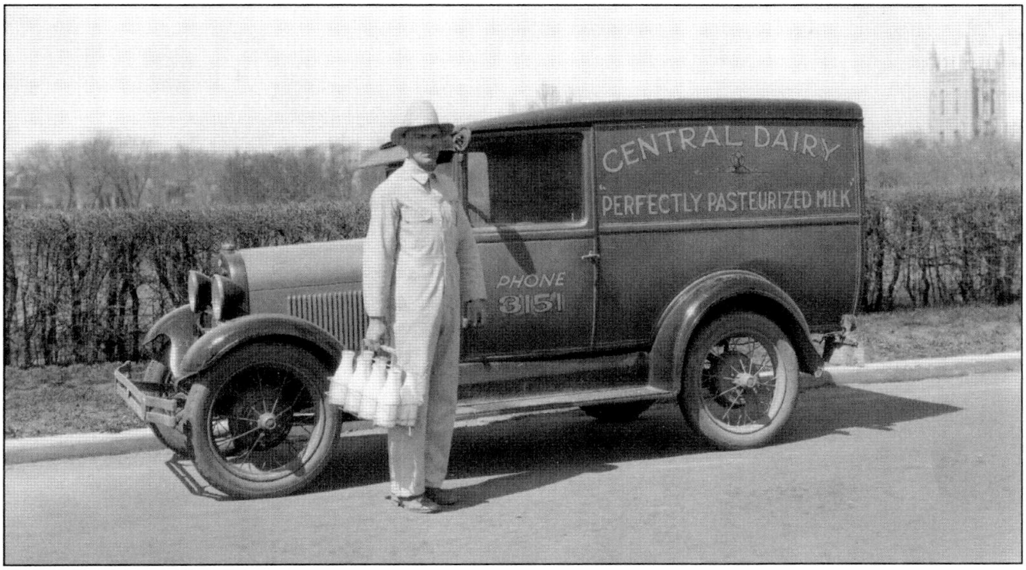

Columbia's Central Dairy was established in 1920. Its bottling facility and headquarters were located on Broadway. Early each morning, uniformed men loaded their trucks with glass milk bottles and made delivery stops throughout town, including to individual homes. Customers placed their empty bottles outside. Milkmen then picked them up and returned them to the plant for cleaning and refilling. The university's Memorial Tower is seen in the distance at right.

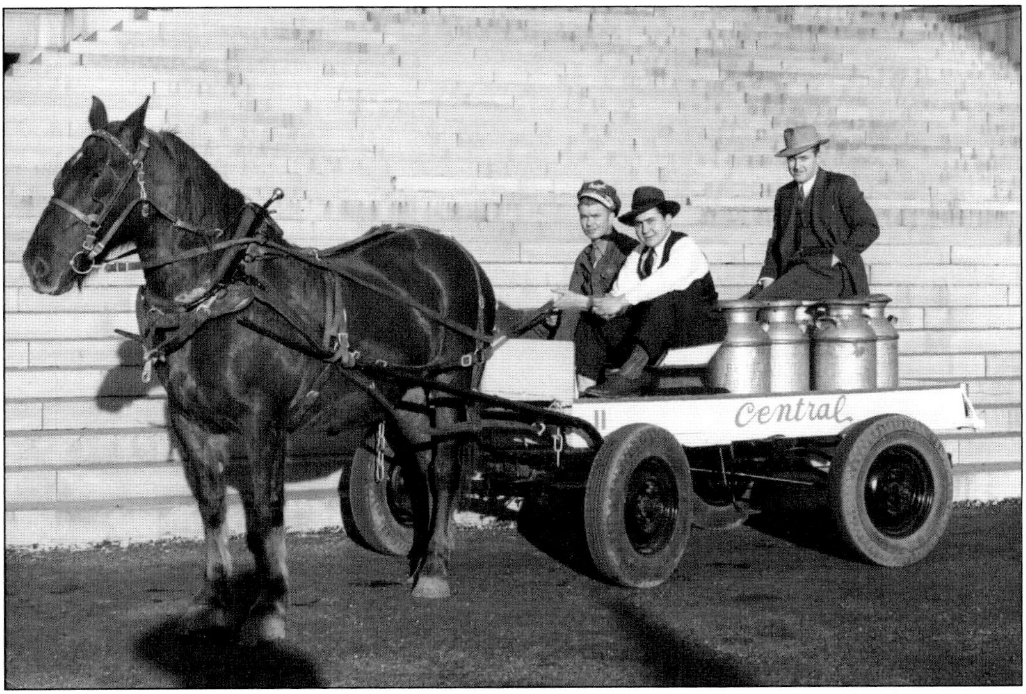

Motorized vehicles and paved roads were becoming more commonplace in Columbia by 1920, but Central Dairy continued to use horse-drawn pickup wagons in some areas. Each morning, dairy farmers milked their cows and poured the rich, creamy liquid into large clean milk cans. Central Dairy employees picked up the cans and then delivered them to the company's facility for processing and bottling.

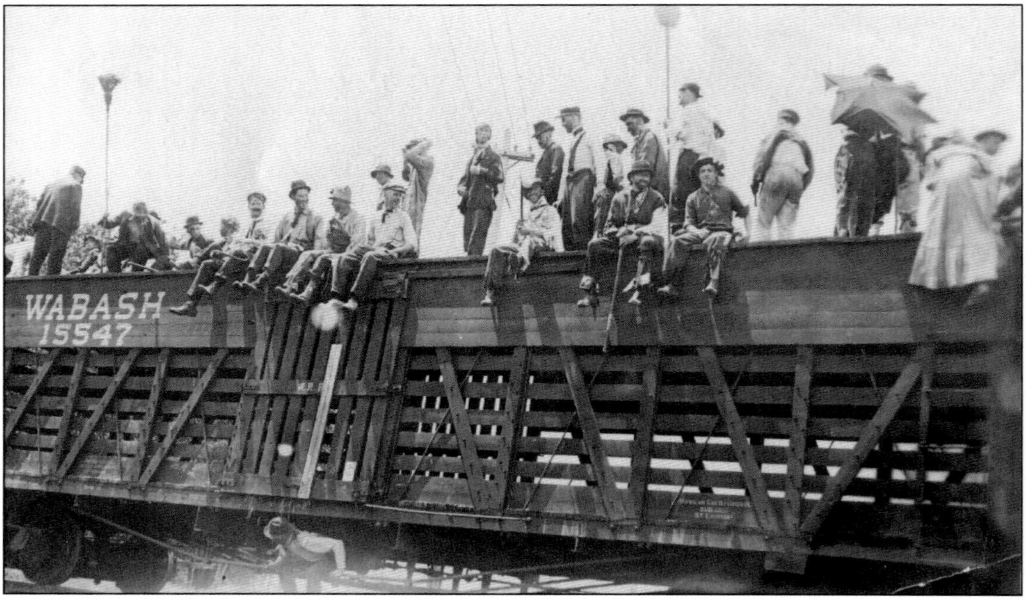

With a uniformed train employee at far left, participants in a Columbia hobo convention stand and sit atop a Wabash Railroad livestock car sometime between 1910 and 1914. The Wabash Railroad ran a short-line connector route between Columbia and Centralia. The markings at lower right on the car identify it as one made by American Car & Foundry Co. at its St. Charles location, in the St. Louis area. The company was for years a major manufacturer of passenger cars, refrigerated rail cars, and trolley cars.

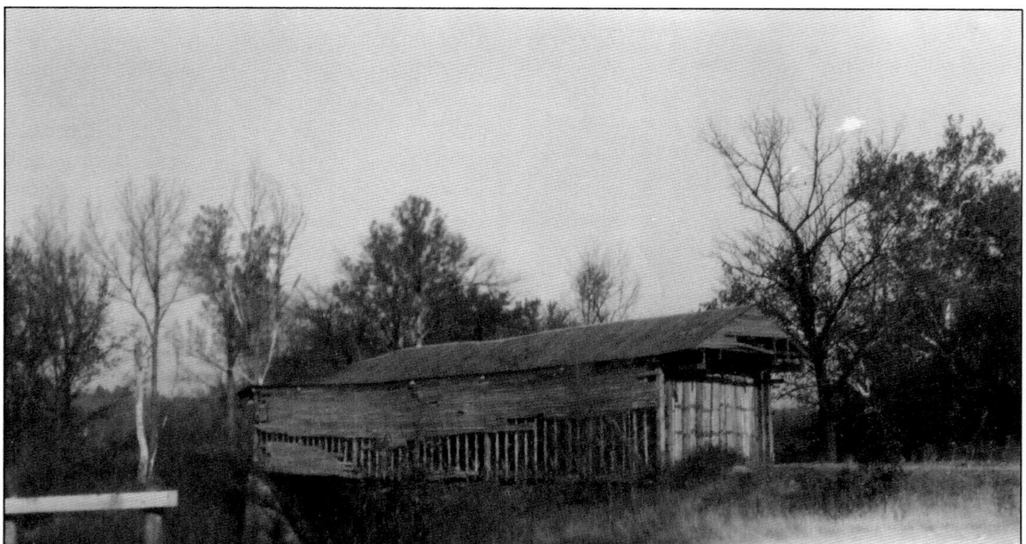

A wooden bridge was built across Perche Creek west of Columbia in 1833. It was well traveled by settlers heading west. Flooding in 1849 destroyed the bridge, hindering the flow of traffic and mail delivery. A replacement covered bridge (pictured) was erected in 1851–1852. It was built to last, with native oak crossbeams, iron support posts forged in Columbia, and rock quarried nearby.

The state improved the road across the bridge in 1912 and made it the first cross-state roadway, Highway 2. It became part of US Route 40 in 1925. Before the Missouri, Kansas & Texas Railroad connector route between Columbia and Rocheport arrived in 1899, a large wagon transported people and supplies from Missouri River boats to Columbia. The bridge closed in the 1920s, and was destroyed in 1931.

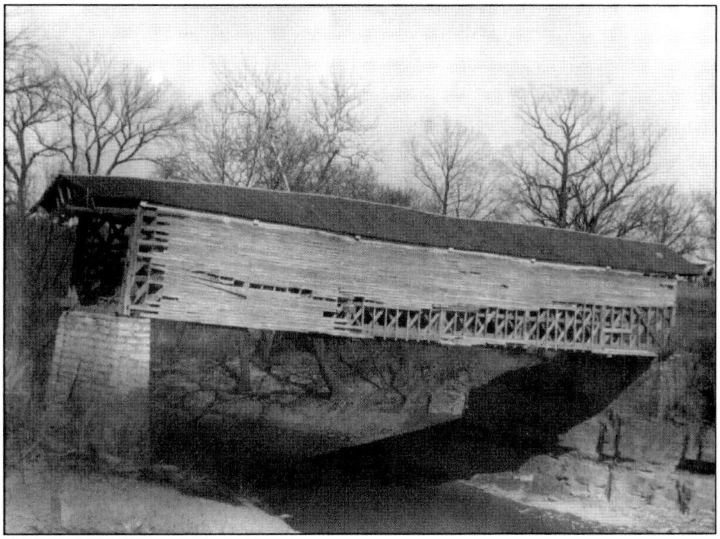

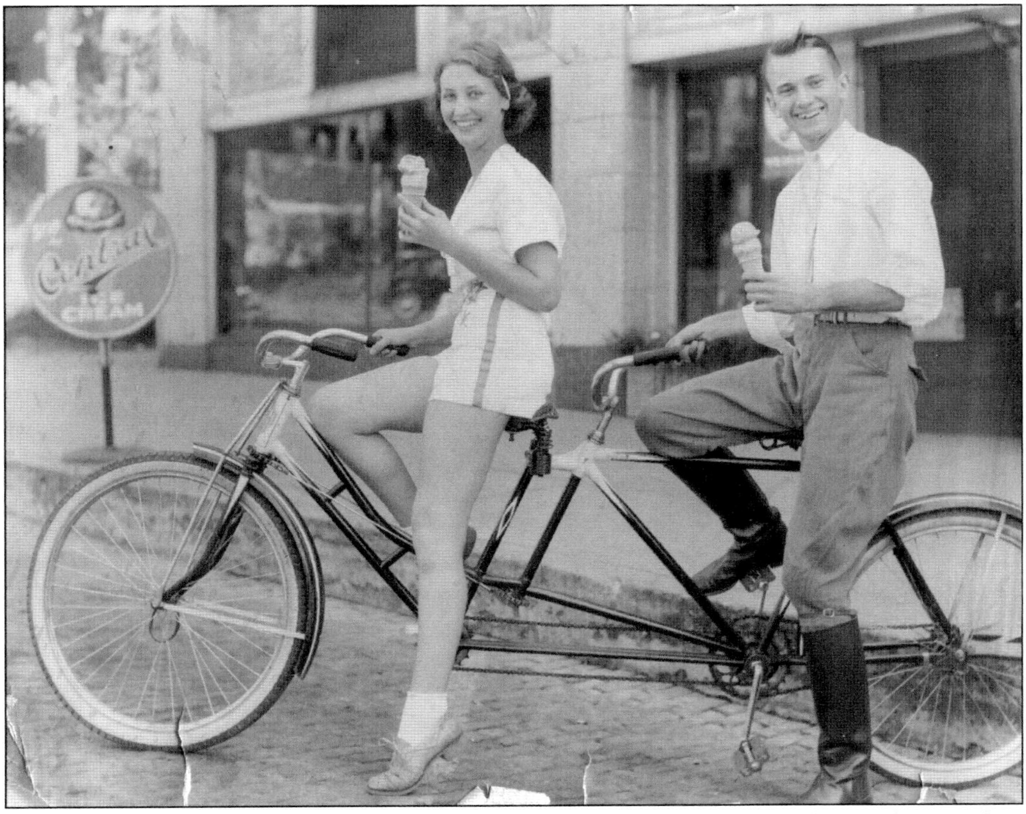

Bicycles have been a popular transportation choice for generations of Columbia residents. When Central Dairy began selling ice-cream cones, students discovered a new favorite hangout. The dairy's downtown location made it convenient to students of Stephens College, Christian College, and the university. This couple enjoys double ice-cream cones after a tandem bike ride.

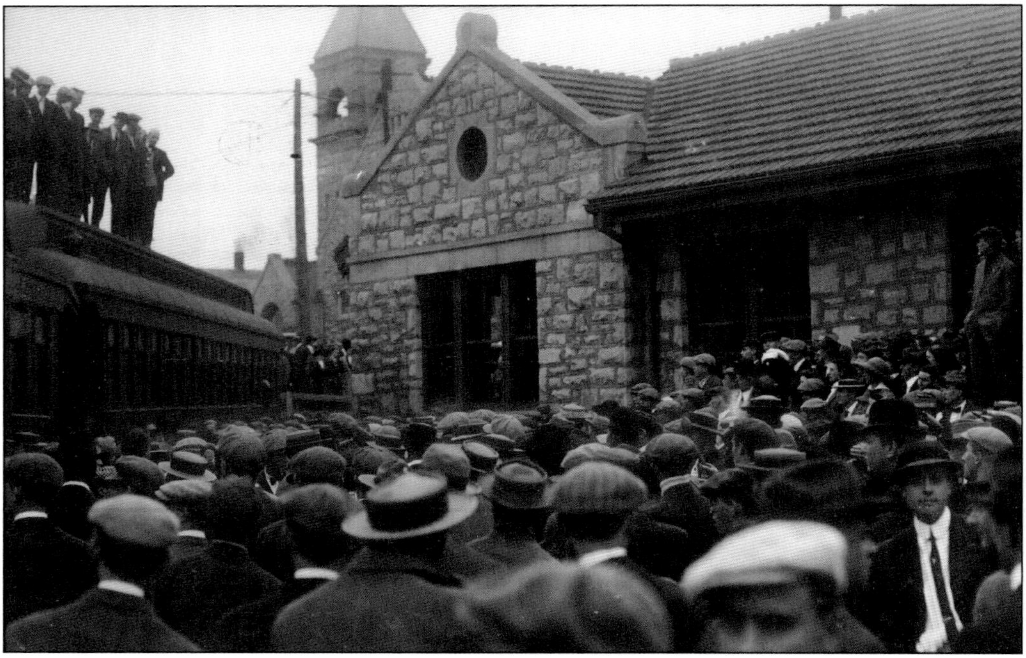

Train service arrived in Columbia in 1867. The Wabash Station and Freight House on North Tenth Street opened in July 1910. It was built of locally quarried stone at a cost of approximately $15,000. The name "Wabash" is carved into the stone on three sides. "Columbia" is carved in stone facing the tracks. It was considered a combination depot, serving both passengers and freight until 1964. Today, it is Columbia's transit station.

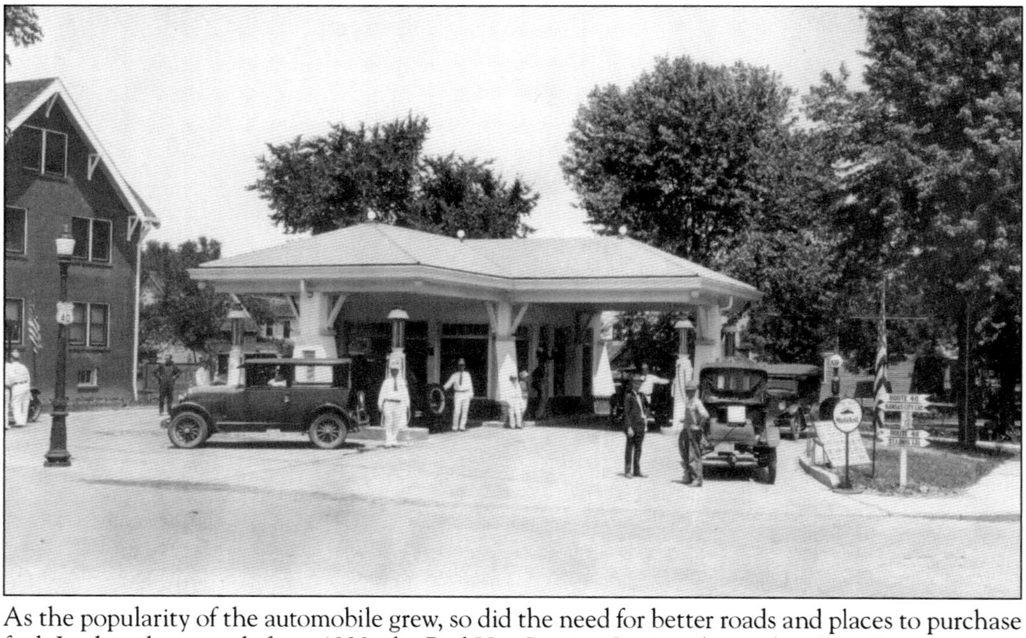

As the popularity of the automobile grew, so did the need for better roads and places to purchase fuel. In this photograph from 1920, the Red Hat Service Station, located on East Broadway, is a busy place. White-uniformed employees are ready to dispense gas and Mobil oil and to provide whatever services drivers needed. It was the first Columbia station with toilets. Small signs show distances to St. Louis and Kansas City.

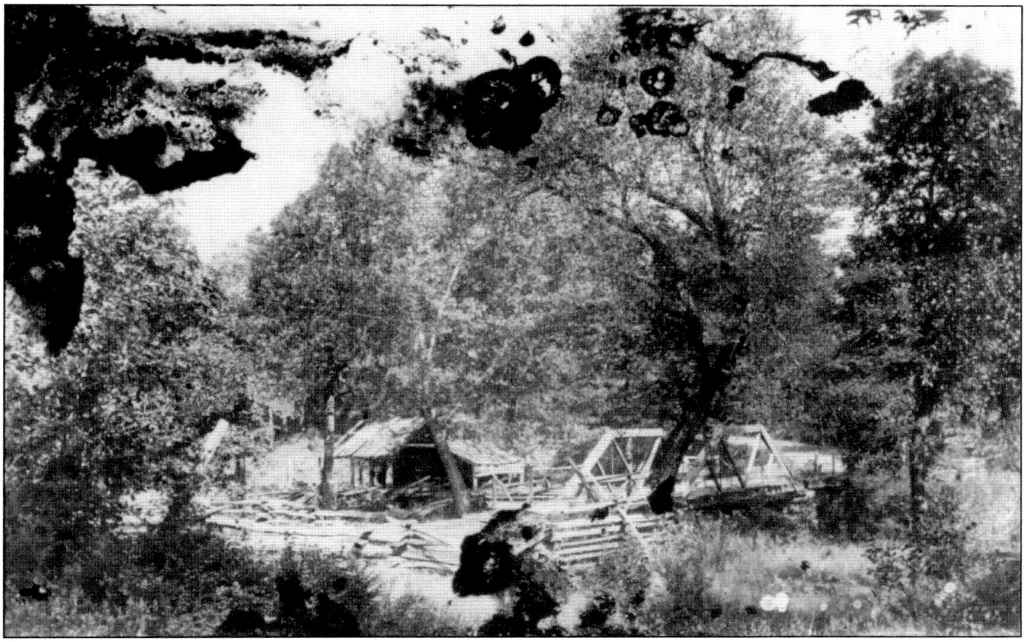

This idyllic scene from around 1920 shows the primitive Bonne Femme Bridge and a split-rail fence near Little Bonne Femme Church. The area is just off Old US Route 63 south of Columbia. This bridge was replaced in 1925 by a concrete tee-beam bridge, which still exists. Bonne Femme Creek and Little Bonne Femme Creek flow southwest, eventually emptying into the Missouri River.

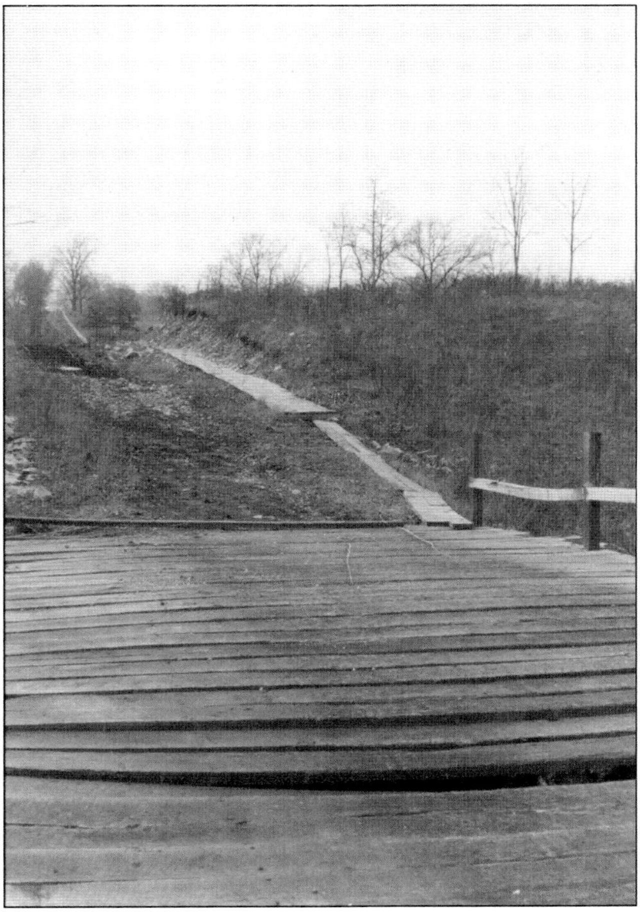

In the late 19th century, all roads leading to Columbia looked much like this. Roadways were mostly unimproved, filled with ruts and rocks. Heavy rains made many of them impassable, as wagon and carriage wheels became mired in the mud. The Columbia and Missouri River Plank Road Company formed in 1856. Bridges across Columbia's various creeks were primitive, made with long planks and wooden supports.

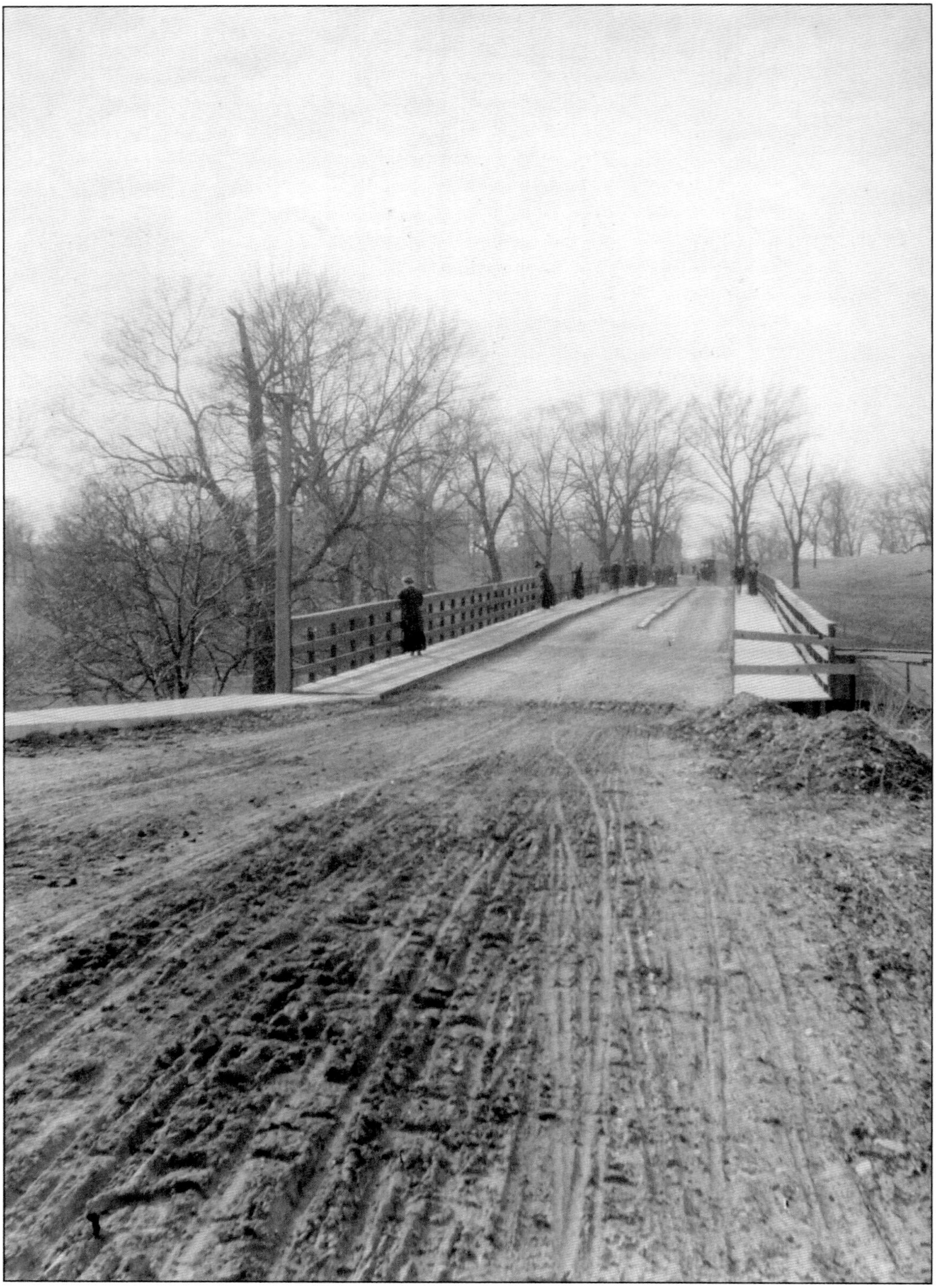

The 20th century brought additional residents, and along with them, the need for improved roads and services. Some bridge decks soon had a smoother finish and sturdy safety railings. This bridge even had pedestrian walking areas and a small divider to help carriages pass safely without colliding, but times were changing. Fred Niedermeyer soon opened Columbia's first automobile dealership on South Ninth Street.

Four

Out and About in the Business Community

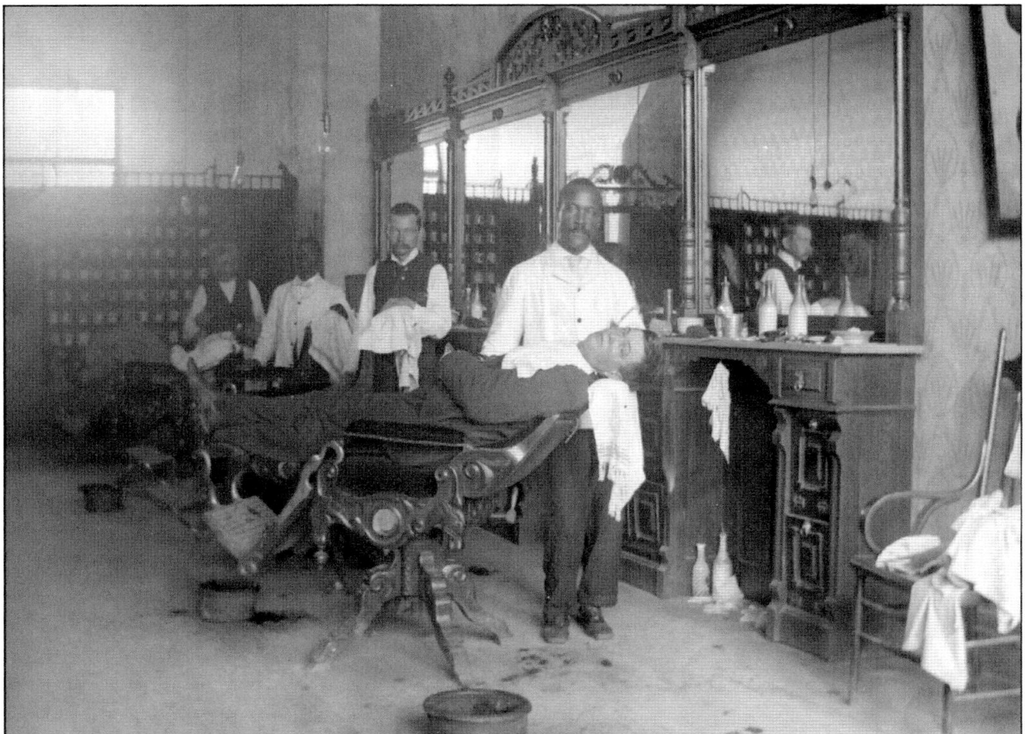

Barbershops were popular places in 1896, when this photograph was taken. Mustaches were in style. Jake Sellinger Barber Shop, located on Broadway between Eighth and Ninth Streets, had numerous regular customers. The back wall is filled with individual shaving mugs. Tools essential to a good shave were a mug of soap worked into lather, a straight razor, and a strop or honing device to keep the razor's blade sharp.

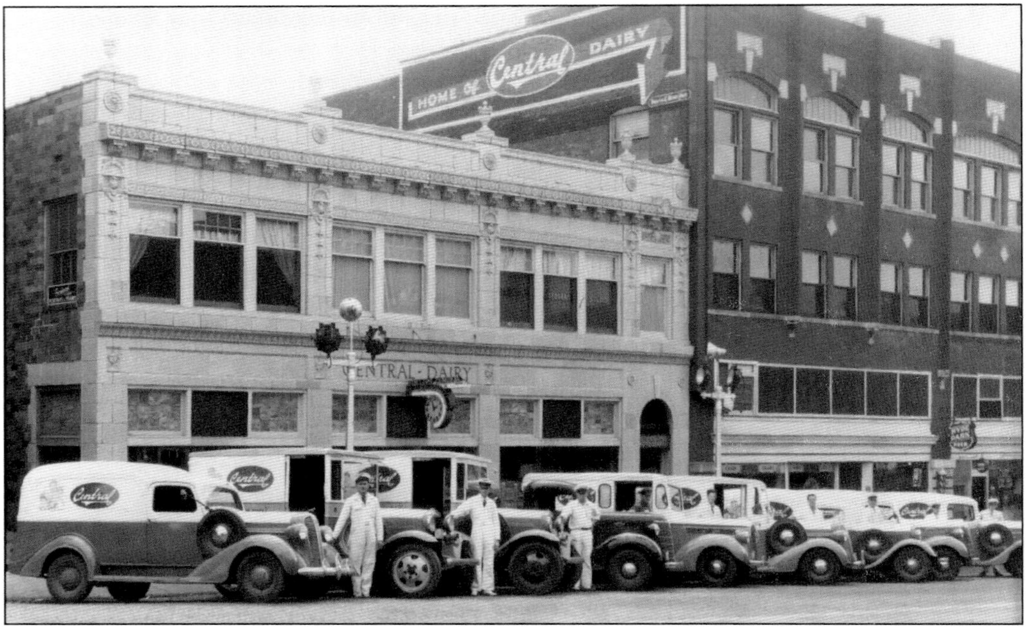

Central Dairy began operations in Columbia in 1920. The building shown here on East Broadway was constructed in 1927 and featured terra-cotta ornamentation. With its close proximity to Columbia's three colleges, it became a favorite student hangout. The company has moved, but this building still exists and is listed in the National Register of Historic Places.

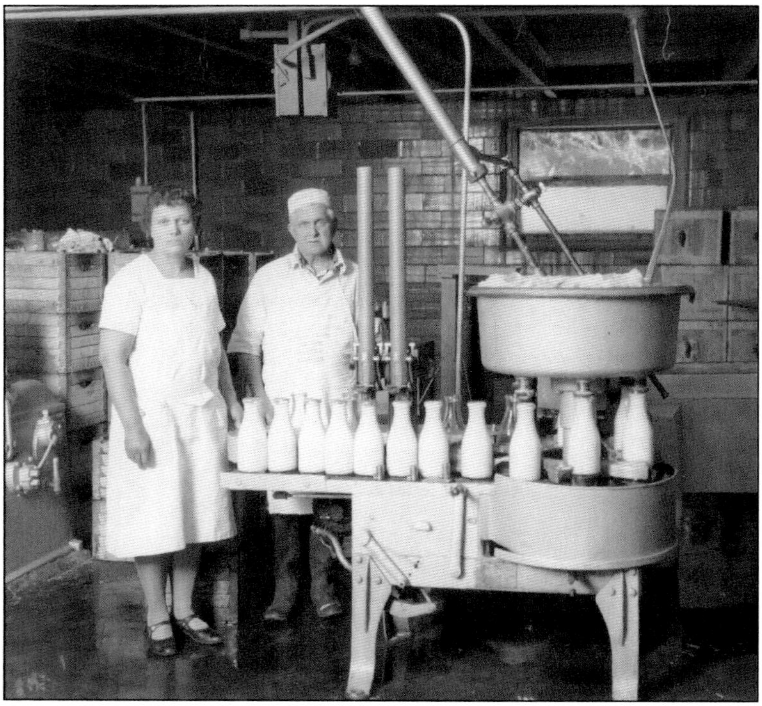

Central Dairy was a small operation by today's standards. As the 20th century progressed, mechanical advances were introduced that saved time and production expenses. These two serious-faced employees washed and sterilized glass bottles before placing them on an automated conveyor to be filled with fresh milk. The bottles were then sealed with paper caps. A company slogan stated: "Central—Perfectly Pasteurized Dairy Products."

Automation and the addition of improved processing equipment increased production capabilities at Central Dairy. Enhanced cooling equipment allowed the company to produce and distribute various dairy products, including ice cream, butter, and cottage cheese. This photograph from the 1930s shows an employee filling canisters with creamy dairy product.

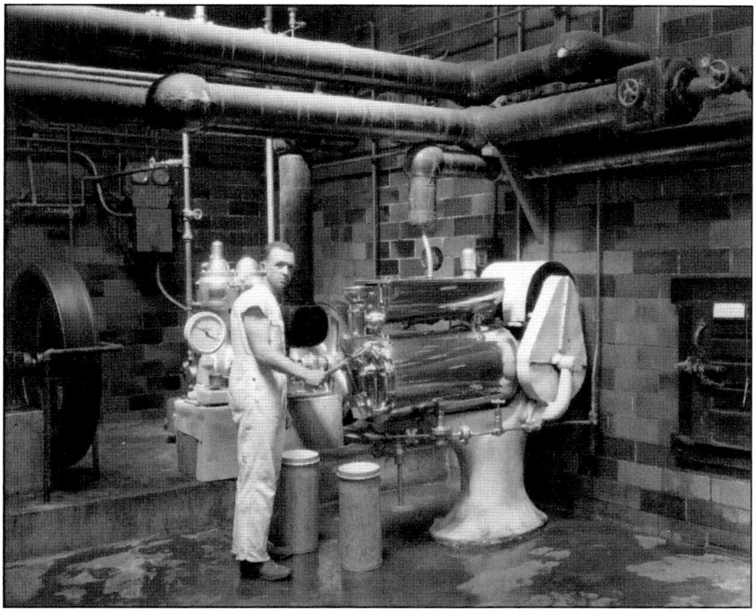

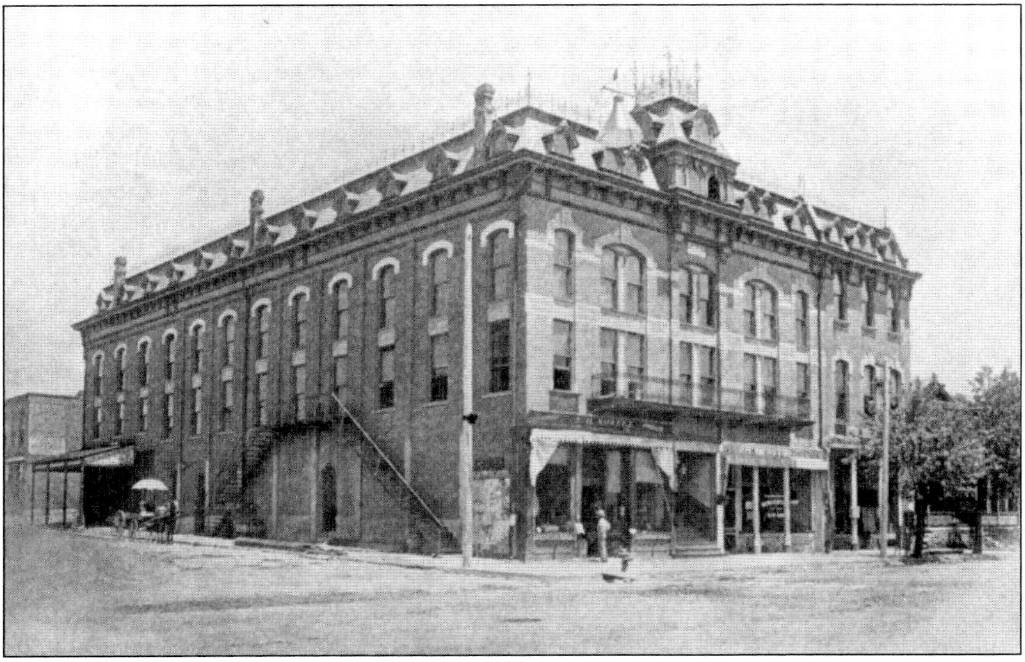

Haden Opera House, located at the corner of Ninth Street and Broadway, was built in 1884. Columbia's first motion picture was shown here in 1897. Columbia's high school held commencement exercises at the opera house in May 1898. The 21 seniors made up the largest graduating class in the school's history. The building was destroyed by fire in 1901.

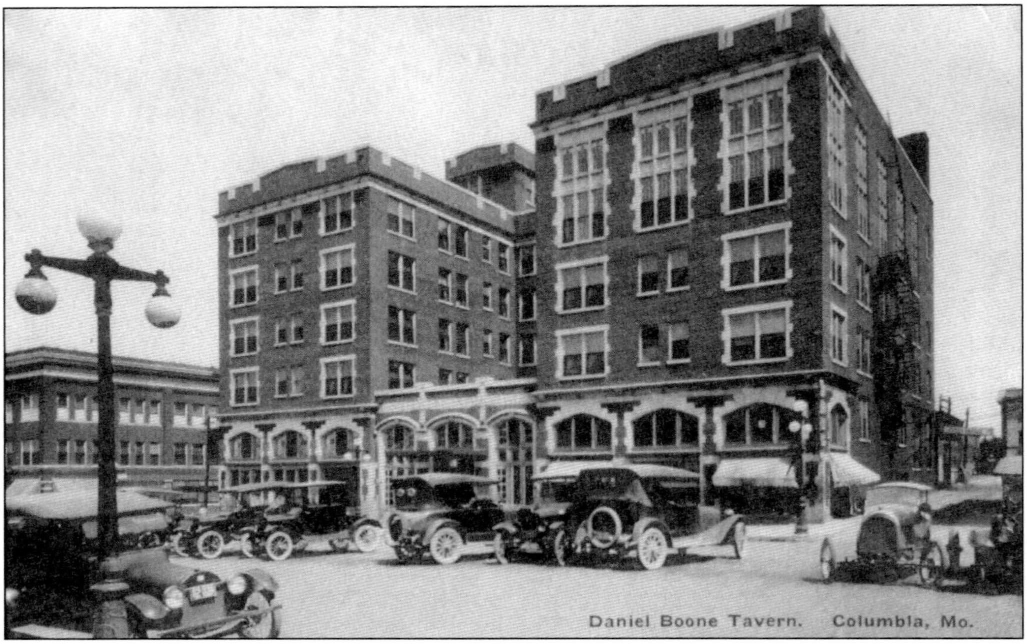

Daniel Boone Tavern/Hotel, located on Broadway, was built in 1917 when city leaders decided Columbia needed an upscale hotel. Citizens raised money to help with construction costs. It featured 100 rooms and 50 bathrooms, and remained a hostelry until the 1970s. Since then, it has housed government offices. The five-story building features limestone detailing. A limestone insert carved with the hotel's name still graces the building's front entry.

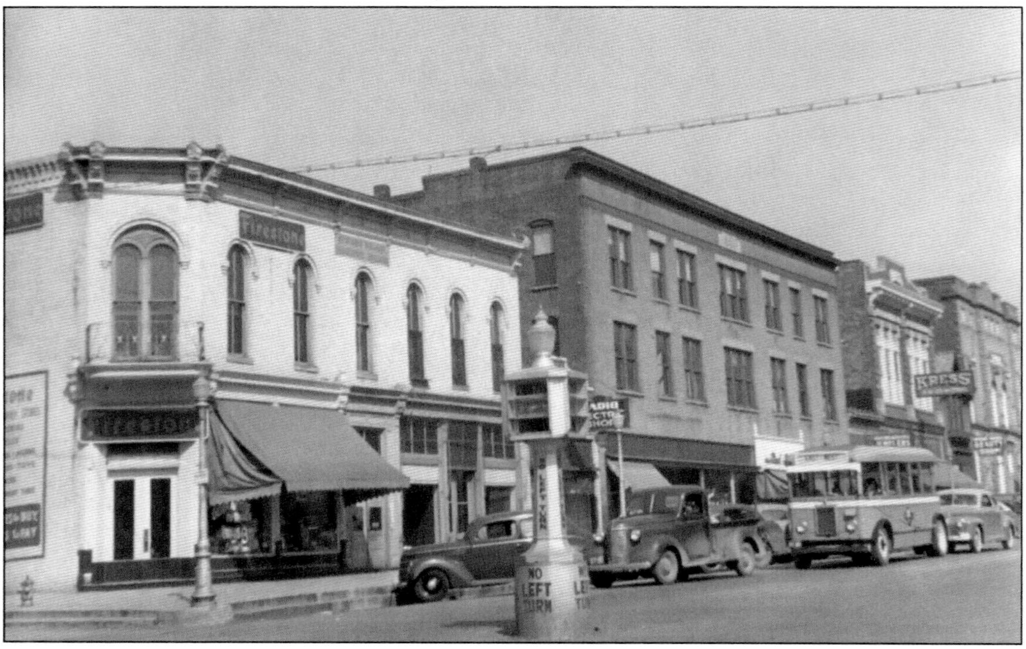

Broadway was a busy place in 1941. Businesses along the block between Tenth and Hitt Streets included a Firestone store, a radio and electric shop, Buchkroeder's Jewelry Store, a Kress store, and a beauty shop. Buchkroeder's, established in 1911, remains in business. The 1909 Kress Building is listed in the National Register of Historic Places.

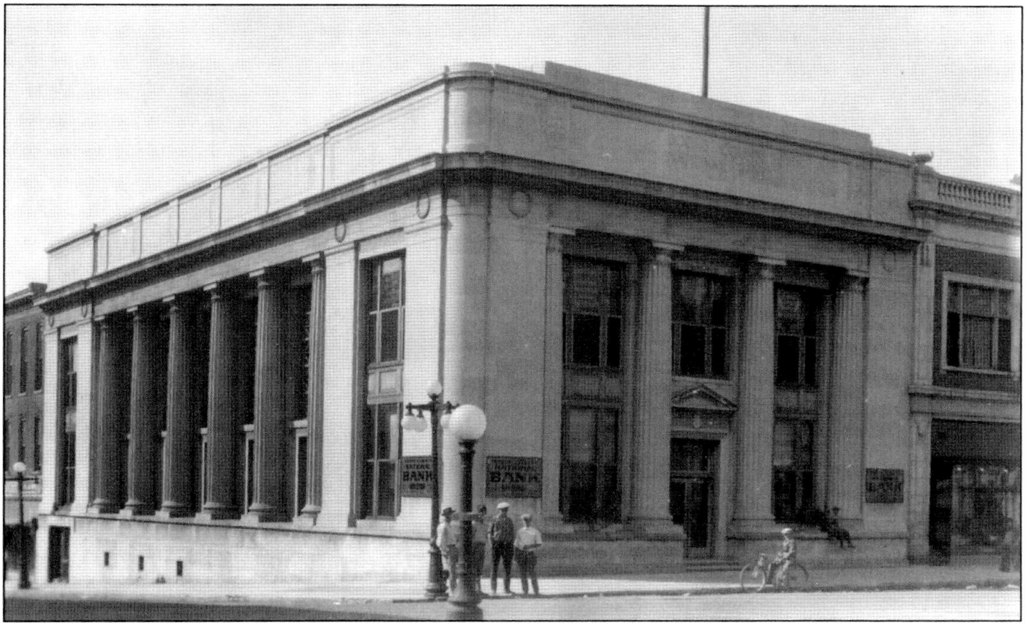

Boone County National Bank has a long history in Columbia. Founded in 1857, it became the first national bank in Missouri in 1871. It sold Liberty Loan Bonds during World War I. The Classical Revival building, shown here around 1927, has stood at the corner of Eighth Street and Broadway since 1916. The building's rows of Doric columns have made it a recognizable downtown landmark for generations of Columbia residents.

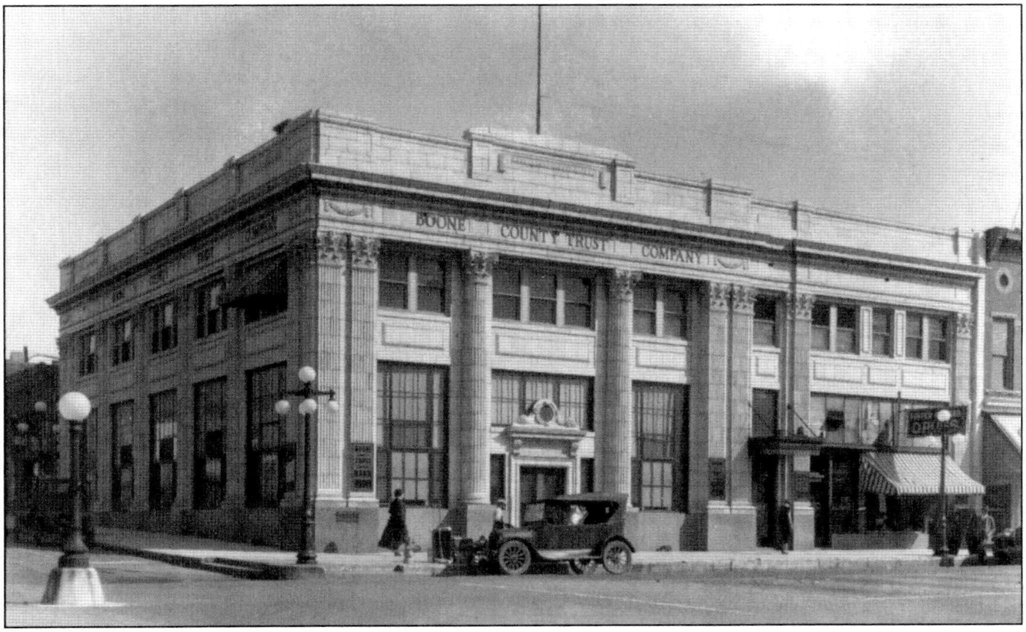

Shown here in 1927, Boone County Trust Company, at Ninth Street and Broadway, has occupied this site since 1921. The location was important in Columbia's history. Settlers built a tavern there in 1833. Female postmaster Anne Hawkins Gentry ran the post office from there for many years. In the 1870s, the site held a theater, followed by a grocery and a drugstore. Today, it operates as Boone National Savings and Loan.

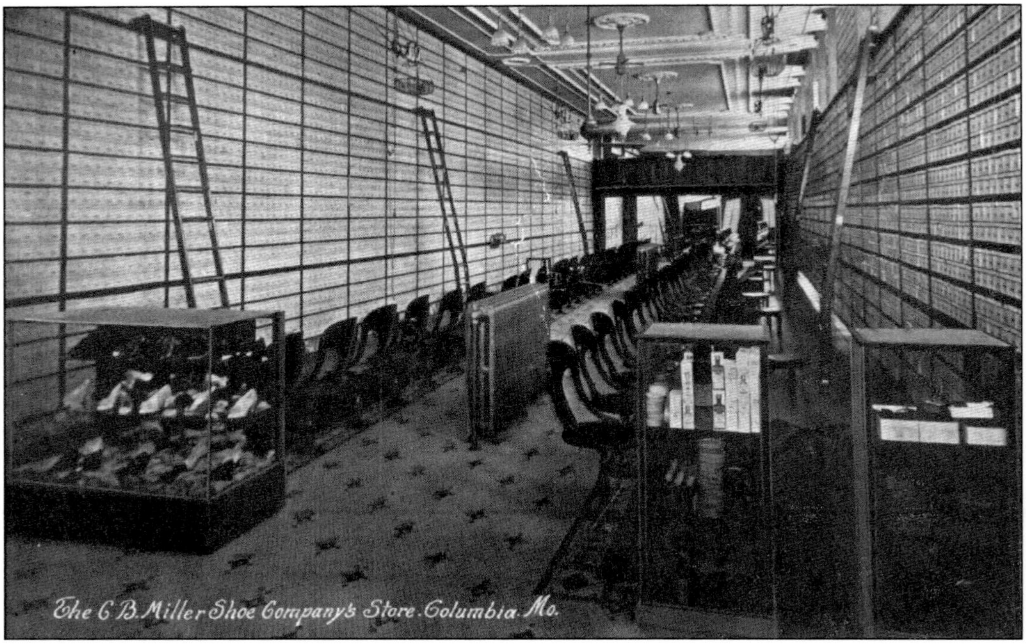

Charles Ballentine Miller, a University of Missouri student, became a shoe-store clerk at age 18. Time passed, and he became a well-known shoe retailer, opening C.B. Miller Shoe Store (pictured) at Eighth Street and Broadway. Miller was active in Columbia's civic life as a member of various organizations and boards of directors. He married Helen Conley, daughter of Columbia pioneer Sanford F. Conley, in 1903.

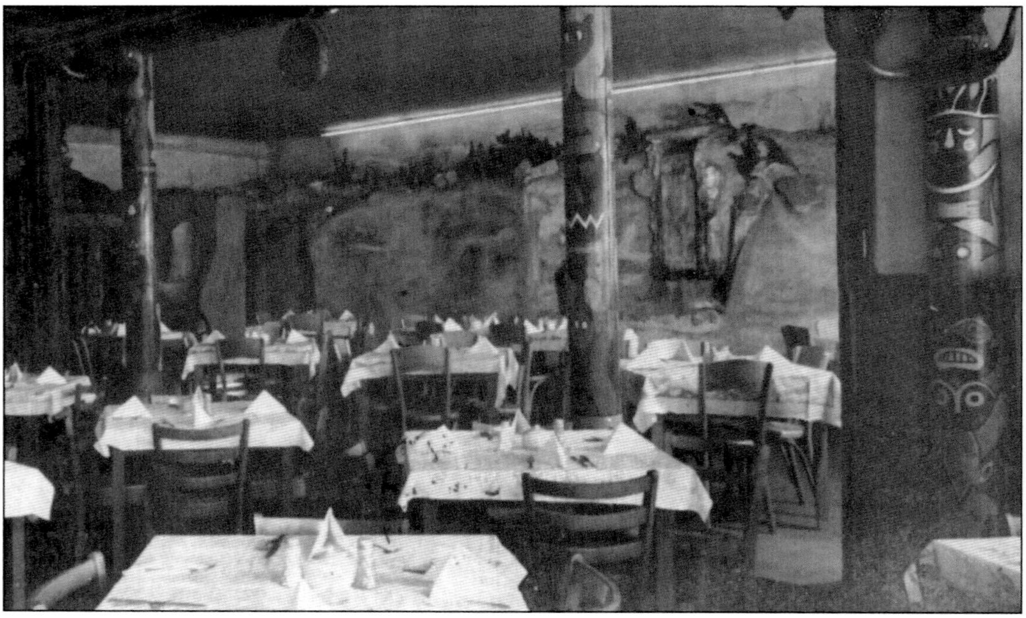

Before Interstate 70, the east-west roadway across Missouri was US Route 40, and it came through Columbia. Automobile traffic meant a demand for restaurants. Columbia's Wigwam Café was located on US 40. Its lavish Native American–themed décor made it a popular stop during the middle of the 20th century. Proprietor Frank Fenton advertised: "At the Sign of the Wooden Indian—Hiway40. Everything to Eat from a Rattlesnake Sandwich to a 2-lb. Porterhouse Steak."

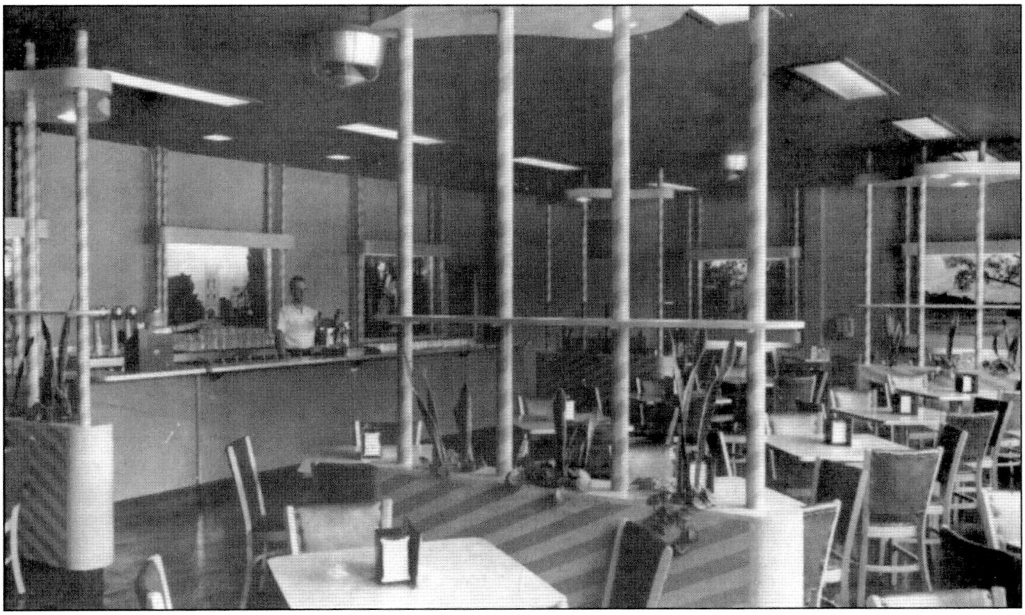

Central Dairy's location on Broadway made it accessible to students from all three Columbia colleges. By the 1940s, the dairy's ice cream was so popular that an ice-cream parlor called The Peppermint Room opened upstairs. Peppermint ice cream was one of the company's popular flavors. With support columns painted like peppermint sticks, the eatery became a local hangout.

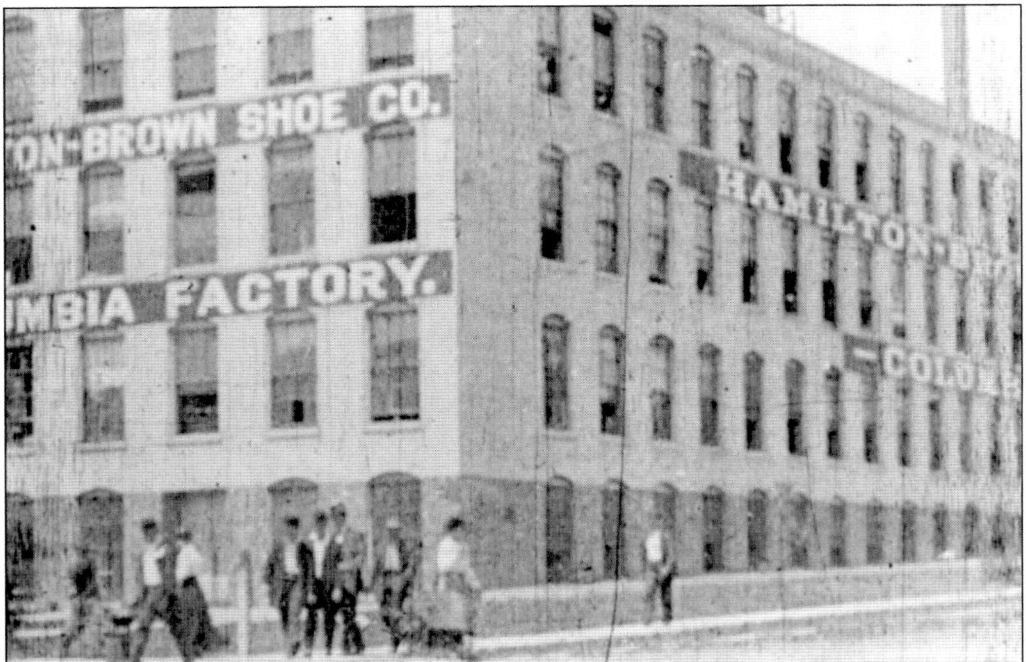

Columbia's first industrial manufacturing operation opened in 1907. Brown Shoe Company of St. Louis built the Hamilton-Brown Shoe Factory, a three-story, rectangular building at the corner of Wilkes Boulevard and Fay Street. It employed approximately 300–350 people. Nearby railroad tracks enhanced distribution. The company remained until 1939, when it became the only local firm to close permanently during the Depression. The building is a National Register property.

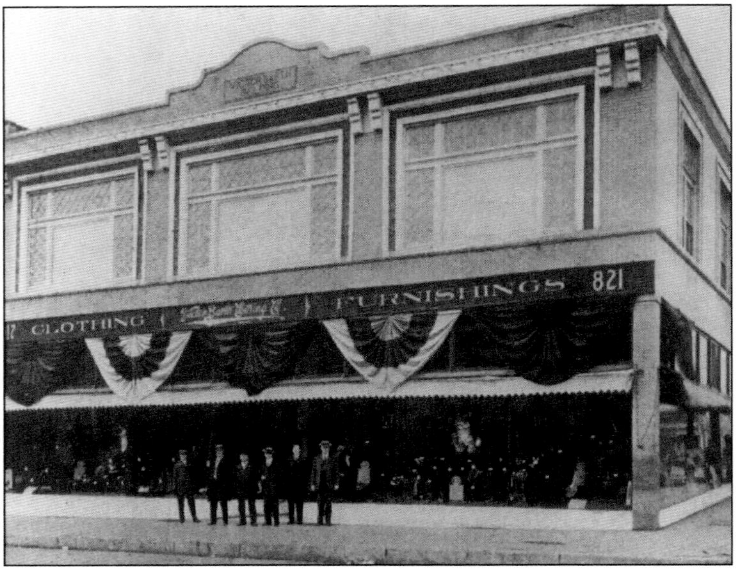

Moses Barth moved to Columbia to open a retail store in 1865; three years later, his nephews Victor and Joseph were running the store. Victor bought out his brother's interests in 1906 and ran the store until his death in 1909. The following year, family members constructed a new building on the Broadway site (pictured) and named it for Victor. Barth's remained in business until 1987.

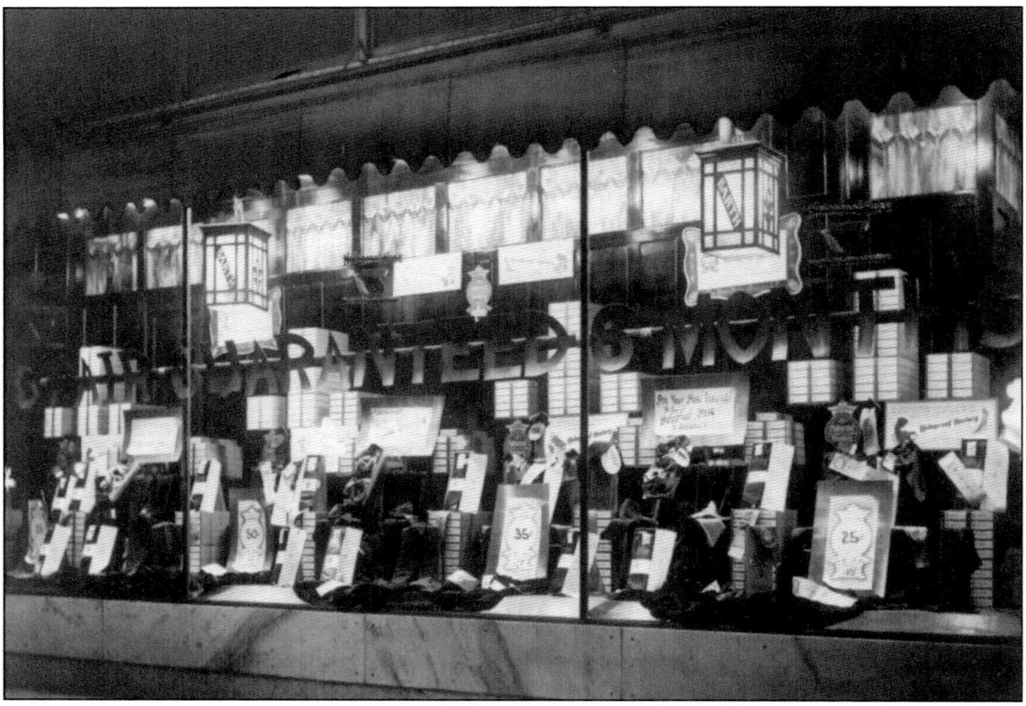

The Victor Barth Clothing Store advertised itself as "Everybody's Store." This c. 1915 photograph shows the store's elaborate Broadway display window. In 1916, the company announced the decision to no longer hold discount sales, claiming that sales "lower the standards of quality" and are "unfair and unjust to the general public." The store said, "We are always desirous of protecting the best interests of our customers."

Victor Barth was a successful Columbia businessman in the 1880s when he posed for a photograph with his son Irvin. A native of Prussia, he arrived in Columbia in 1866. He quickly rose from peddling wares on horseback, to clerking, then to owning his own company. Irvin graduated with honors from the university in 1897 and from Harvard University. He left Columbia and the family business to practice law in St. Louis.

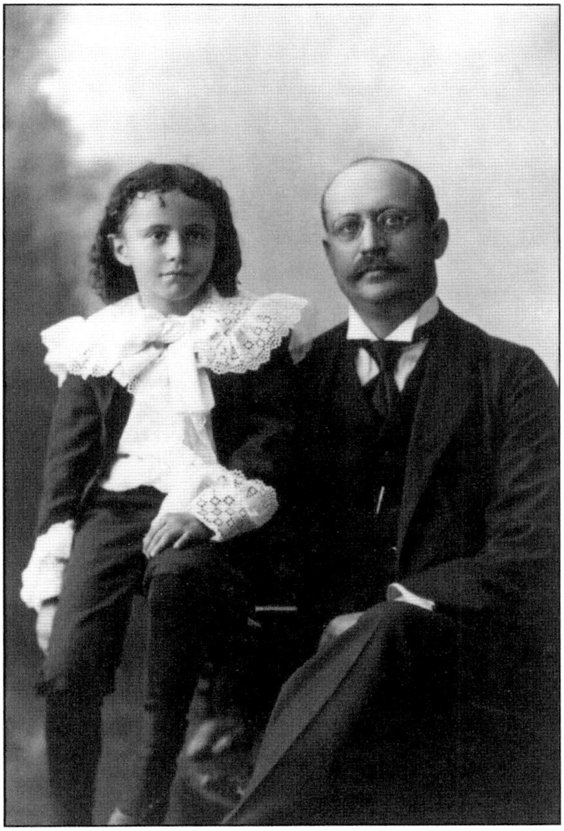

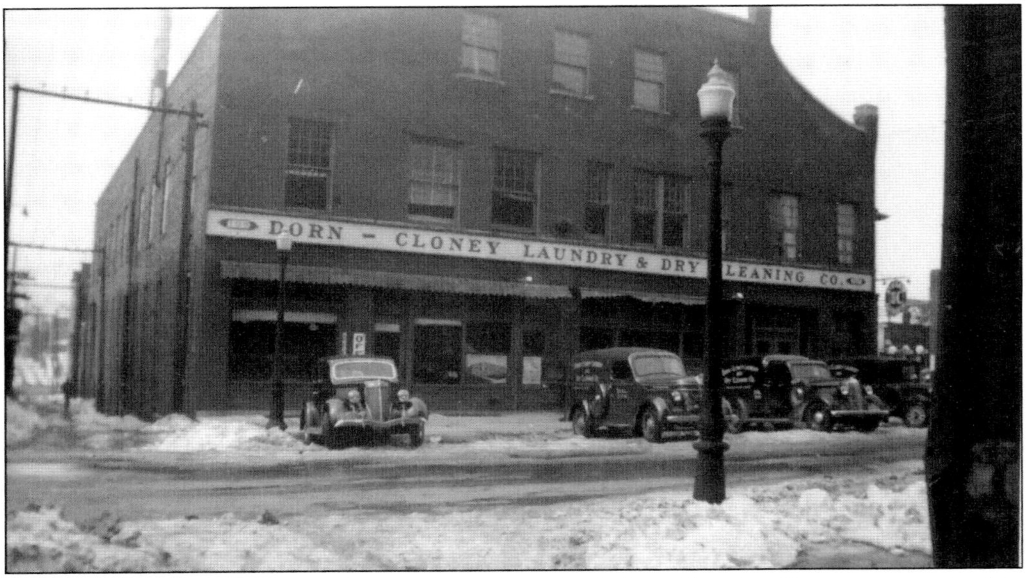

Established in the early 1900s, Dorn-Cloney Laundry & Dry Cleaning Company remained in business more than 100 years. To attract student customers, the company in 1921 offered a cash prize to the university journalism student who submitted a winning advertising idea. The company's advertisement in a 1922 Kiwanis Club program read, "Life is too sweet to kill yourself doing the family washing—We can satisfy you with one of our many services."

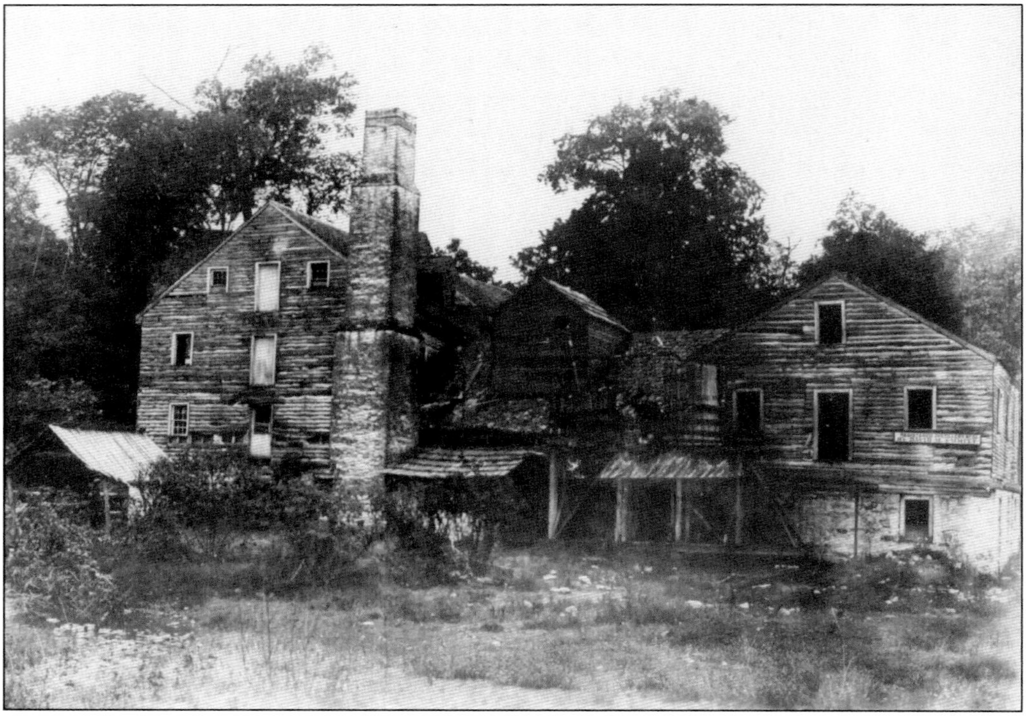

A natural, 100-foot-wide rock bridge spans Little Bonne Femme Creek south of Columbia. Early residents soon harnessed the power of the water and built a mill there. By the 1860s, a distillery had been built. David Martin Emmitt moved to Boone County from Ohio, and in 1872 bought the Rock Bridge property, which included the distillery (shown here in the 1880s), a store, and 800 acres of land.

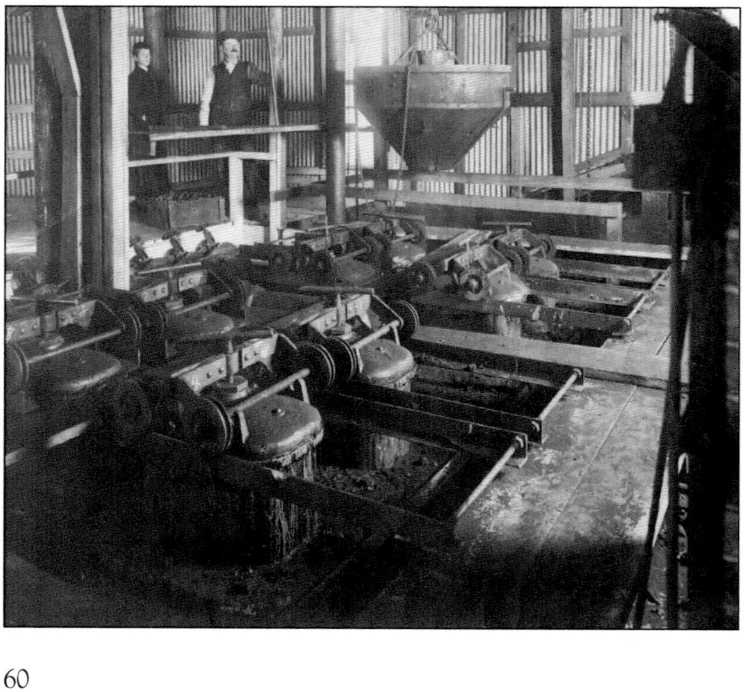

Before the days of natural-gas pipelines, power plants heated coal with steam and produced a burnable gas. Columbia Coal Gas Company, owned by Odon Guitar, provided the city with gas for heat and light from 1875 until 1932. The company was located on the banks of Flat Branch, a good water source near the Wabash Railroad Station. Coal shipments for the company arrived on railroad cars.

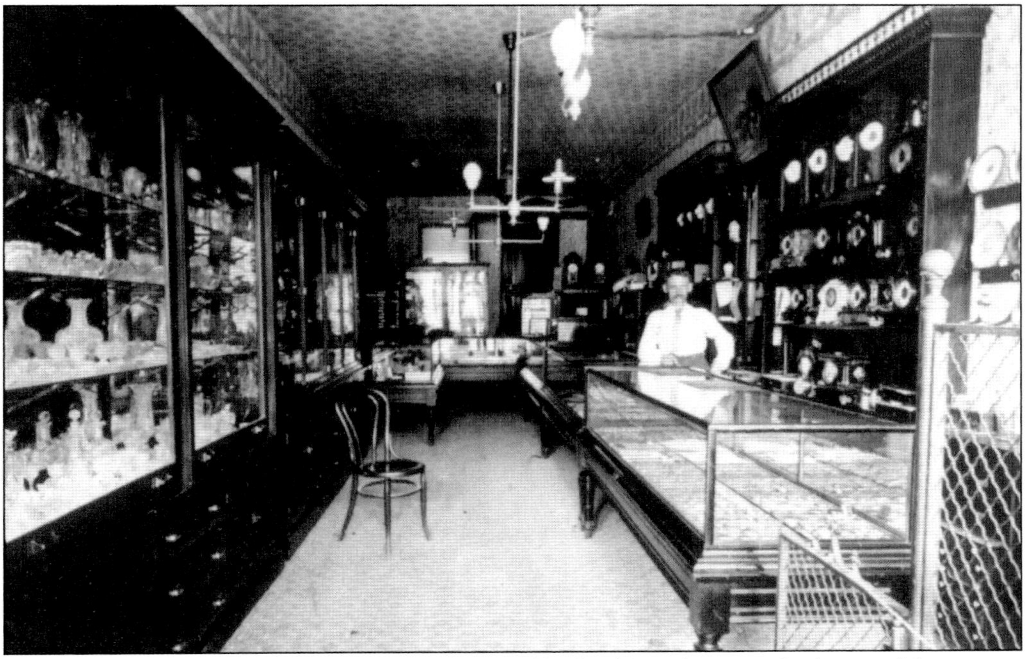

Henninger Jewelry Store was located in the 800 block of Broadway, in the heart of downtown Columbia. Owner Frederick Albert Henninger poses beside a display case in 1902. Henninger was also an inventor. He applied for and was granted patents in 1889 and 1902, including one for eyeglass frames.

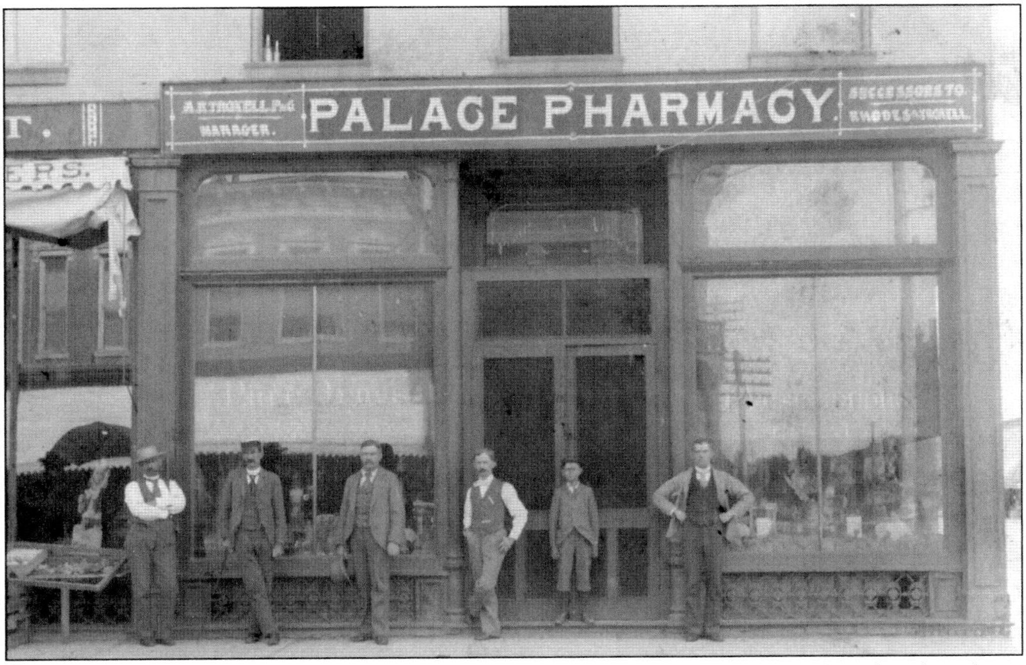

A.R. Troxell's Palace Pharmacy had the words "purity" and "accuracy" painted on the glass above the front door. Before the days of large drug manufacturers, pharmacists mixed and packaged their own medical compounds. According to the *Columbia Daily Tribune*, Columbia had 23 practicing physicians and five dentists in 1901.

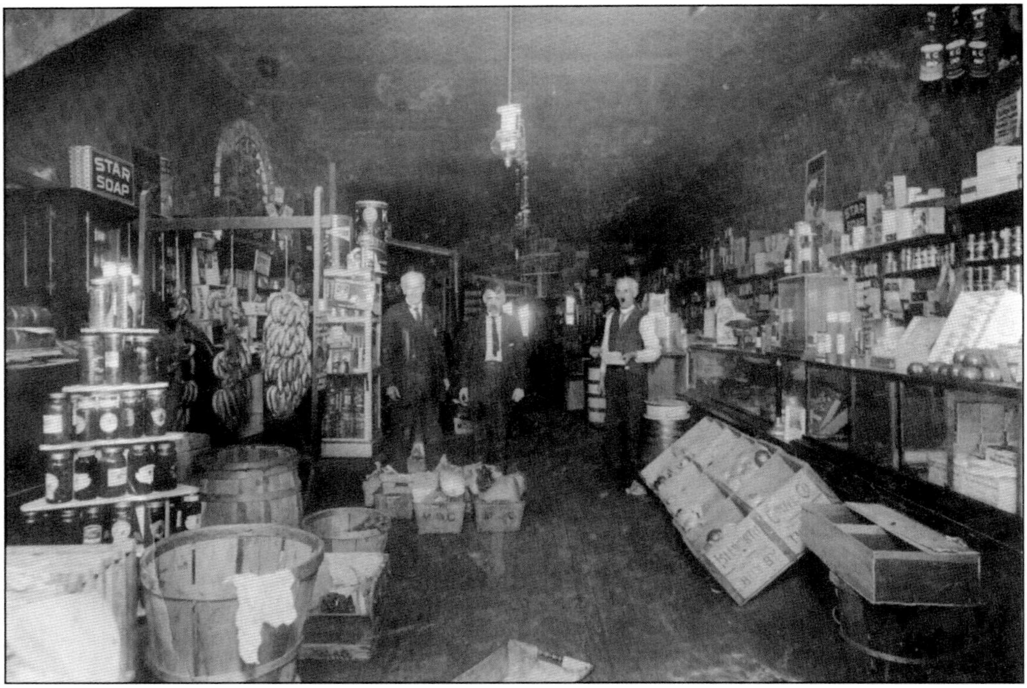

Baker, Shaeffer & Scott Grocers was located at 812 East Broadway. This 1916 photograph shows a fully stocked store, complete with displays for Crisco, Aunt Jemima products, Quaker Oats, and Star Soap. Baskets and crates filled with fresh produce line the store's narrow wooden floor. Before the days of self-service supermarkets, store employees personally helped customers select their purchases. Columbia had numerous groceries and meat markets.

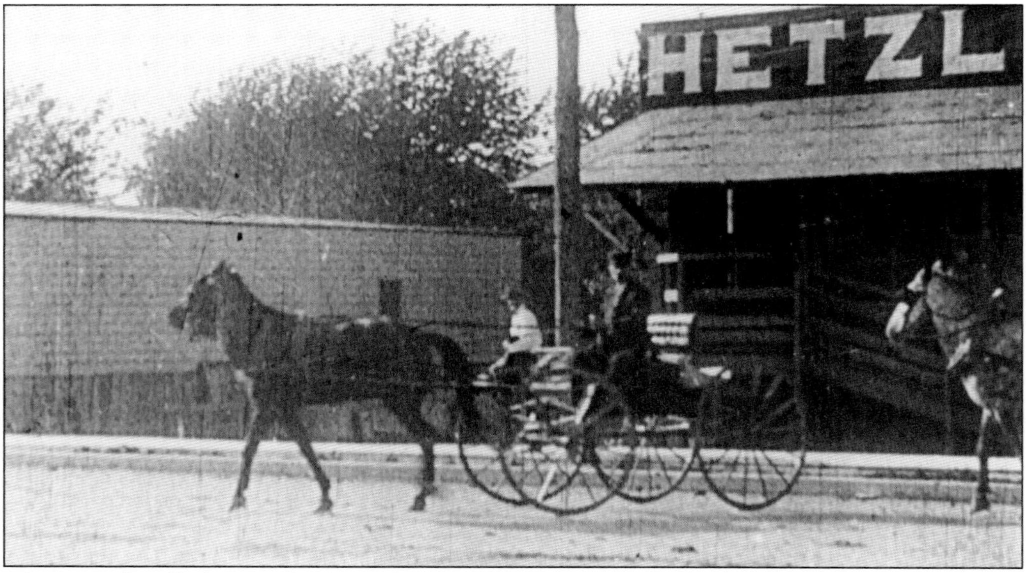

Johann and Wilhelm Hetzler formed Hetzler Brothers' Ice Plant and Packing House in 1905. A 1916 issue of the trade publication *Ice and Refrigeration Illustrated* reported on Hetzler Brothers' big news: the addition of a refrigerating machine and brine cooler. The company slogan was "Hetzler Products, where quality and sanitation reign supreme." Wilhelm was elected mayor in 1927. The brothers were active in The Commercial Club, the chamber of commerce's predecessor.

J.A. Hudson established the Columbia Telephone Exchange to provide telephone service to local subscribers. An operator sat at this switchboard and manually connected calls from one subscriber to another. Columbia had 85 subscribers when this photograph was taken around 1898. Also that year, the Missouri Independent Telephone Association was formed by 30 telephone exchanges throughout the state. J.A. Hudson was selected chairman. He added switchboards and long lines as needed.

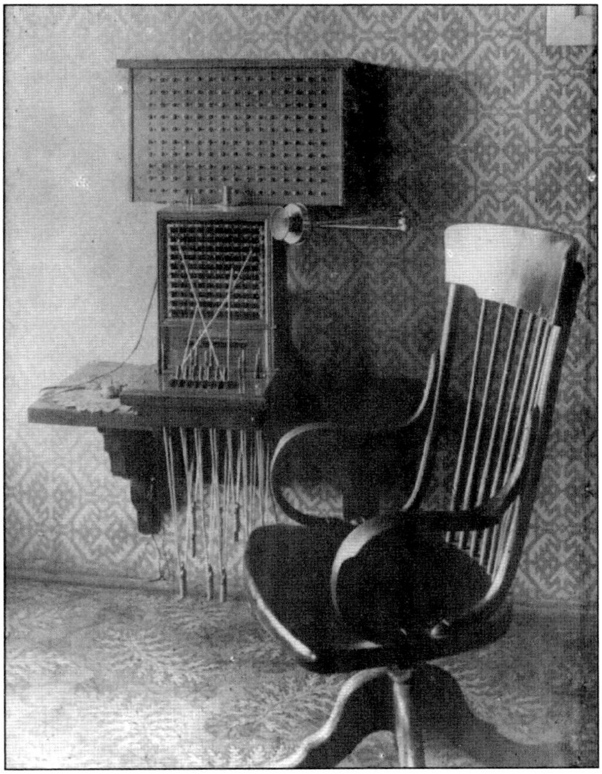

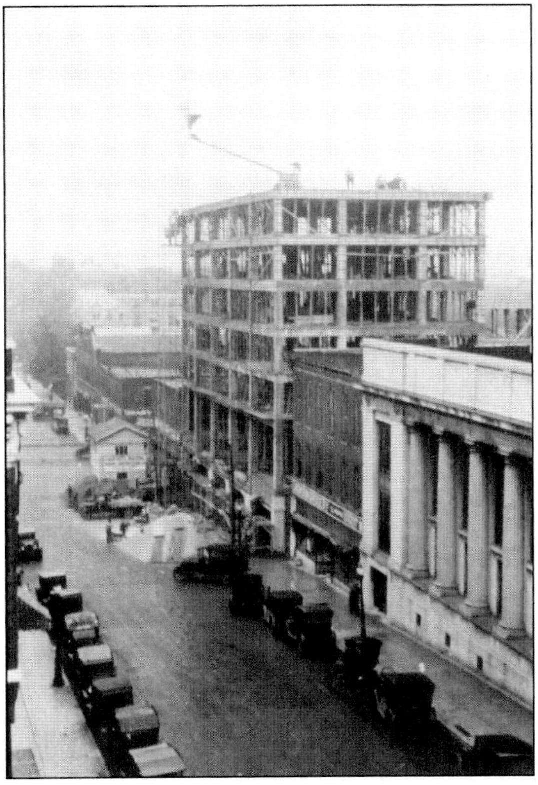

The Tiger Hotel, at 23 South Eighth Street, was under construction when this photograph was taken in 1924. Boone County Bank and Jackson Grocery can be seen nearby. When it opened in 1928, the Beaux-Arts hotel was Columbia's tallest building, at 10 stories. It provided shelter during countless parents' weekends and home football games. Today, the Tiger Hotel is a luxury boutique hotel with 62 rooms.

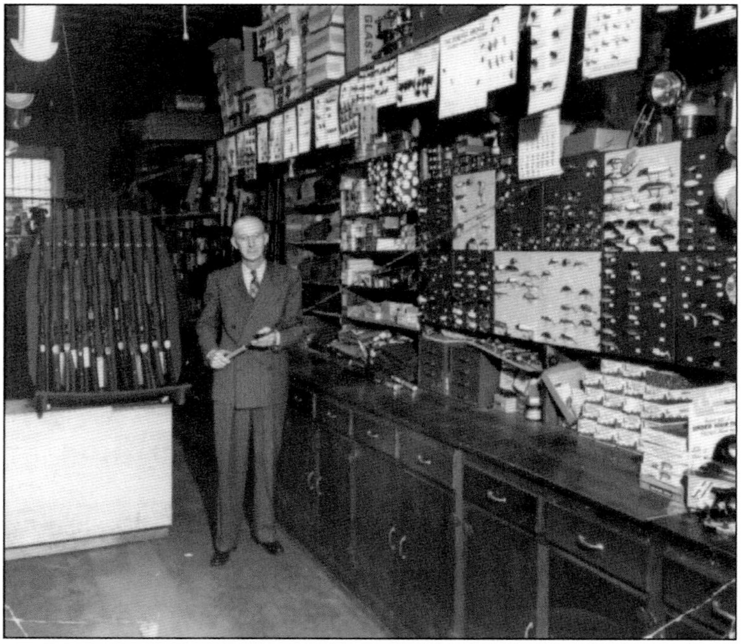

Orlie Anderson's Hardware & Appliance Store, located at Ninth and Walnut Streets, offered a variety of merchandise including sporting goods and student room supplies. Fishing lures, guns, washing machines, coffee pots, trash cans, lightbulbs, and General Electric appliances also could be found there.

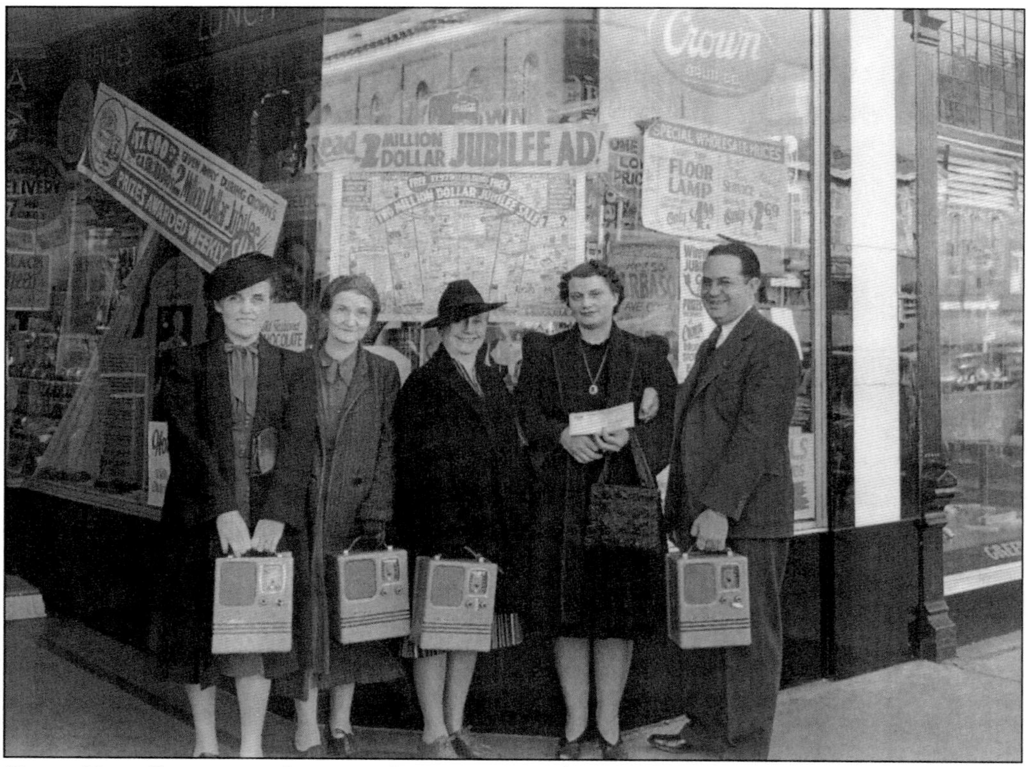

Crown Drug Company, a longtime fixture on Broadway, was part of the regional Crown Drug Company chain. Then as now, promotions and sweepstakes were successful in drawing customers to stores. The Columbia residents shown here around 1940 were winners in the company's 2 Million Dollar Jubilee. Prizes included a check and Detrola radios. Detrola was a popular brand from 1931 until 1948.

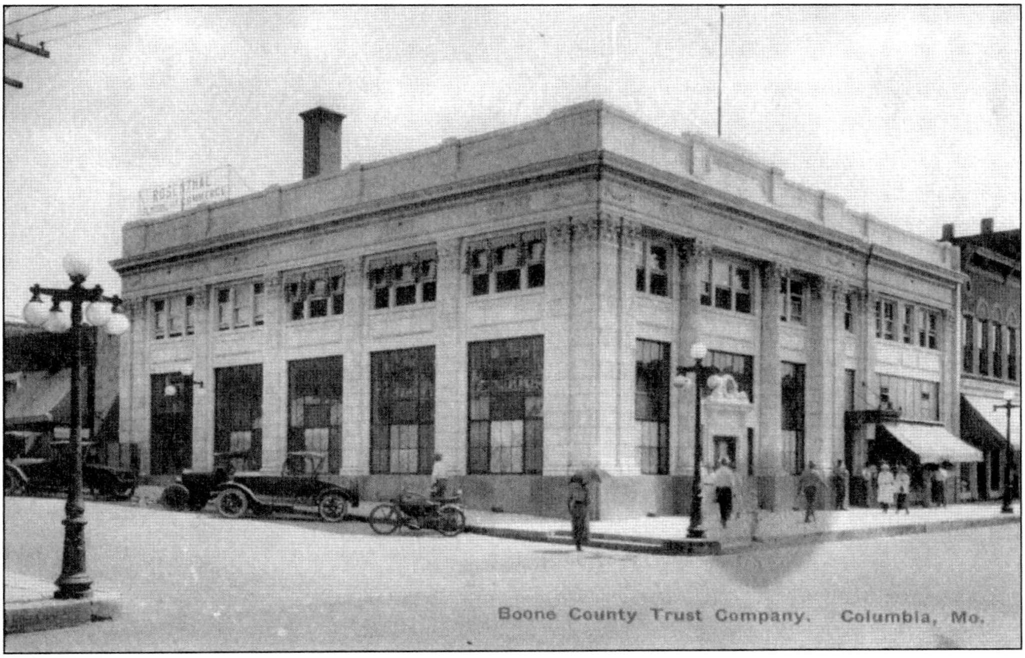

Boone County Trust Company was established in 1903 by Sanford Hunt and his father-in-law, William A. Bright. Hunt served as vice president and then president of the company until his death in 1934. A community leader, Hunt is credited with contributing to Columbia's growth in the early 20th century. The Trust Company, located at Ninth Street and Broadway, is seen here in 1920.

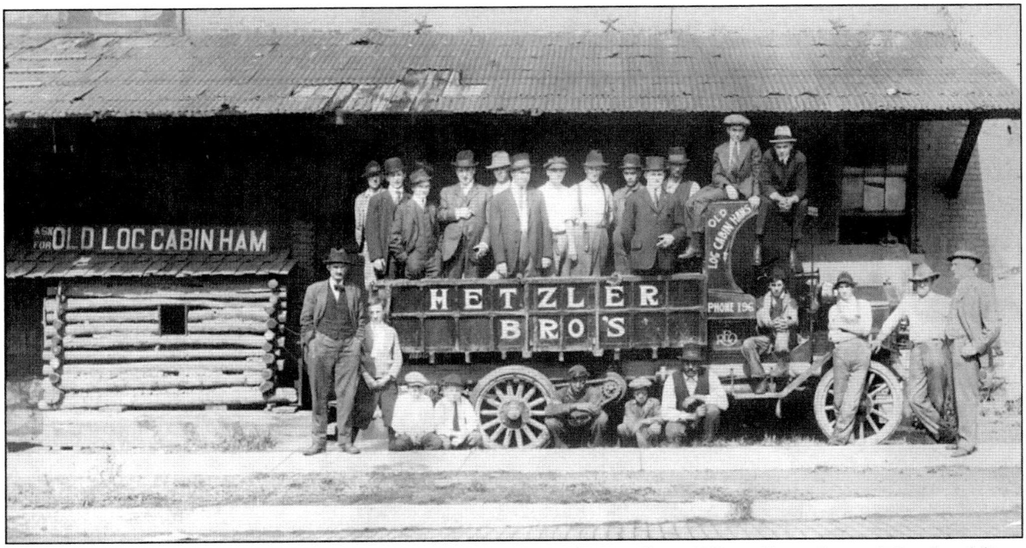

Hetzler Brothers' Ice Plant and Packing House was located on West Broadway. The building bearing the Hetzler name still stands. In October 1911, the *University Missourian* reported that the company wanted to build a slaughterhouse at this location near Flat Branch. Many community residents opposed the idea, citing unpleasant odors and unsanitary conditions, particularly in warm-weather months.

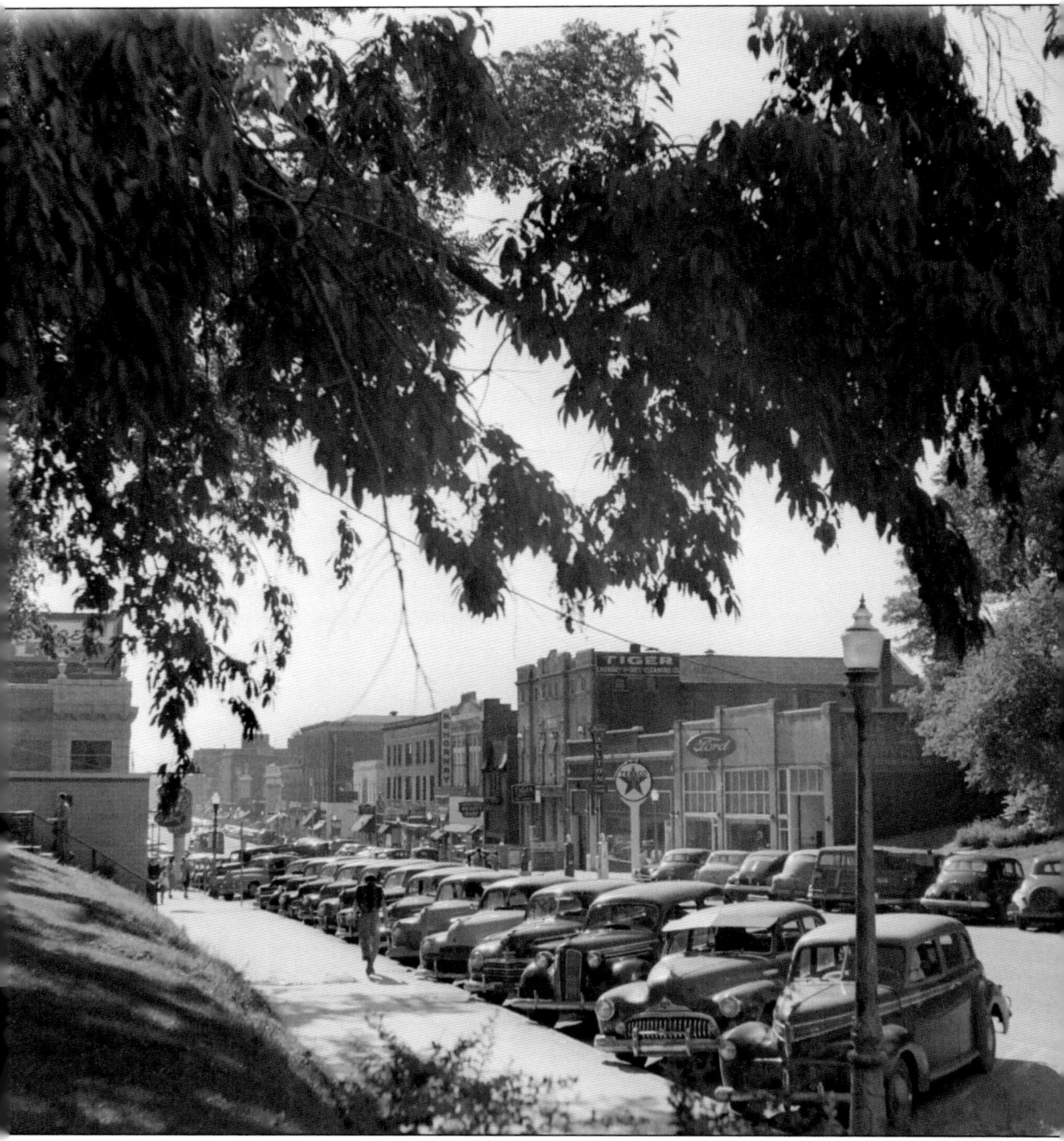

Columbia's settlers made the main thoroughfare, today's Broadway, wide enough to accommodate heavy wagon traffic. Once automobiles replaced horses and wagons, the extra width made it possible to park cars at an angle rather than parallel. This 1949 photograph shows Central Dairy on the left and Tiger Laundry and Dry Cleaning Company across the street. Texaco gas pumps stand in front of the Allton Ford dealership.

Five

People around Town

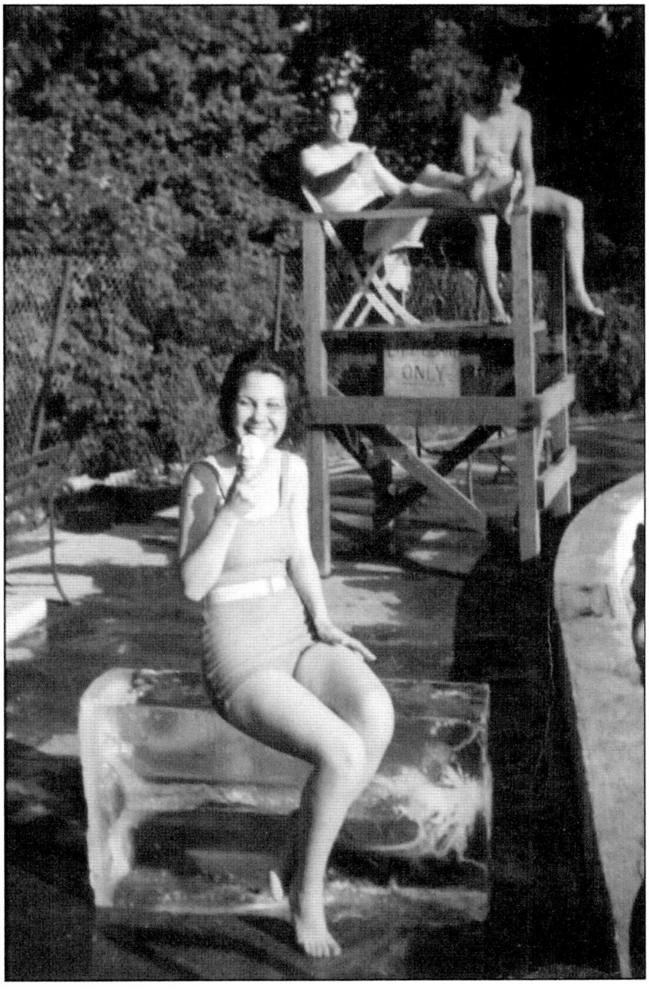

Summers in Columbia are hot and humid. Daily temperatures often reach 100-plus degrees. In the days before air conditioning, residents sought relief from the heat on front porches and at swimming pools and nearby lakes. Here, in an attempt to cool down on an extremely hot day, a coed sits on a large block of ice beside a pool. A refreshing ice-cream cone makes the heat more tolerable.

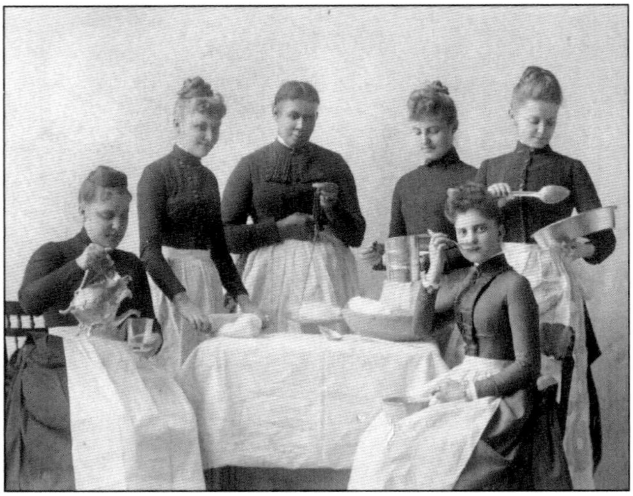

The Rollins family was one of Columbia's most prominent families. Land and money donations by businessman, lawyer, and activist James Sidney Rollins (1812–1888) led to the establishment in Columbia of the first public college west of the Mississippi River. He fathered 11 children, seven of whom lived to adulthood, including five sons. This portrait, by Columbia photographer Joe L. Douglass, shows Rollins women on baking day measuring butter, sifting flour, and rolling dough.

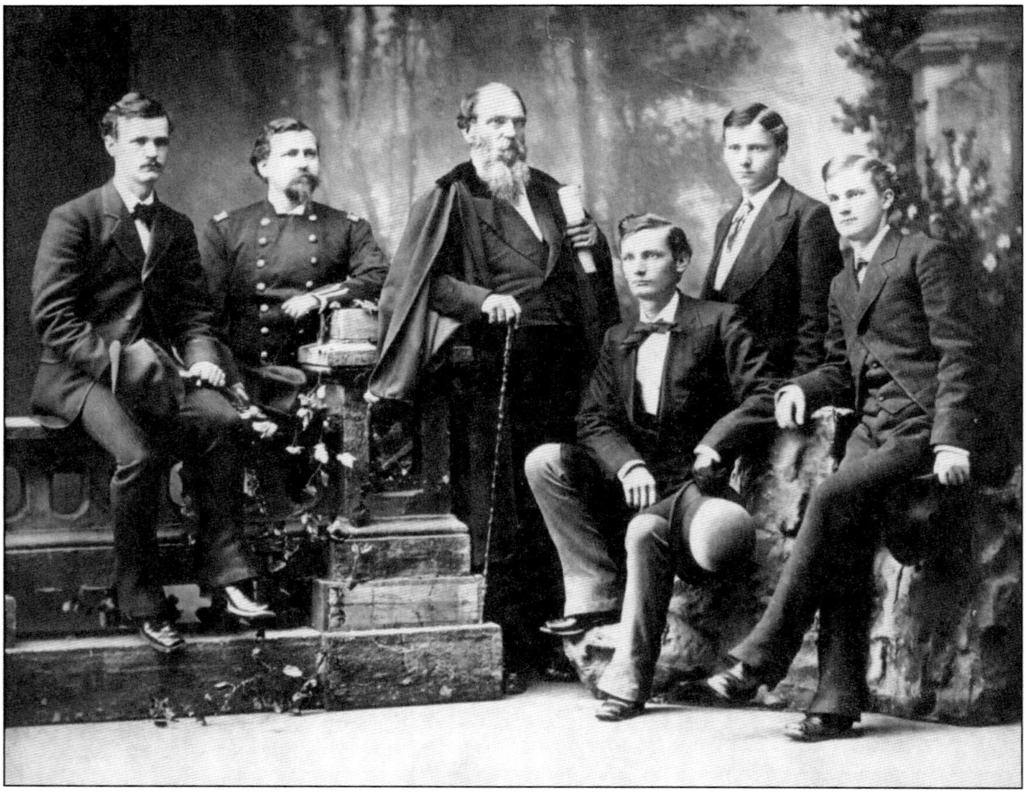

Kentucky-born James Sidney Rollins was a lawyer and landowner. He served in the Missouri legislature and two terms in the US Congress. He worked tirelessly to get the university located in Columbia and pushed for railroad and river improvements. He is shown here at center with his five sons, from left to right, George Bingham Rollins, James Hickman Rollins, Curtis Burnam Rollins Sr., Edward Tutt Rollins, and Frank Blair Rollins.

Odon Guitar moved with his family from Kentucky to Columbia in 1827. He graduated from the university in 1843, served in the Mexican-American War, and was a Union cavalry commander during the Civil War. He married, returned to Columbia, and practiced law for more than 40 years. Guitar served on the university's board of curators and was the alumni association's first president. Columbia photographer Joe L. Douglass photographed him in 1905.

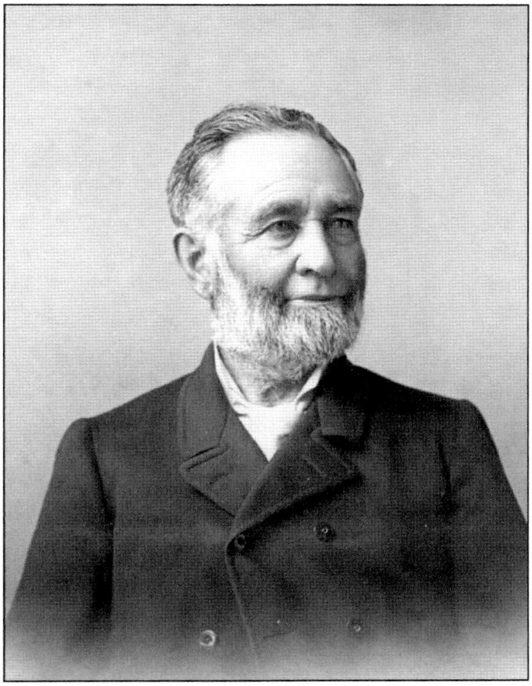

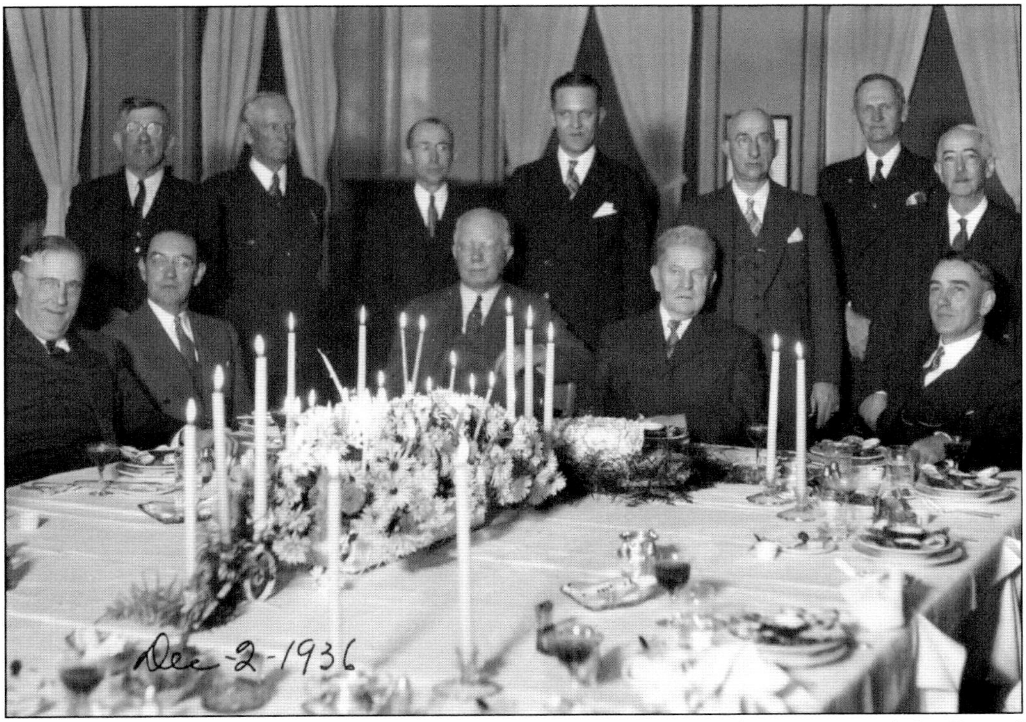

In 1918, Walter Williams, dean of the university's School of Journalism, organized the Round Table Club. Modeled after King Arthur's knights of the round table, the club's members included educators, businessmen, and civic leaders. They met for lunch at a café's large, round table. Membership was limited to the men who could fit around the table. The group, shown here in 1936, collected no dues and kept no meeting minutes.

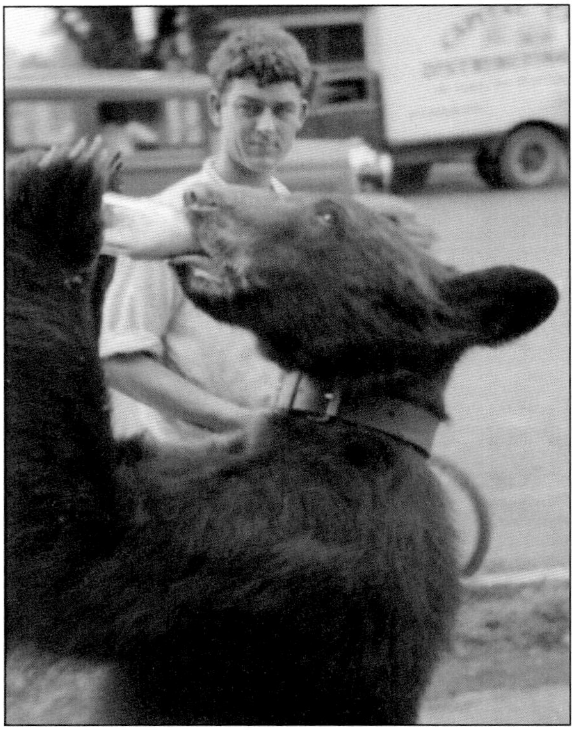

Anything's possible in a city nicknamed College Town, USA, including pranks, oddities, and unusual behavior. Here, a black bear sporting a collar and exceptionally long claws pauses downtown on his back haunches to enjoy a refreshing swig of bottled milk. No further information was available regarding the bear's preference for dairy products.

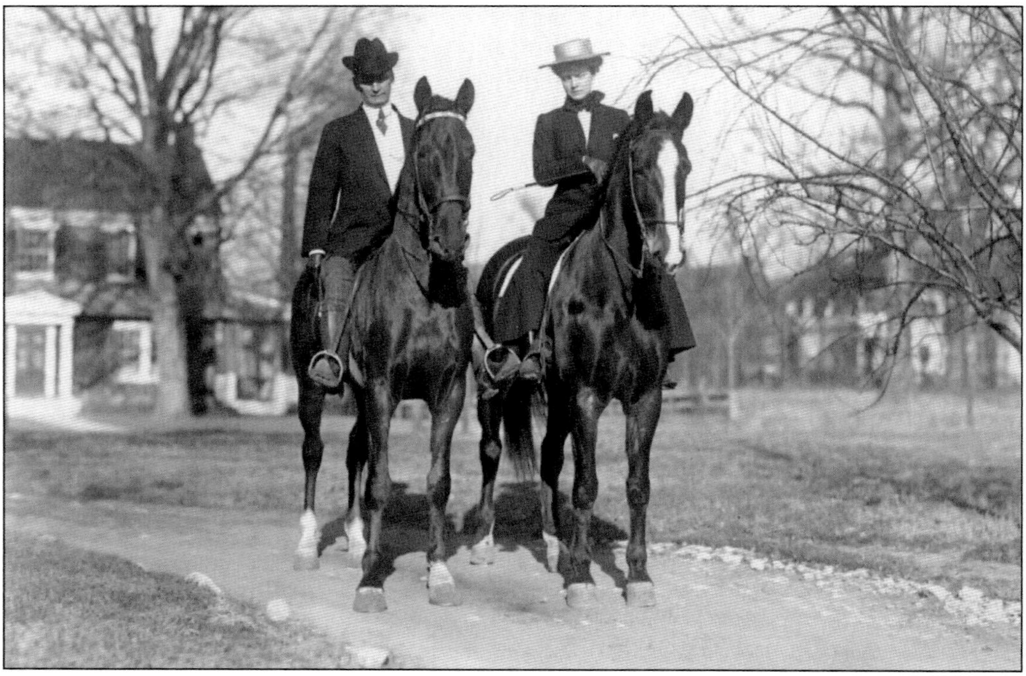

The Rollins family maintained a strong presence in Columbia for several generations. Shown here are Ruth Rollins and Curtis Burnam Rollins (1853–1940), son of James Sidney Rollins. Note that Ruth is riding her horse, Morgan, astride rather than sidesaddle. She also is wearing riding breeches rather than a skirt. Sidesaddle riding for women was falling out of favor at the time of this photograph.

William Franklin Switzler was editor and publisher of the *Missouri Statesman* newspaper from 1843 until 1885. He served three terms in the state legislature and was a supporter of the university. In 1882, he wrote *History of Boone County*, chronicling the county's early settlement. The university's oldest academic building, Switzler Hall, was named for him.

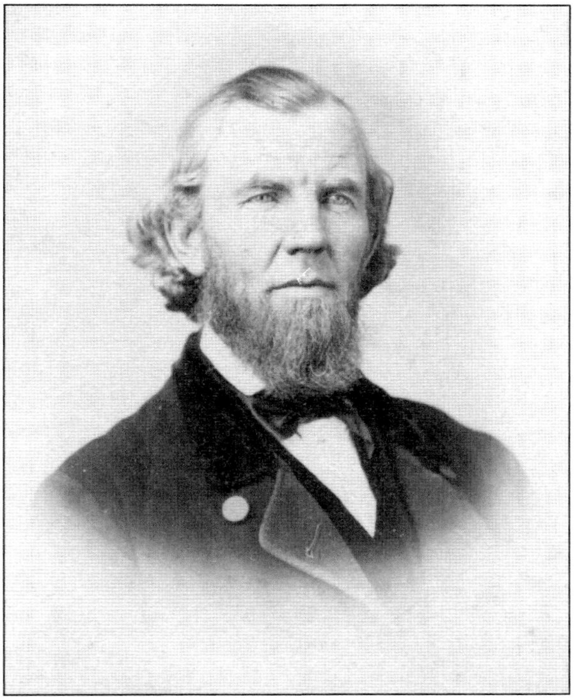

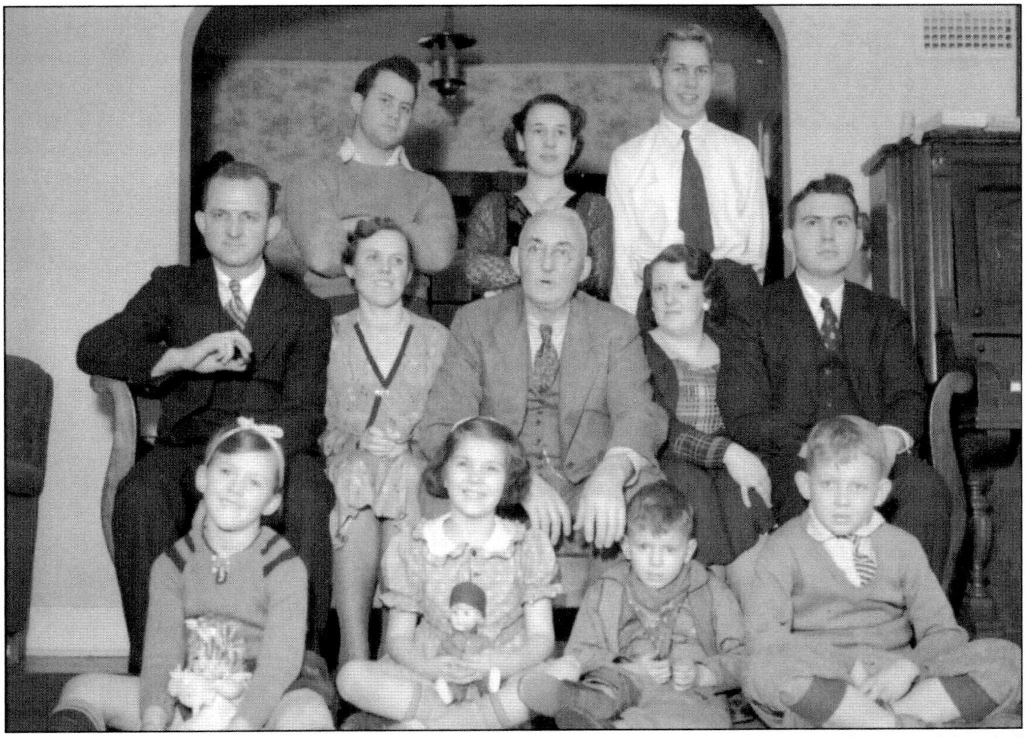

Central Dairy cofounder and president Dot Sappington and his wife, Bessie, had a large blended family. They married in 1921, one year after Sappington opened the dairy in Columbia. She had four children; he had seven. All the children spent time working at the dairy. This Christmas photograph from the 1930s shows Dot, Bessie, and 10 of their children.

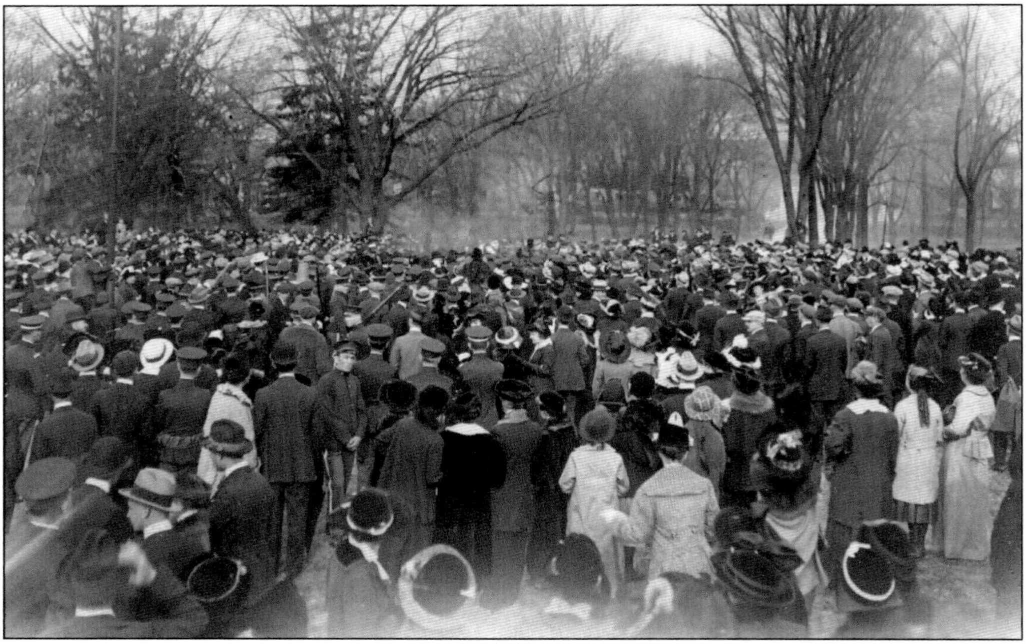

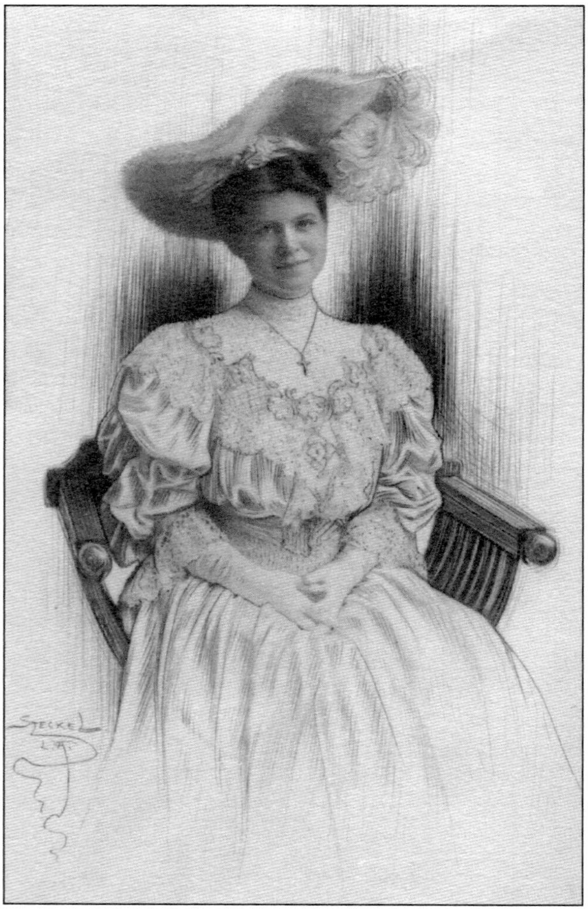

Then and now, college athletic events can bring out the best and worst in people. For reasons unknown, tempers flared and spectators stormed the university's Rollins Field at an early 1900s sporting event. Prim and proper women spectators, with their hats adjusted just so, observed the action with hands in their laps. The dome of Jesse Hall can be seen in the background.

Columbia had a state university and two colleges, but it was still a small town in the heart of the Midwest. Eulalie Bowman married into Columbia's first family when she wed James Hickman Rollins, son of James Sidney Rollins. James Hickman Rollins died in 1898. In 1899, Eulalie moved to Los Angeles, citing "societal reasons" for the move. This combination sketch and photograph of Eulalie is from 1906.

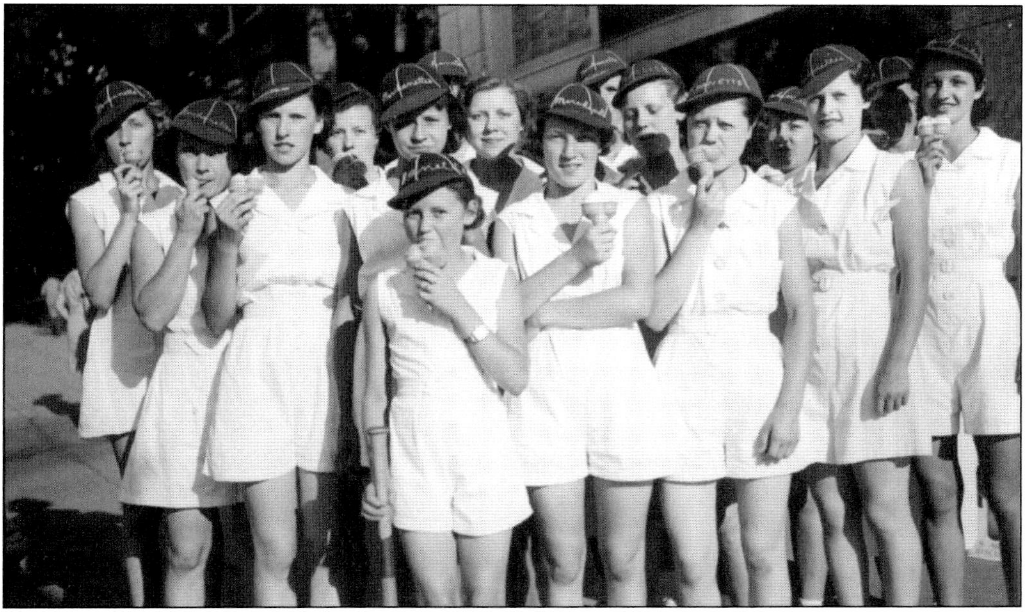

Summer, softball, and ice cream make a winning combination. This image from the 1930s shows The Merchanettes softball team enjoying double-scoop ice-cream cones outside Central Dairy. In the days before air conditioning, Central Dairy was a popular place for people of all ages to stop and cool down with a frozen treat.

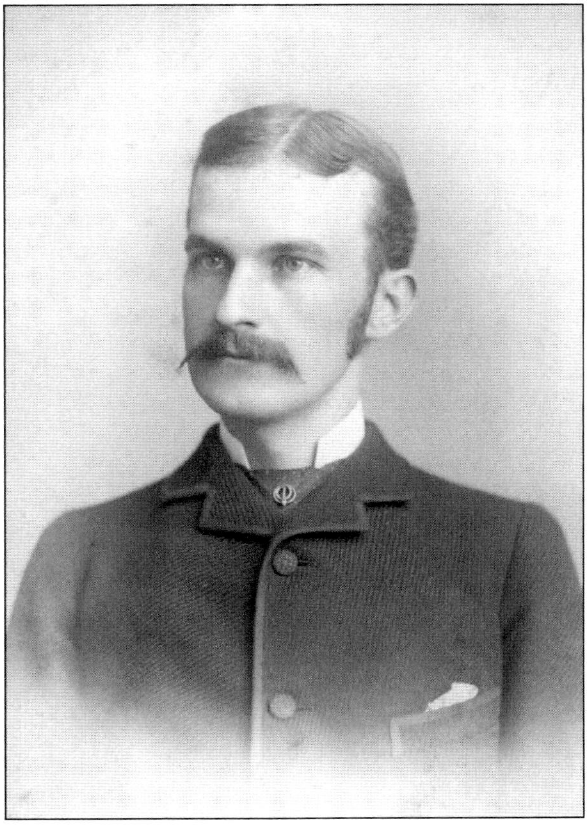

Frank Blair Rollins was one of the five sons of James Sidney and Mary Hickman Rollins. Born in Columbia in 1857, he attended the university and Harvard University. He graduated from St. Louis Law School in 1882 and was admitted to the bar association. He had a successful law practice until he died in 1884 of appendicitis.

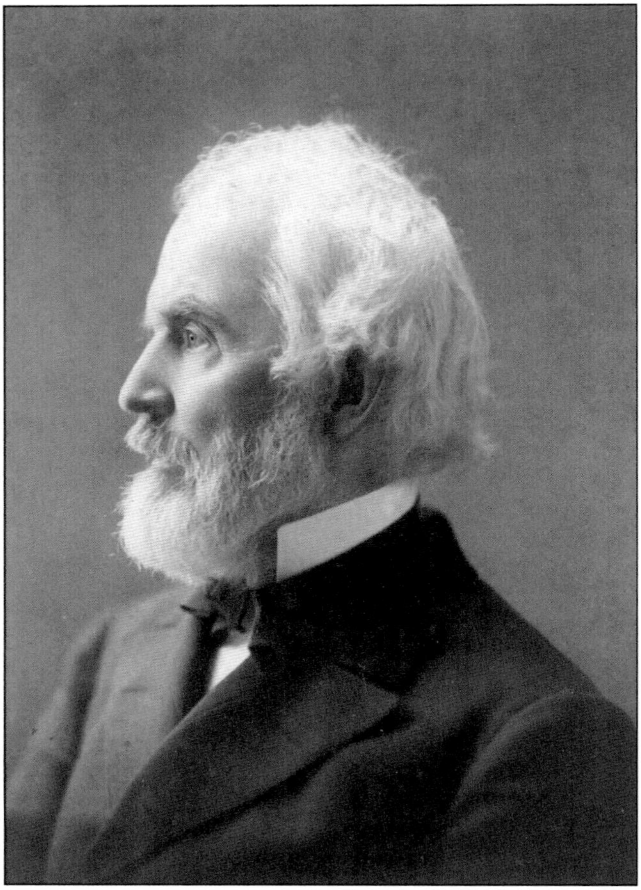

Philemon Bliss was a state supreme court judge. He was a member of the university's board of curators in 1867 when the idea for a law school was suggested. He agreed to establish the School of Law in 1872 when he retired from the bench. The school enrolled 25 students that first year. Tuition was $40.

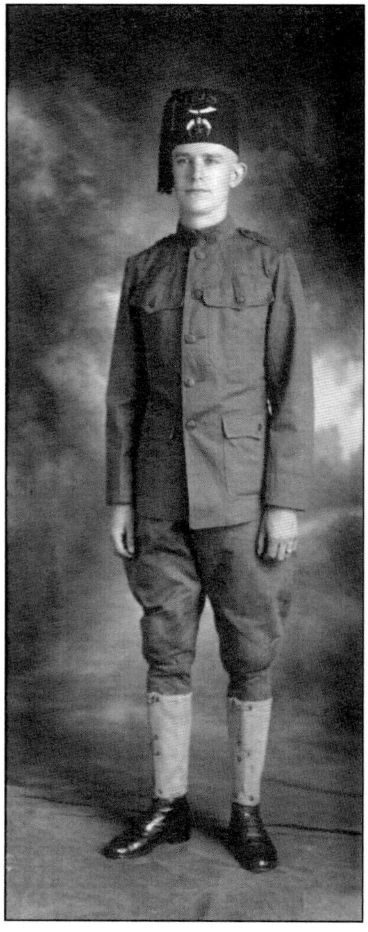

The Ancient Arabic Order of the Nobles of the Mystic Shrine (Shriners), established in 1870, is part of Freemasonry. This Boone County resident, attired in his World War I uniform, wears his Shrine fez. During the war, *The Columbia Missourian* listed names of Missourians who died, whether in active duty or from disease. This man returned from the war, remained a Shriner, and was buried with his fez.

Columbia's first paid fire department was organized in 1893. When this photograph was taken in 1911, horses were still used to pull department wagons. The city was divided into five districts. When an alarm came in, a whistle on top of a downtown building sounded. The number of whistle blasts indicated the district where the fire was located.

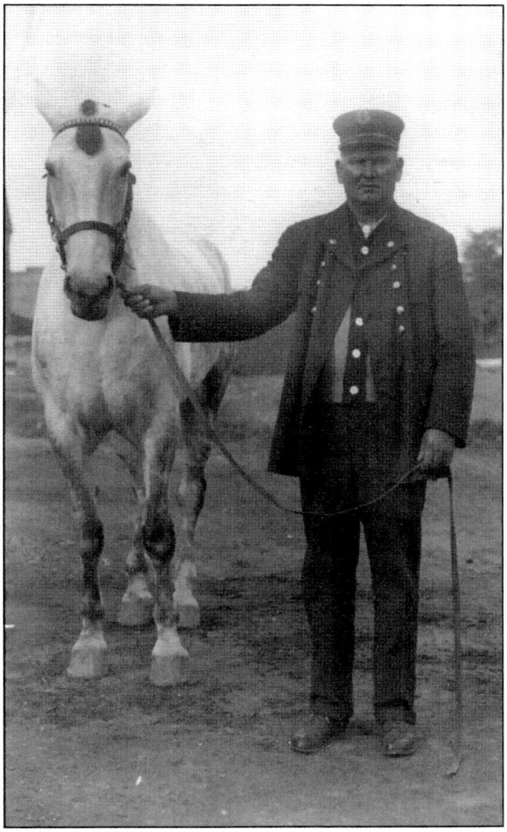

Women's clubs have long been a popular way for women to keep up with each other. Literary clubs, garden clubs, quilting clubs, and church-affiliated clubs provided opportunities to exchange ideas, discuss current events, and support each other. Members of the 42 Club posed for this photograph more than 100 years ago.

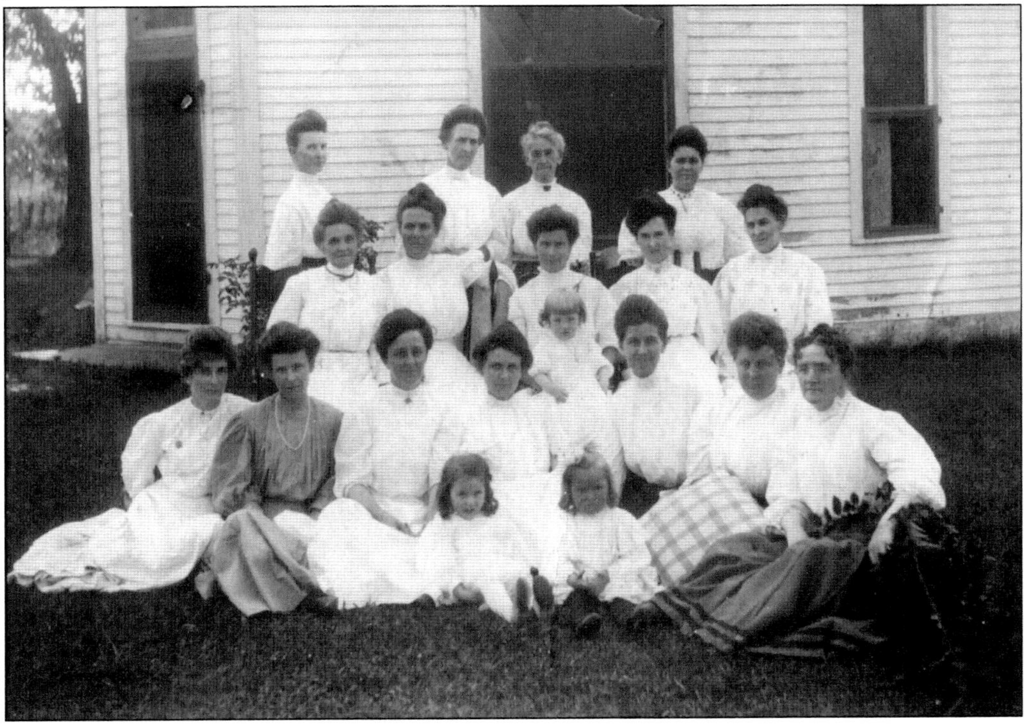

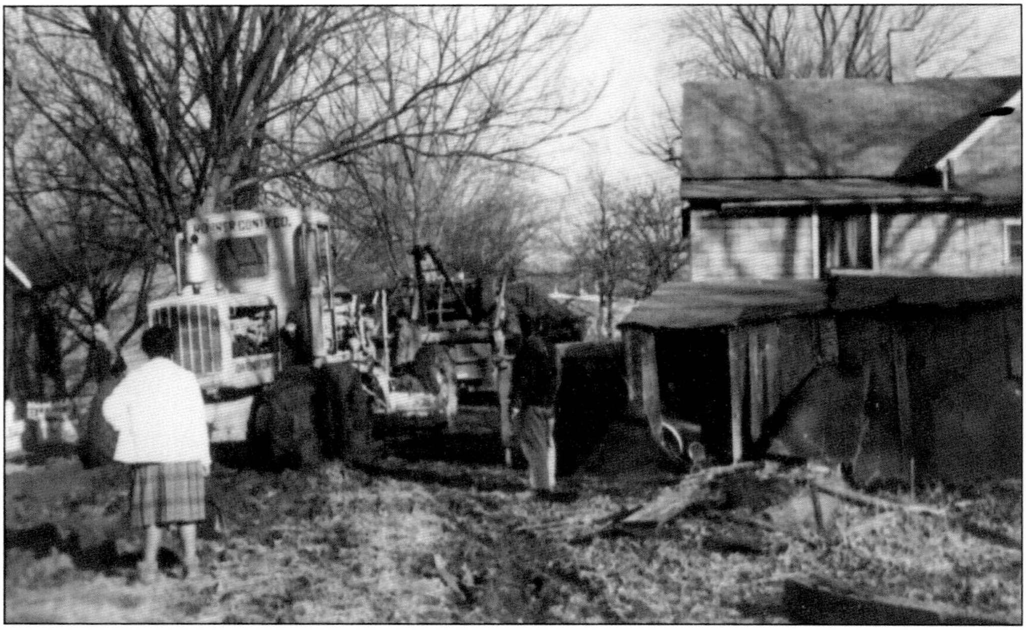

Amanda Estes opened Columbia's first nursery school for African Americans in 1933. The Nora Stewart Memorial Nursery, named for Estes's foster mother, remains in operation as the Nora Stewart Early Learning Center. When urban renewal was discussed in Columbia, Estes was an outspoken advocate. Her goal was to establish a community where all people could work, play, and build with a sense of honor and dignity.

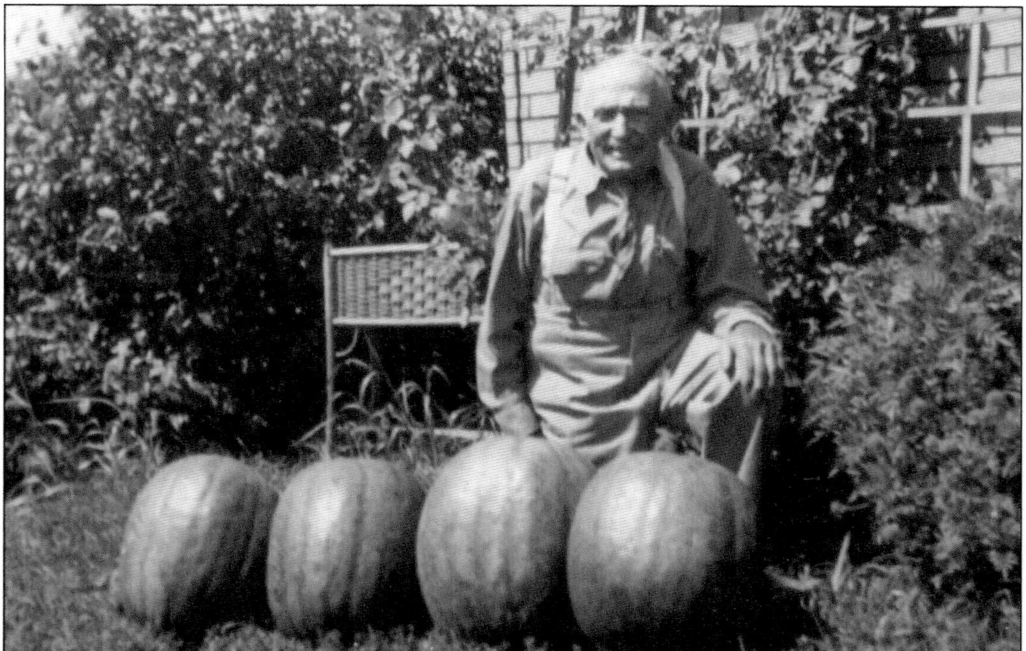

Few things taste as good during the hot days of summer as a slice of watermelon. This Columbia resident, identified only as Mr. Hancock, The Watermelon Man, poses with four melons from his garden. He was known for the quality and size of the watermelons he grew each year.

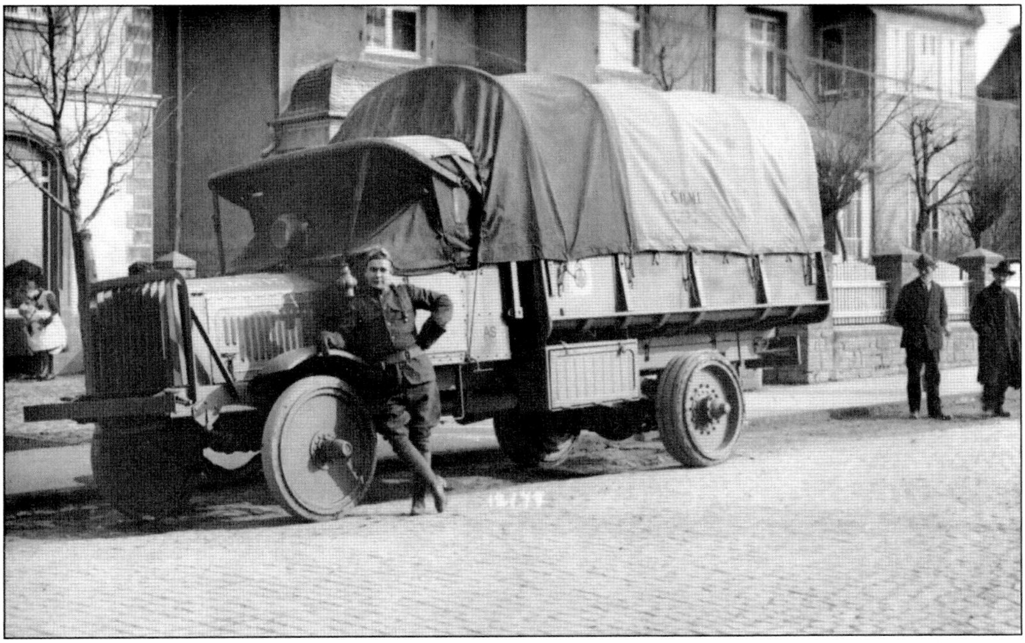

A World War I Marine poses with his truck. During the war, university students and faculty enlisted in the military or went to work in war-related industries. More than 100 of them died during the conflict. In addition, a worldwide flu epidemic brought travel and gathering restrictions to Columbia as the illness hit students and residents.

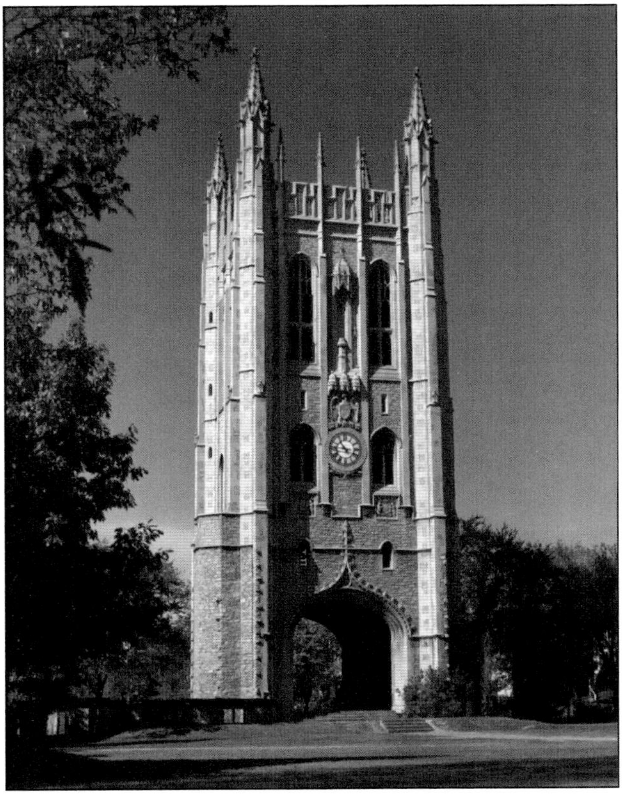

In 1921, a pledge program was initiated to raise money to build a memorial union and memorial stadium to honor those who died in the war. The Gothic-style Union Tower was completed in 1926, but plans for additional construction ended with the start of the Great Depression. The tower stood alone until the north and south wings were completed in 1952 and 1963.

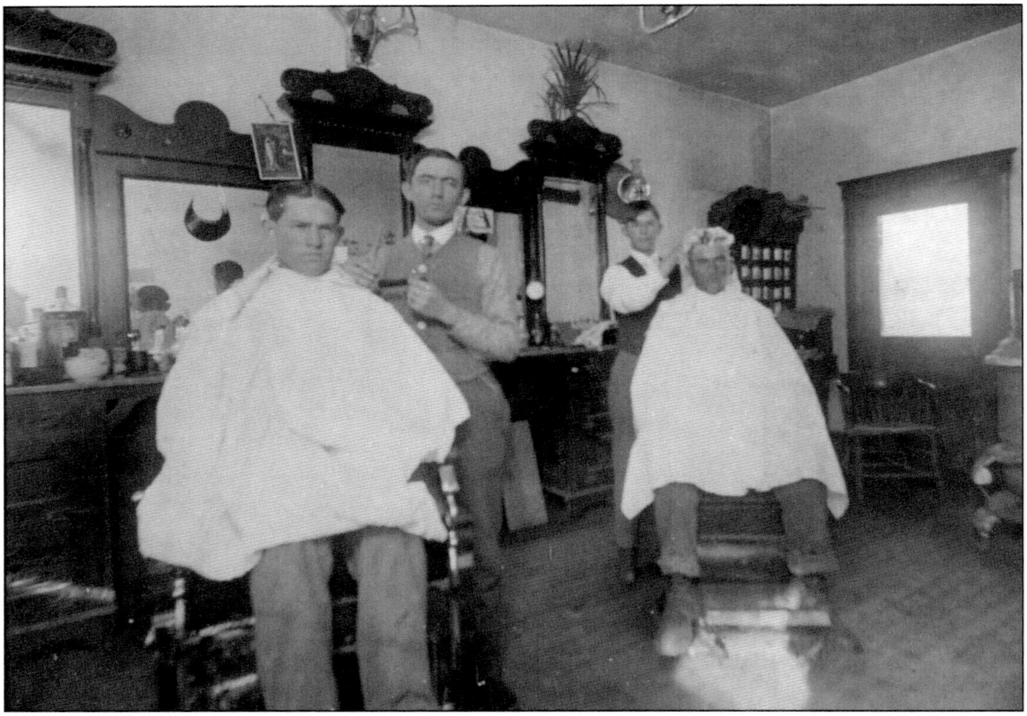

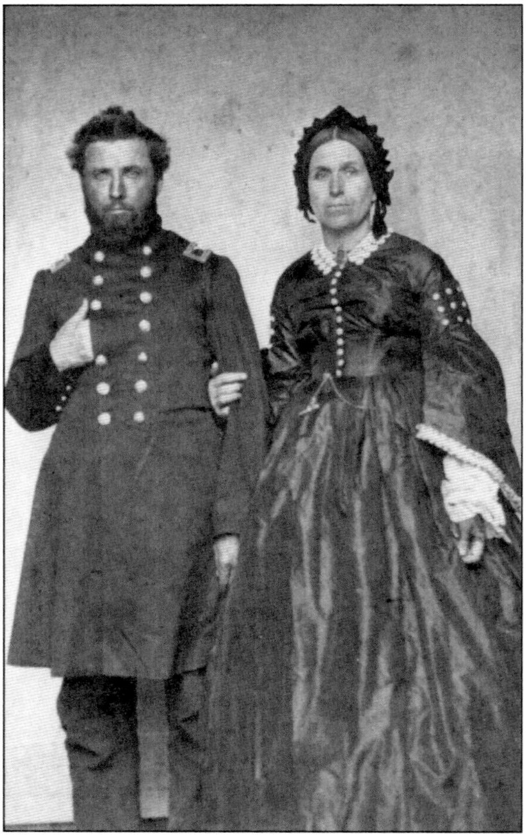

Before the days of unisex hair salons, men visited barbershops. There, a man could get a shampoo, have the hair on his head and face trimmed, and sometimes splurge on a shoeshine. He also could catch up on the latest happenings around town. Frank Girdner, shown here shampooing a customer, began his barber career as a teenager. He kept generations of men looking their best.

Odon Guitar moved to Columbia from Kentucky in 1827. An early graduate of the university, he studied and practiced law and served two terms in the Missouri House of Representatives. In 1862, Guitar was commissioned as a colonel of the 9th Cavalry, Missouri State Militia. After the war, he was president of the local bar association and a university curator. He and his wife, Kate, are shown here in the 1860s.

An unidentified Columbia dentist checks a patient's teeth in the 1940s. The tidy office features equipment of the day along with organized shelves and cabinets. Frequently used tools were kept in the drawers behind the doctor. A few personal items are seen on top of the cabinets, including a photograph of a young man in a military uniform. A portrait of George Washington hangs on the wall.

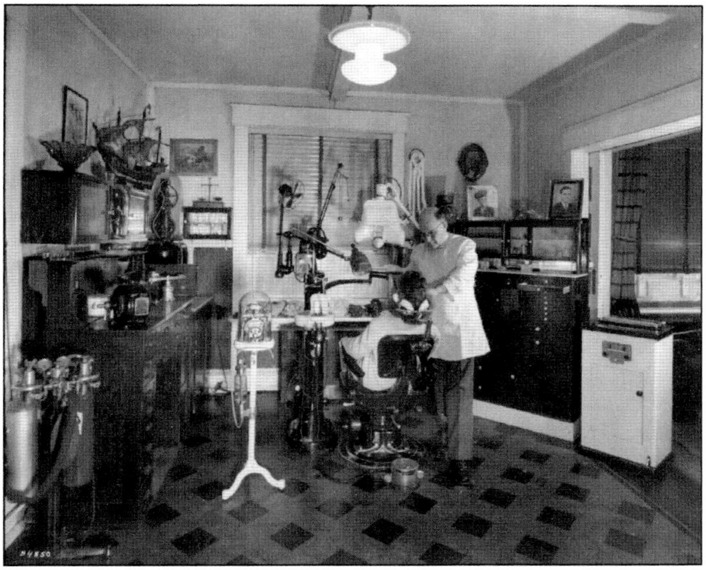

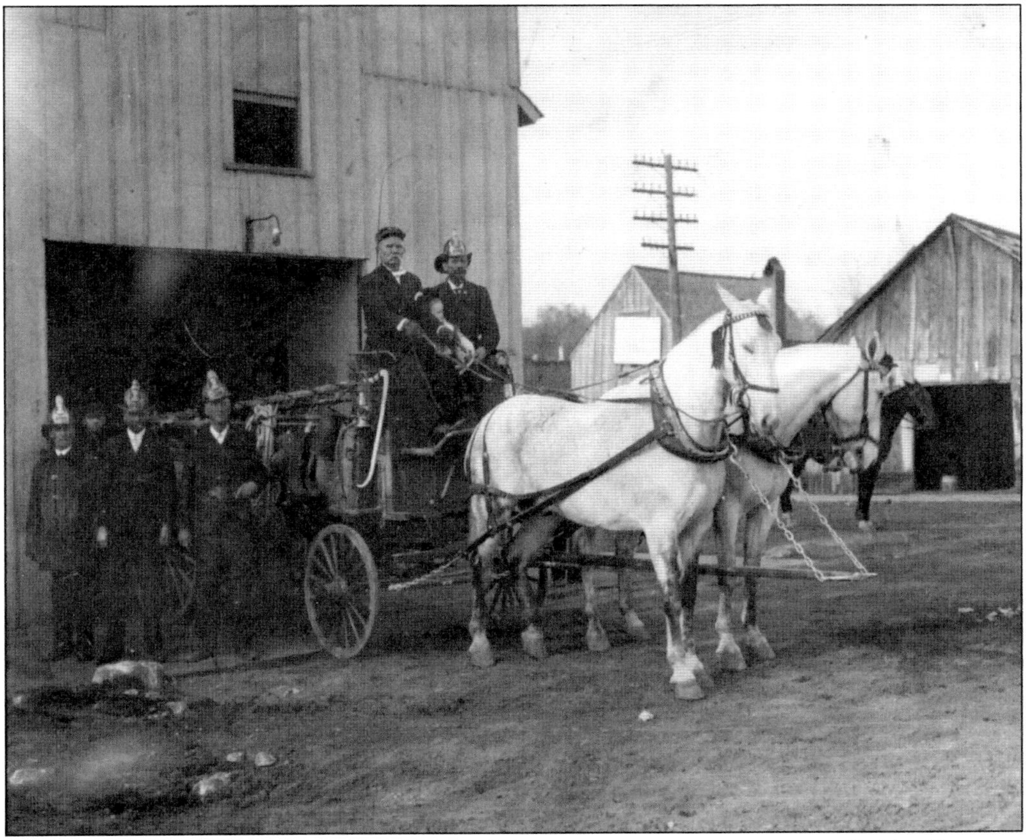

This 1910 photograph shows Columbia's firefighting equipment—a wagon pulled by Dan and Prince, two matched white horses trained to "harness" when a fire bell sounded. The fire wagon and horses were housed in a building at Eighth and Ash Streets. Motorized fire equipment did not come to Columbia until 1913. Today, the Boone County Fire Protection District operates 14 fire stations and approximately 120 emergency vehicles.

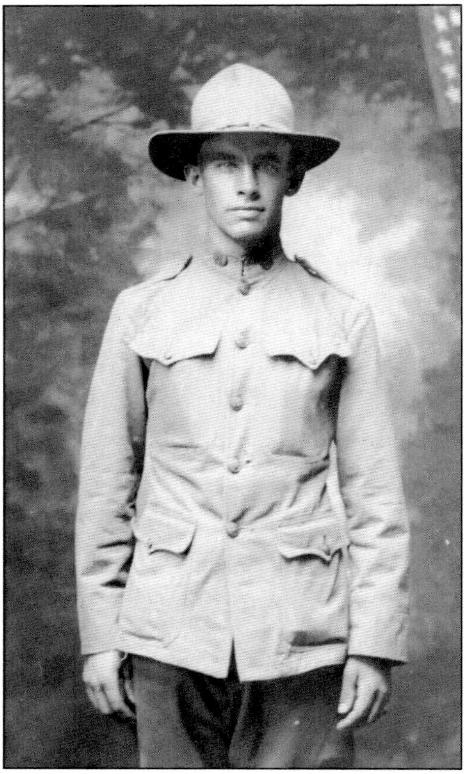

An unidentified Columbia man poses in his military uniform in 1917. County records show that more than 1,500 Boone County men registered to serve in World War I. Most came home; 45 did not.

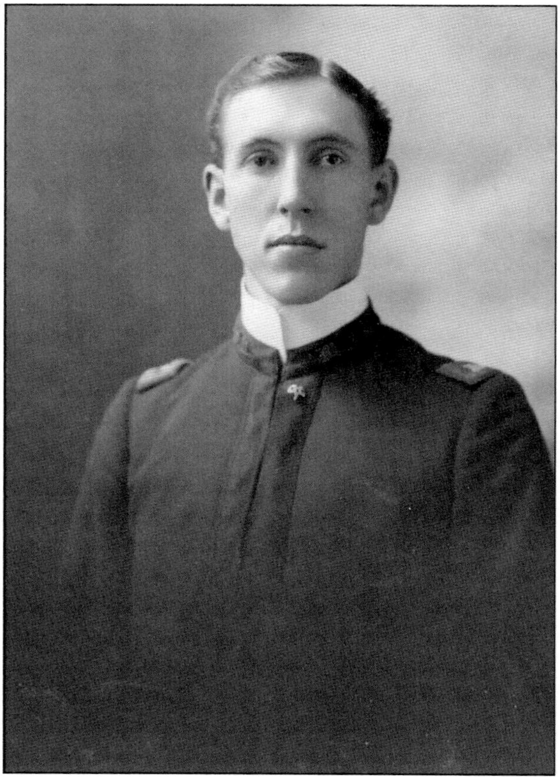

The university's military science cadets routinely practiced marching through the quadrangle. From 1899 through 1902, W.H. Turner was an instructor in military science and tactics. This portrait of Turner, a member of the university's class of 1898, was taken by Columbia photographer J.L. Douglass. Turner also served in the Spanish-American War.

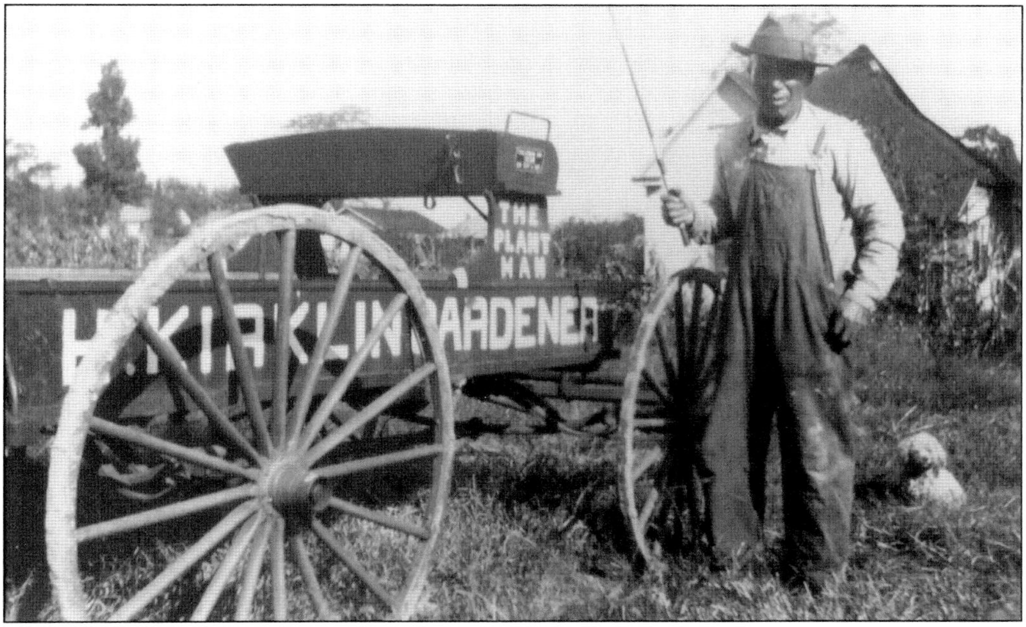

Henry Kirklin was born a slave. He had little education, but was a gifted gardener. Known in Columbia as The Plant Man, Kirklin grew impressive vegetables. He sold his produce first from a wheelbarrow and later from a wagon. So good were his skills that a university professor asked Kirklin to provide hands-on training to horticulture students. His produce also won awards.

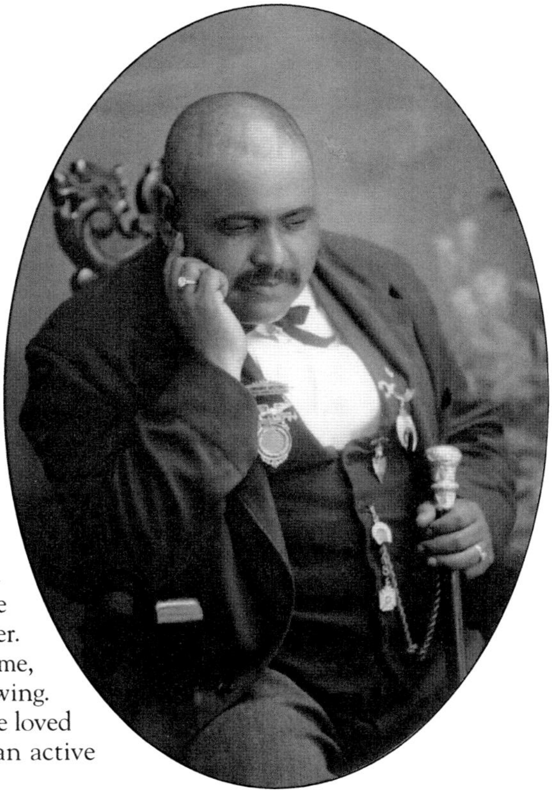

John William "Blind" Boone was born a slave. He overcame blindness, poverty, and prejudice to become a celebrated pianist and composer. While he loved classical music, he played ragtime, a predecessor to jazz, and established a following. Although he performed around the world, he loved Columbia. Boone returned here and was an active philanthropist during his lifetime.

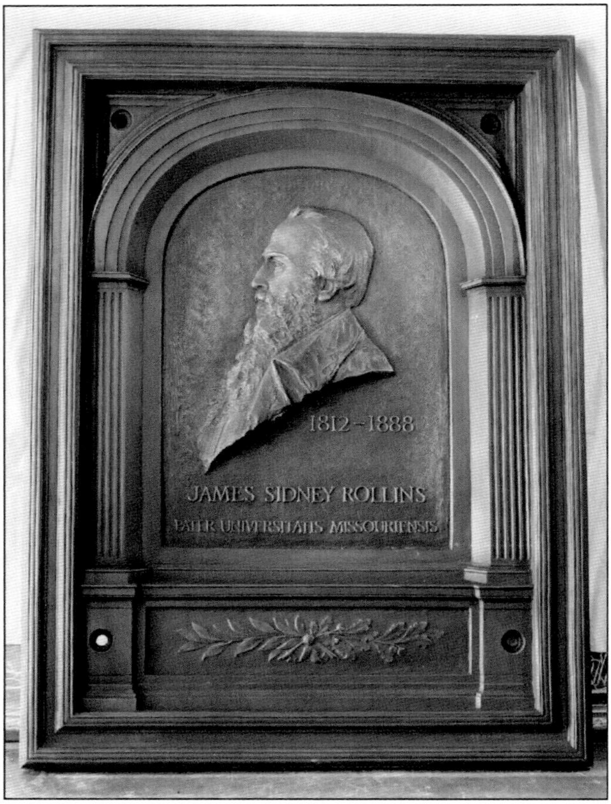

James Sidney Rollins's wealth and personal influence are said to have positively impacted the decision to locate Missouri's state university in Columbia. His efforts to have the university located in Columbia earned him the nickname "Pater Universitatis Missouriensis," Latin for Father of the University of Missouri.

Francis Quadrangle's Switzler Hall is the university's oldest classroom building. Completed in 1872, it was named for Col. William Switzler, an editor and university patron. The building has housed various programs and witnessed historic moments through the years. In this c. 1908 photograph, engineering students stage a St. Patrick's Day pageant in front of Switzler Hall.

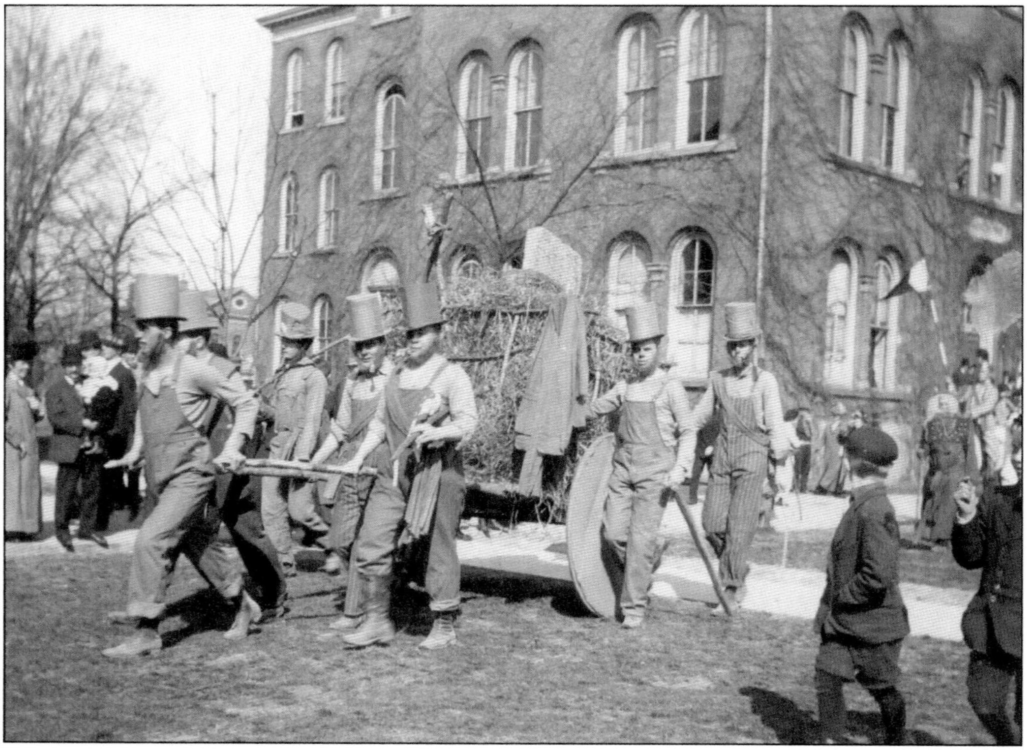

Six

Celebrations, Fairs, and Gathering Spots

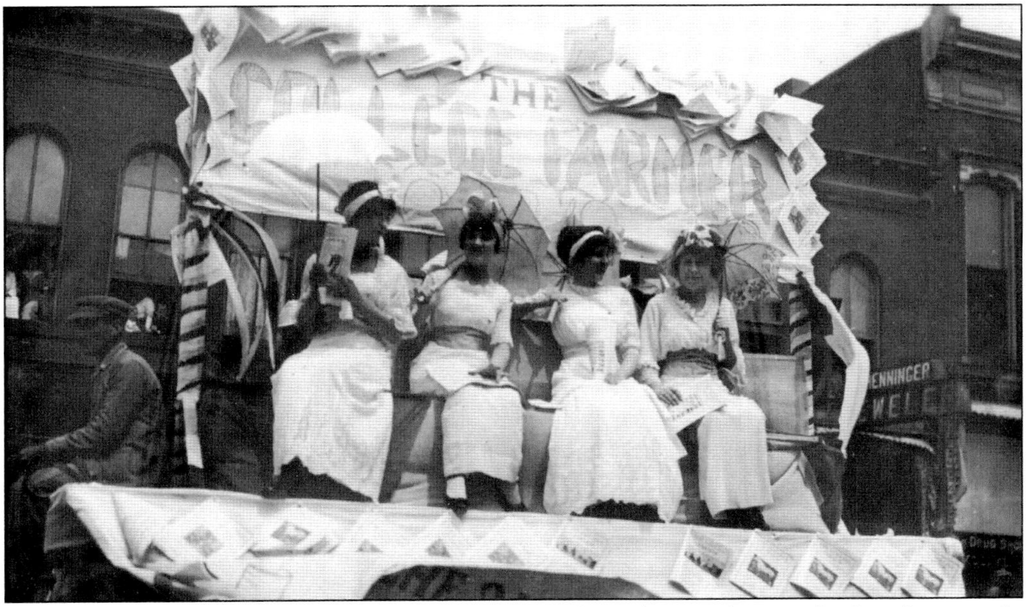

Broadway has remained a major artery in Columbia throughout its history. In this photograph, taken sometime between 1909 and 1914, a horse-drawn float titled The College Farmer carries women down Broadway. The parade was held in conjunction with the university's annual College of Agriculture Farmers' Fair. A sign for Henninger's Jewelry, located in the 800 block of Broadway, can be seen in the background.

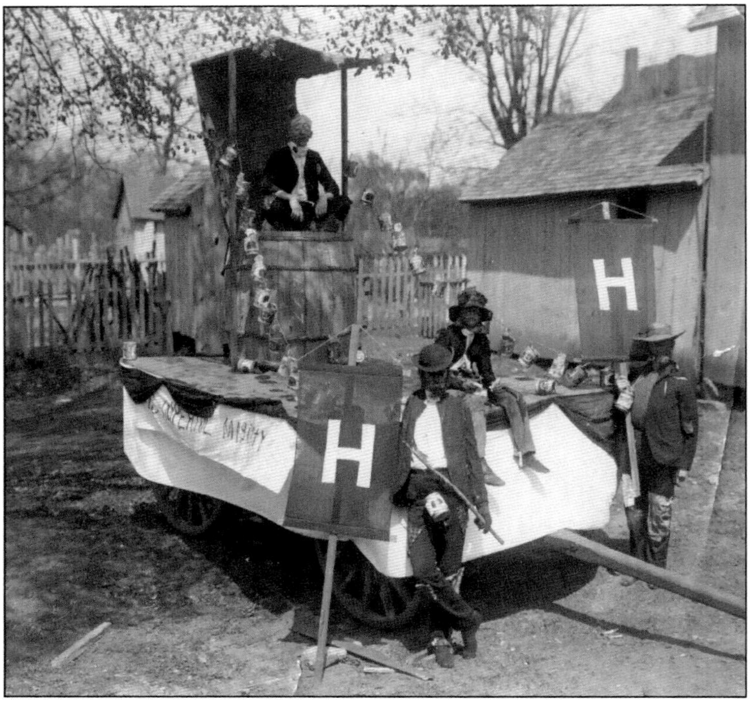

A float waits to participate in a Columbia Hobo Convention parade in 1905. A sign identifies the man seated on the barrel as Hobo Imperial Majesty. Hobos have been defined as migratory itinerant workers, people who wander and work. In the late 19th and early 20th centuries, hobos frequently hopped trains to travel. A hobo organization remains active, holding conventions in Britt, Iowa.

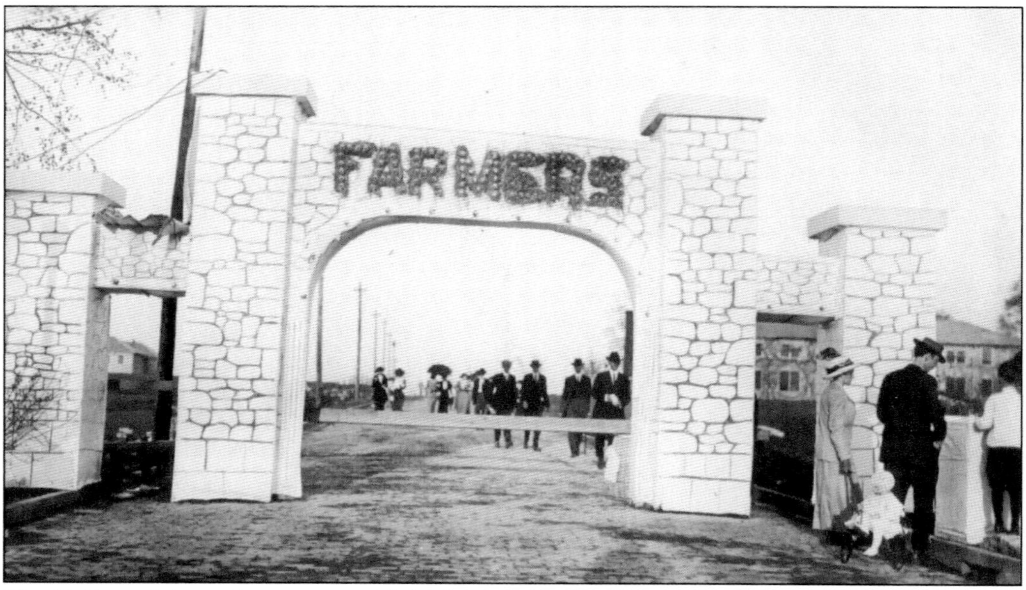

The College of Agriculture was established in 1870 and remains an integral part of the university's educational system. The Farmers' Fair began in the spring of 1905 as a student-organized agricultural activity. It became an annual event and was held each year until 1957. This gate on Rollins Street was decorated for a fair sometime between 1909 and 1914.

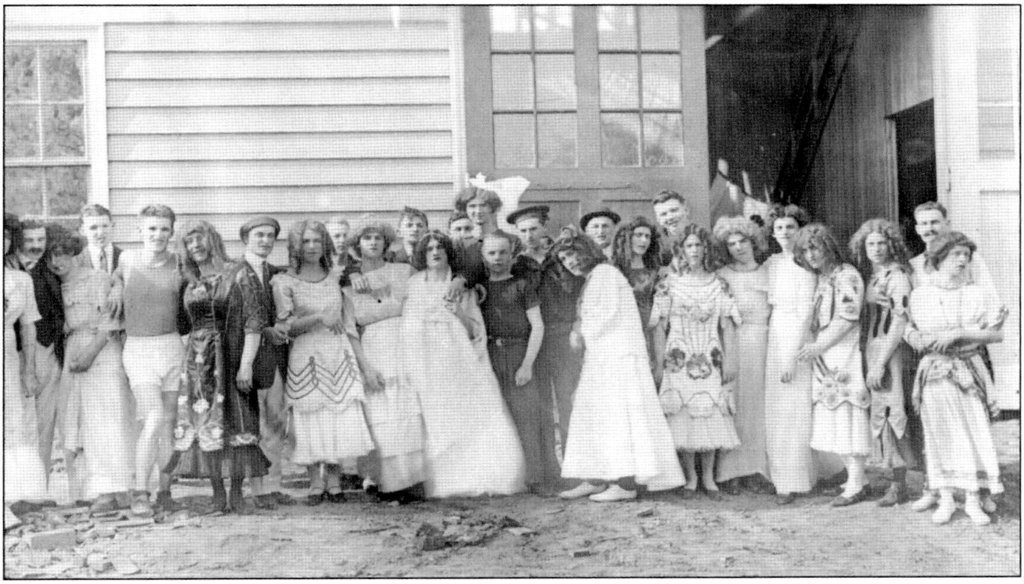

University student photographer Volney McFadden caught a group of agriculture students taking a break from their studies to prepare for Columbia's Hobo Convention between 1909 and 1914. Some donned wigs, dresses, and women's shoes. Then as now, the behavior of college students was sometimes unpredictable.

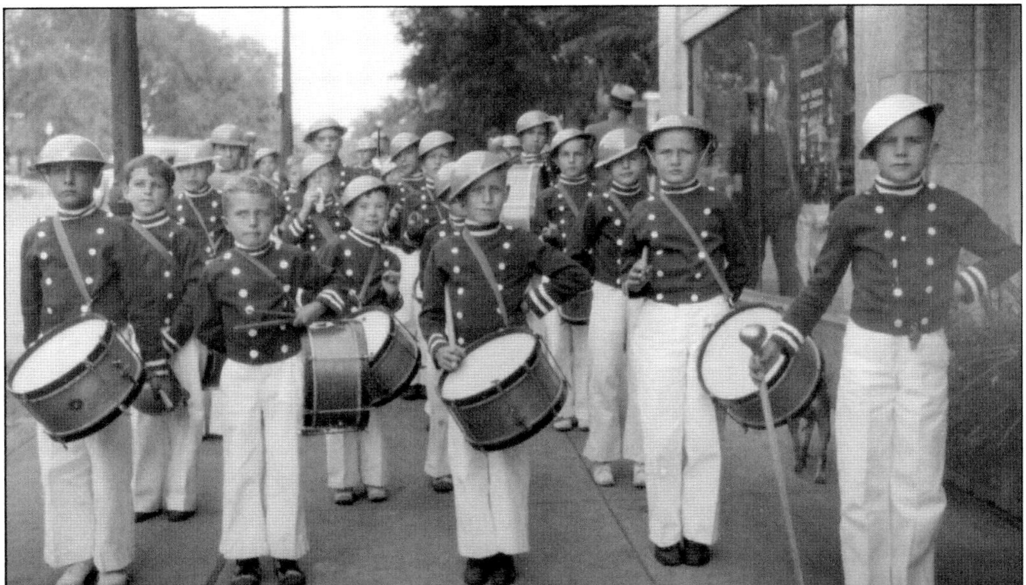

A group of unidentified young men, perhaps from a Missouri military academy, stop marching and beating drums long enough to pose for a photograph in downtown Columbia. Note the various angles of the helmets, plus the absence of helmets on some heads. The photograph dates to the 1930s.

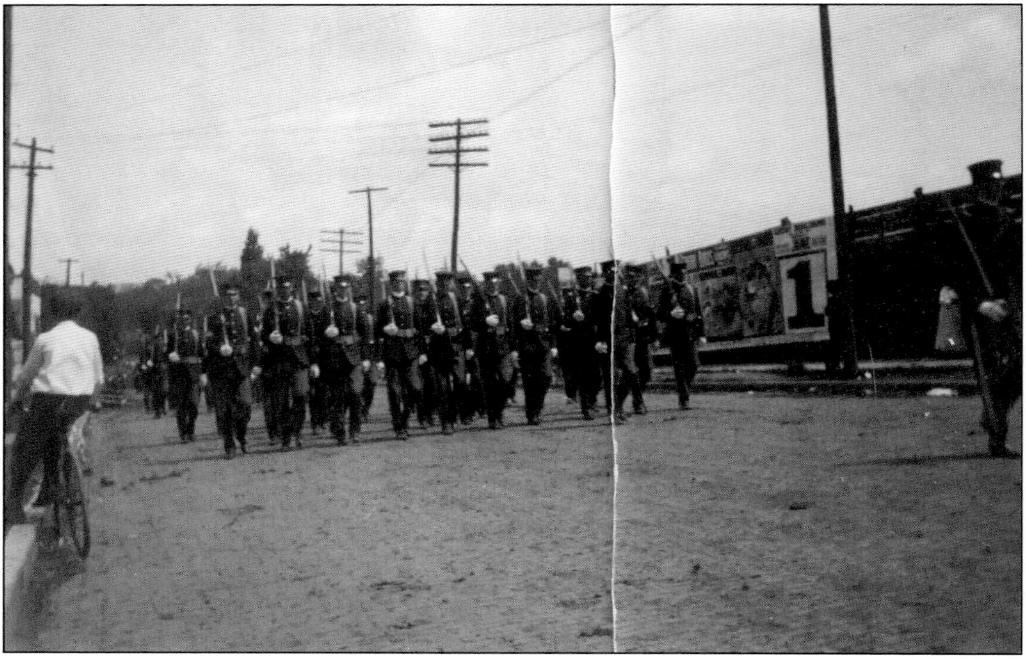

In the years after the Civil War, the university became one of 20 US schools to teach military science. Lt. Enoch H. Crowder became professor of military science and tactics in 1884. He brought innovative ideas to the program. Cadets frequently marched around the quadrangle. Here, cadets march down a cobblestone street in an early-20th-century Knights Templar parade.

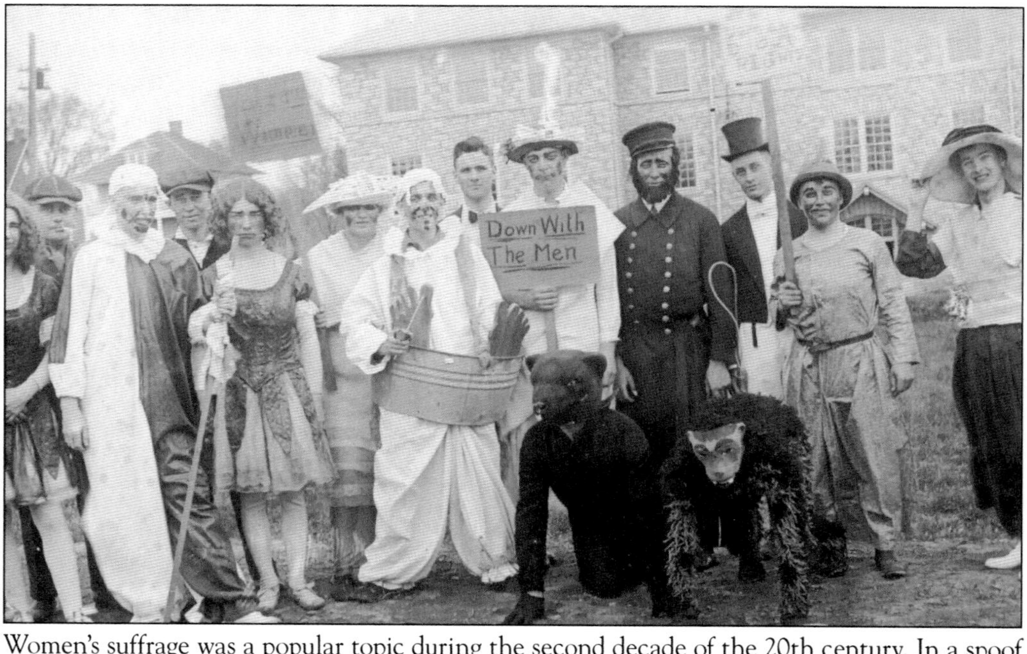

Women's suffrage was a popular topic during the second decade of the 20th century. In a spoof of suffragettes, the university's College of Agriculture students dressed as women during the Farmers' Fair. They carried signs stating, "We Demand Our Rights," "Votz To Wimmen," and "Down With the Men." The Columbia Equal Suffrage Association was organized in 1912 and became the League of Women Voters in 1919.

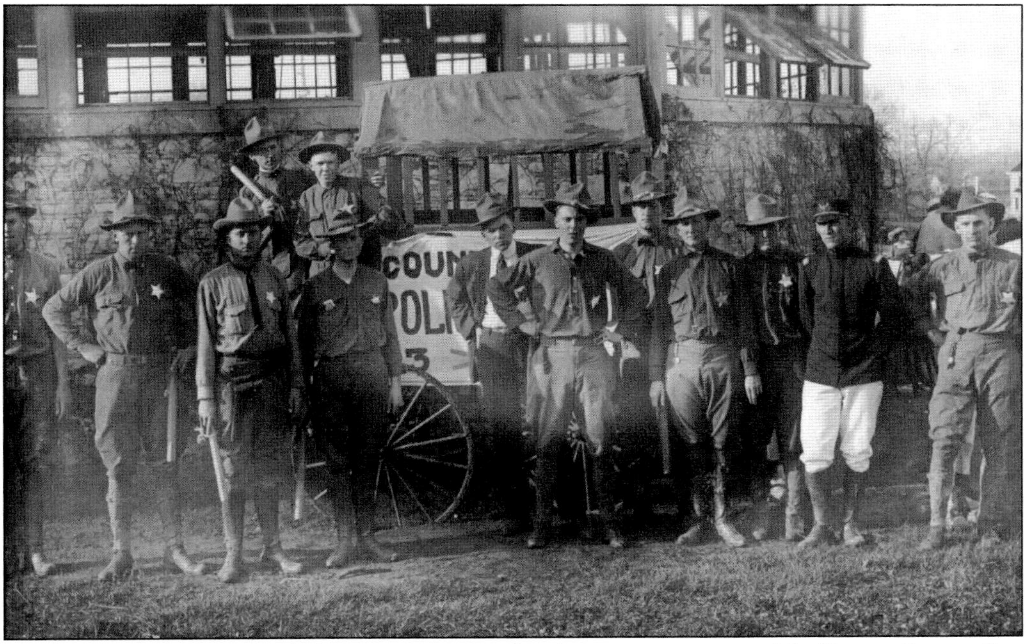

Looking somber and official, these men were outfitted as representatives of the Boone County Fair police patrol. Badges, clubs, whistles, guns, and a paddy wagon were the tools used to maintain order among fairgoers. The Boone County Fair was first held in 1835. It was the first such fair west of the Mississippi River. This photograph was taken around 1910.

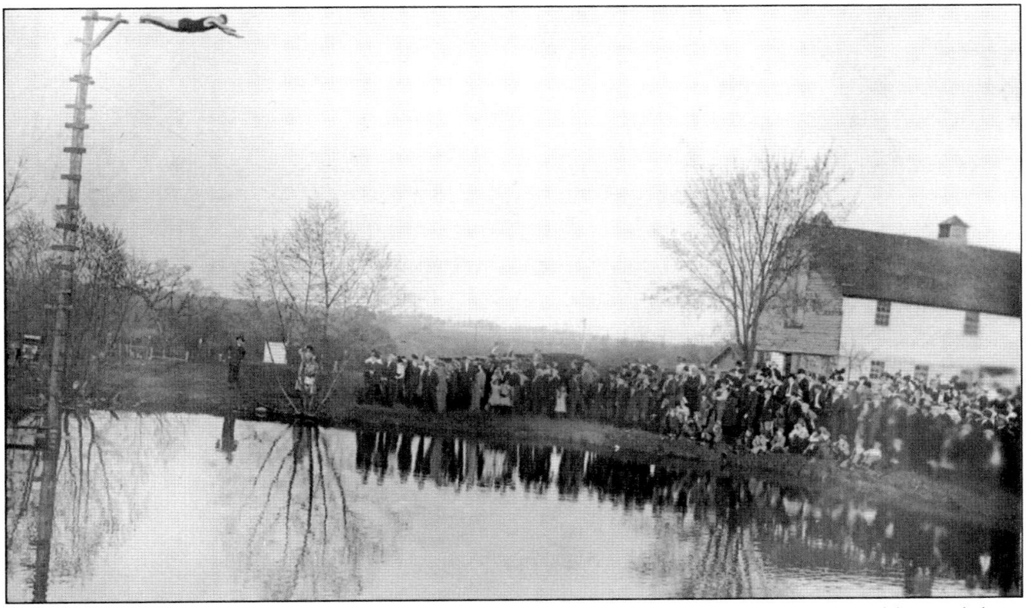

All eyes were on this man in the two-piece swimming suit as he climbed a crude ladder and dove into what was called the university's agriculture pond. Student photographer Volney McFadden captured the moment sometime between 1909 and 1914. Nearby trees are bare, and the spectators are wearing coats and hats. No information is available on the water temperature or the outcome of the dive.

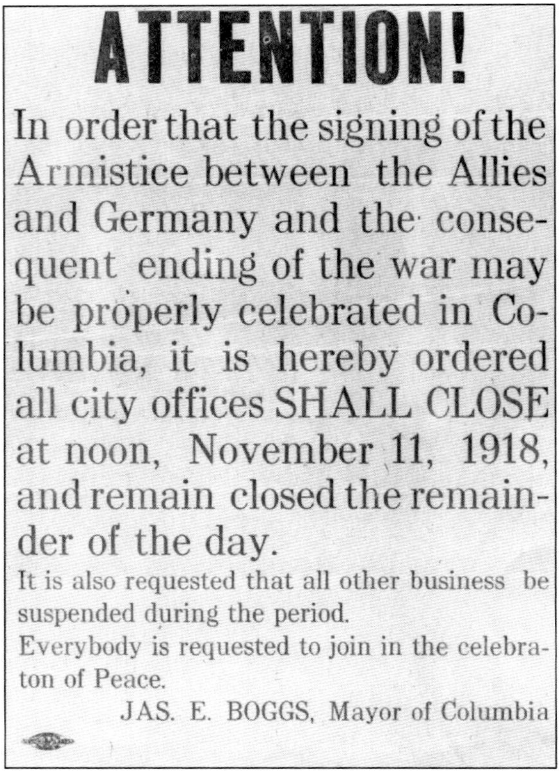

ATTENTION!

In order that the signing of the Armistice between the Allies and Germany and the consequent ending of the war may be properly celebrated in Columbia, it is hereby ordered all city offices SHALL CLOSE at noon, November 11, 1918, and remain closed the remainder of the day.

It is also requested that all other business be suspended during the period.

Everybody is requested to join in the celebraton of Peace.

JAS. E. BOGGS, Mayor of Columbia

Christian College students were important to the US effort during World War I. They rolled bandages, knitted, and promoted Liberty Loans by riding on Liberty Loan parade floats through Columbia. Columbians, like people throughout the country, were ready to celebrate when it was announced on November 11, 1918, that the war was over. This Armistice Day broadside was posted throughout Columbia by Mayor James E. Boggs.

The return of soldiers from the battlefields of World War I was cause for a celebration. This group of returning uniformed soldiers gathered outside the university cafeteria on February 22, 1919, in an event sponsored by the Boone County chapter of the American Red Cross.

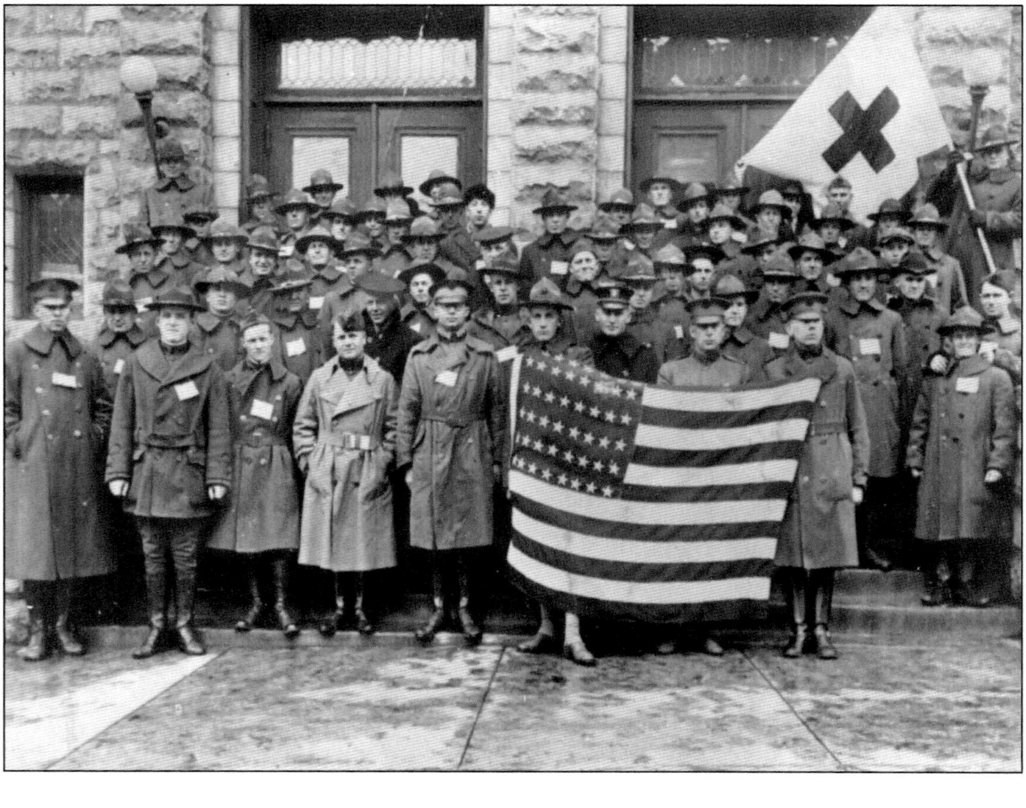

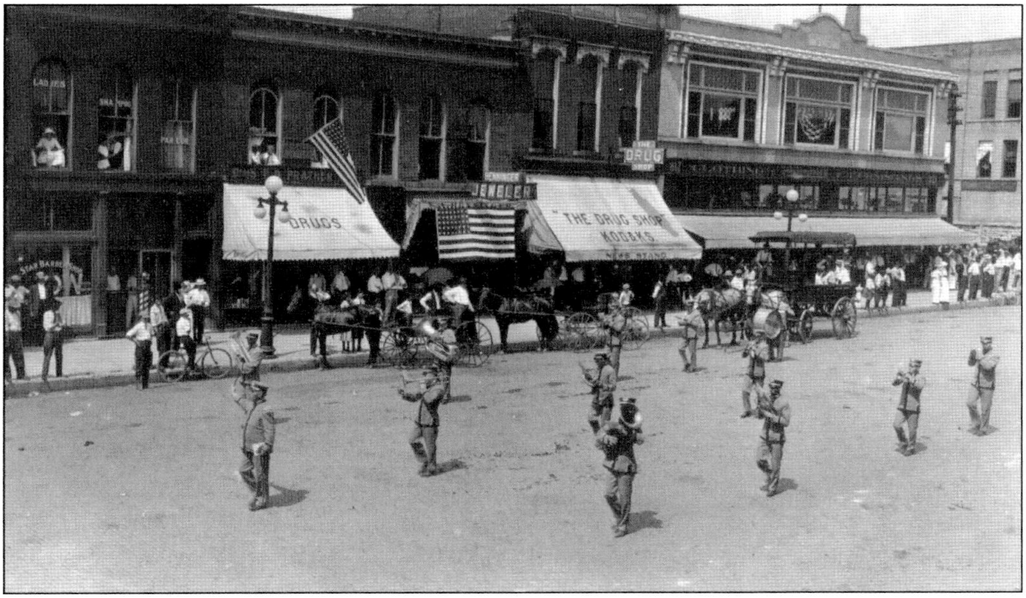

In the early 20th century, parades were a popular way for groups to promote civic pride. Through the years, Columbia's main thoroughfare has hosted parades for schools, bands, and fraternal and social organizations. Here, an unidentified band marches down Broadway. The Victor Barth Building, which still exists, can be seen on the right. The American flag has 48 stars, which means the photograph was taken sometime after February 1912, when Arizona became a state.

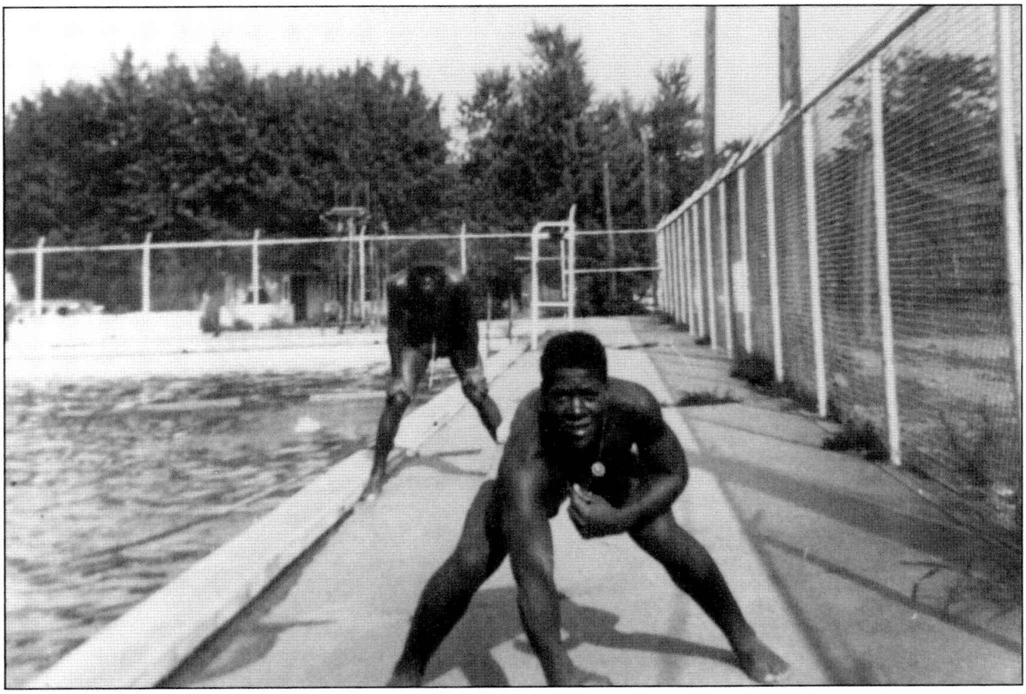

Douglass Park sits north of Douglass High School off Providence Road. With its swimming pool and ball fields, it was for many years a hub of social activity for Columbia's African American community. In 1948, a young swimmer strikes a football pose before jumping into the water. Today, the park's outdoor pool facilities feature a water slide, water jets, and a splash zone.

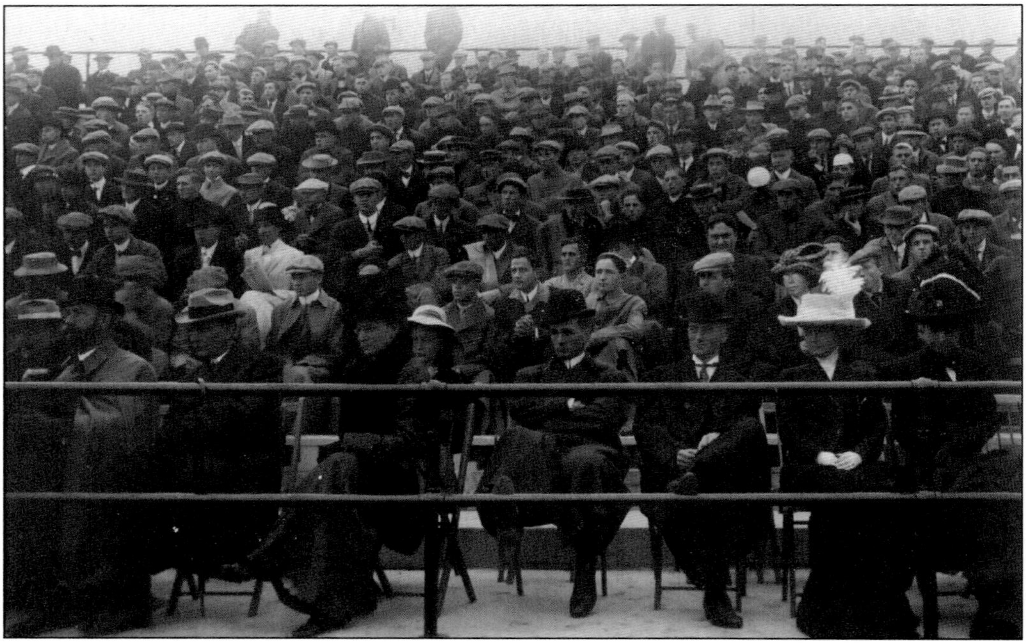

The university's football team has attracted crowds of fans and spectators for more than 100 years. This 1909 photograph was taken at Rollins Field on a cold fall day. Dr. and Mrs. Albert Ross Hill are seated at left in the front row. Dr. Hill was the university's ninth president, serving from 1908 until 1921. Hill Hall, built in 1952, was named for him.

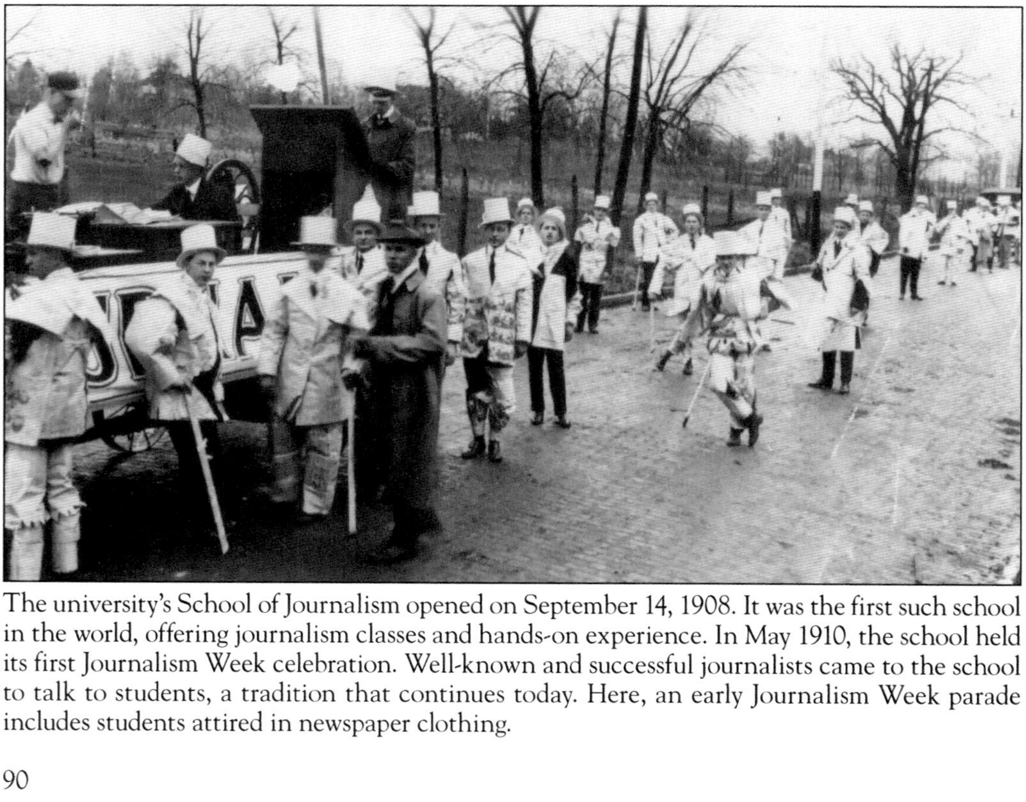

The university's School of Journalism opened on September 14, 1908. It was the first such school in the world, offering journalism classes and hands-on experience. In May 1910, the school held its first Journalism Week celebration. Well-known and successful journalists came to the school to talk to students, a tradition that continues today. Here, an early Journalism Week parade includes students attired in newspaper clothing.

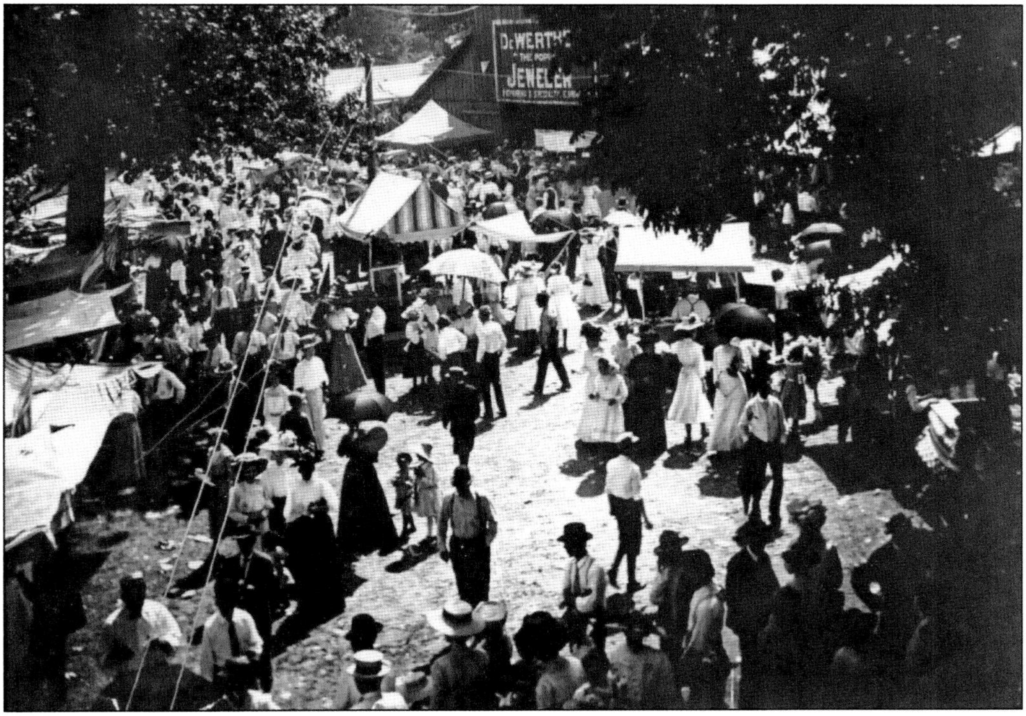

In 1835, the Boone County Fair became the first such fair held west of the Mississippi River. Throughout its history, the fair has attracted crowds who come for the displays, competitions, food, and socialization. The fair has been held at six locations in Columbia. This photograph shows the fair midway, on the grounds of what is now Hickman High School.

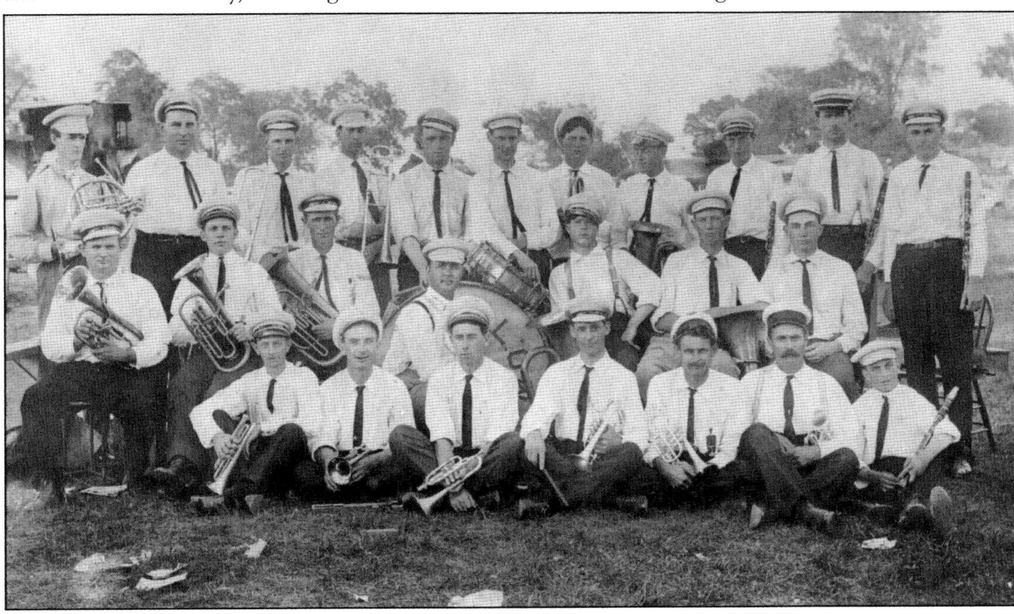

Through the years, bands and their music have remained popular at the Boone County Fair. Here, members of an unidentified band pose with their musical instruments prior to a performance in 1905. The fair, held each summer, promises events and attractions for all ages and interests. The fair was suspended in 1917 during World War I. It did not resume until 1947.

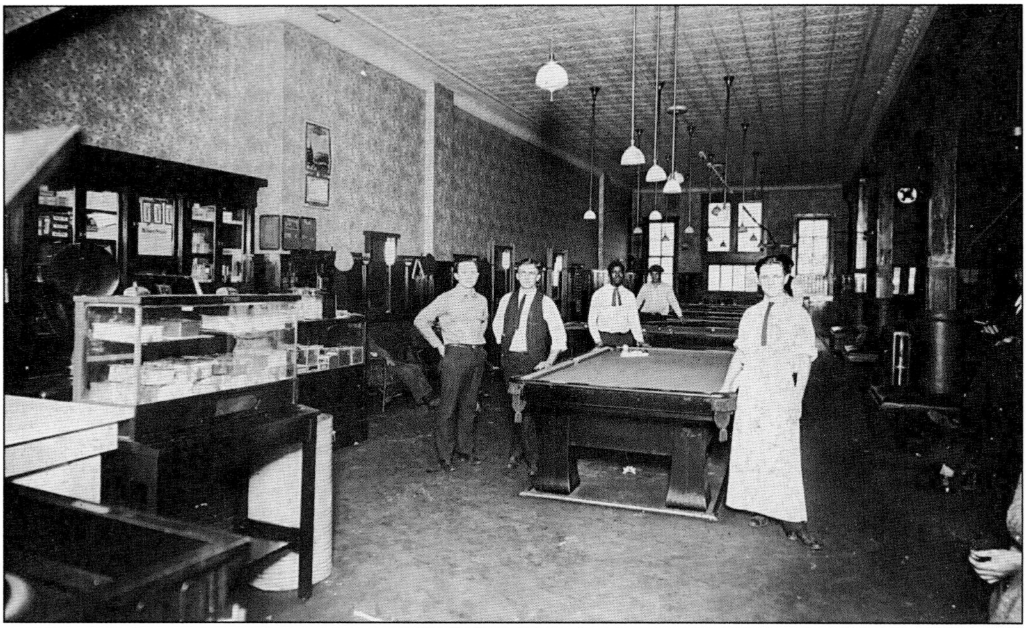

Since the 1880s, generations of Columbians have entered the doors of Booches Billiard Parlor. With full-size pool tables, snooker tables, and a no-pocket billiard table, this is no family-friendly establishment. Booches supposedly received its name from original owner Paul Blucher "Booch" Venable. In 1920, a barbershop adjoined the second-floor South Ninth Street billiard hall. Today, Booches is known for its hamburgers and as a student hangout.

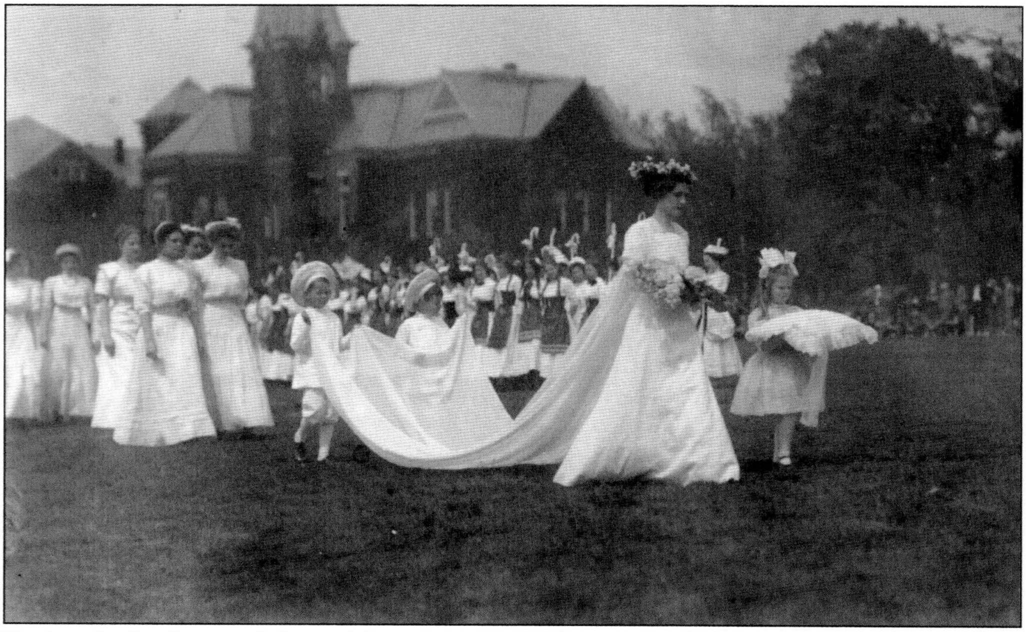

For hundreds of years, Celts and Saxons recognized May 1 as the start of planting season and an agricultural holiday. Traditional May Day celebrations usually included flowers, dancing, and weaving streamers around a May pole. May Day was celebrated at the university's quadrangle in 1910 by women only, with the selection of a queen from the senior class and attendants. The university's celebrations ceased by the 1920s.

Seven

Schools and Churches

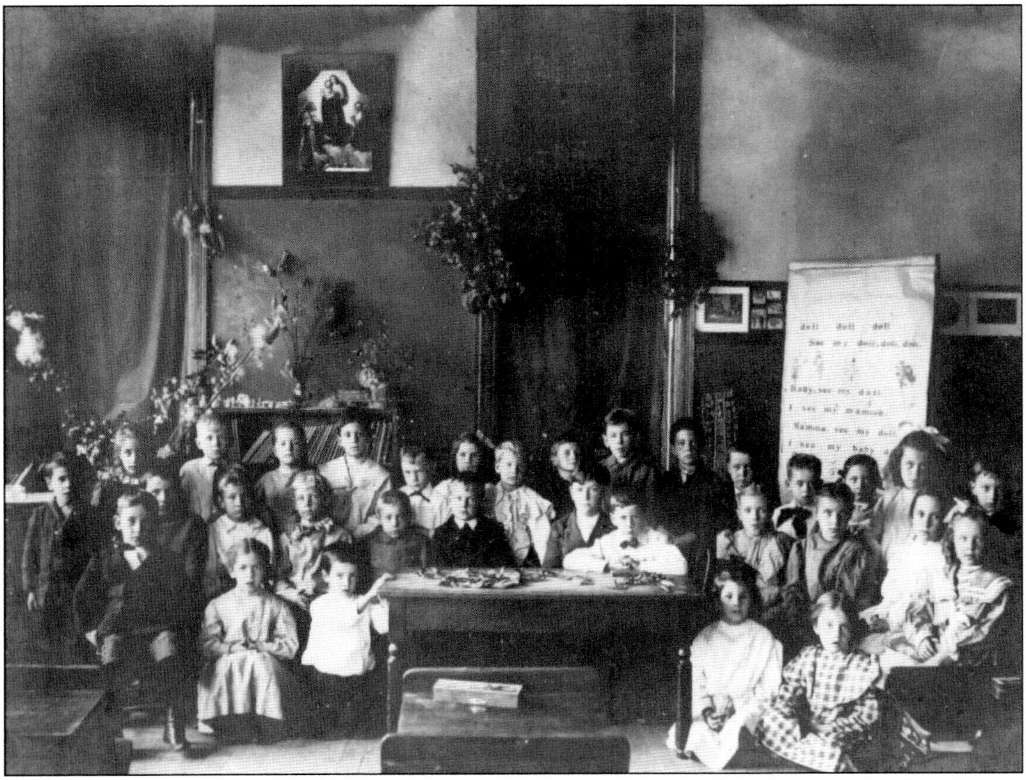

These children were students in Joy Fewsmith's primary room at Robert E. Lee School on Locust Street. The school was established in 1904 in the heart of downtown Columbia. The original building shown here was replaced with the school's current building in 1934. Today, the school is known as Lee Expressive Arts Elementary School. It serves approximately 300 students. Fewsmith taught for 50 years.

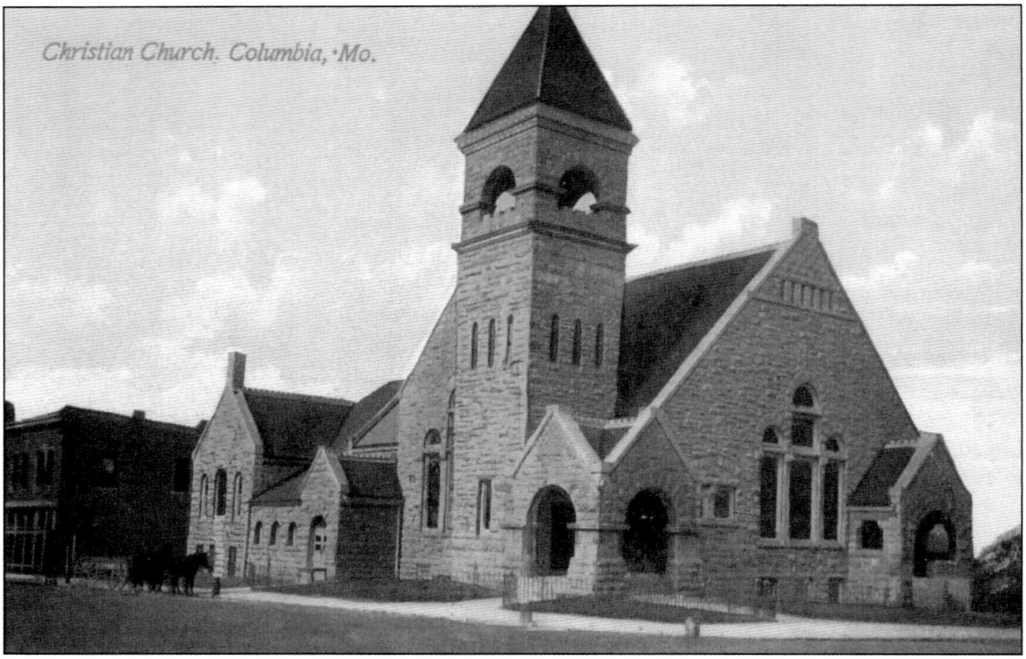

Columbia's First Christian Church, at Tenth and Walnut Streets, traces its history to 1832. In its infancy, it held worship services in the Boone County Courthouse. The building shown here is the congregation's second structure. It was designed by a Chicago architect, built in the Richardson-Romanesque style, and dedicated in 1893. It is listed in the National Register of Historic Places.

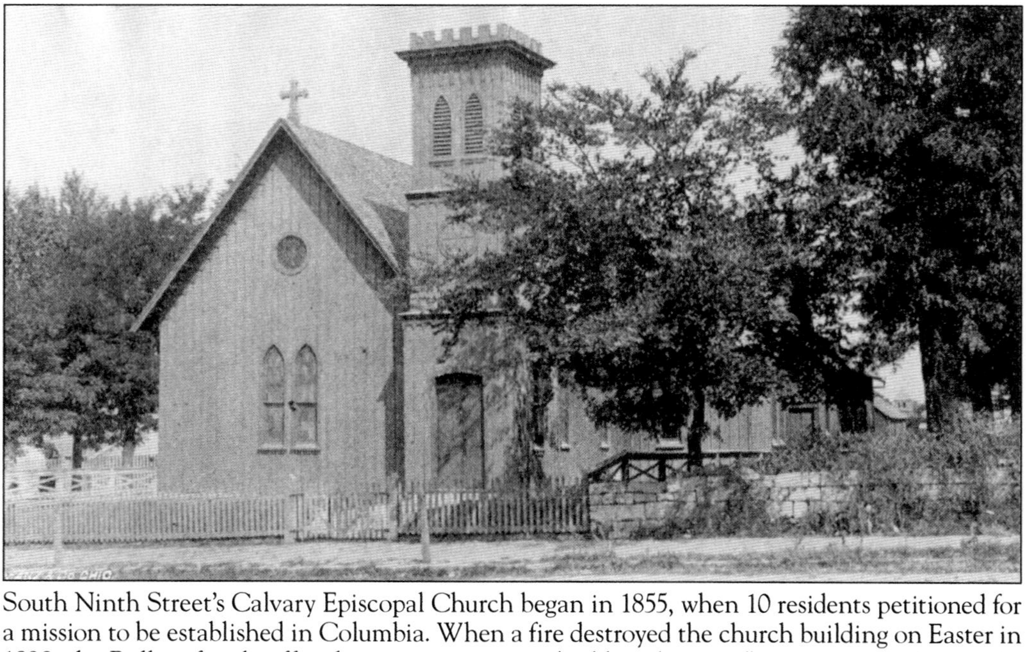

South Ninth Street's Calvary Episcopal Church began in 1855, when 10 residents petitioned for a mission to be established in Columbia. When a fire destroyed the church building on Easter in 1898, the Rollins family offered to construct a new building (pictured). In an unusual move for that time, the family chose a female architect, Mary Louise Hale. She successfully salvaged and reused materials from the old building.

Rogers Street's Jefferson School opened as a high school in 1911. When David H. Hickman High School opened in 1927, the Jefferson school became Jefferson Junior High School. It was renamed Jefferson Middle School in 2013 and is referred to as "Columbia's oldest new middle school."

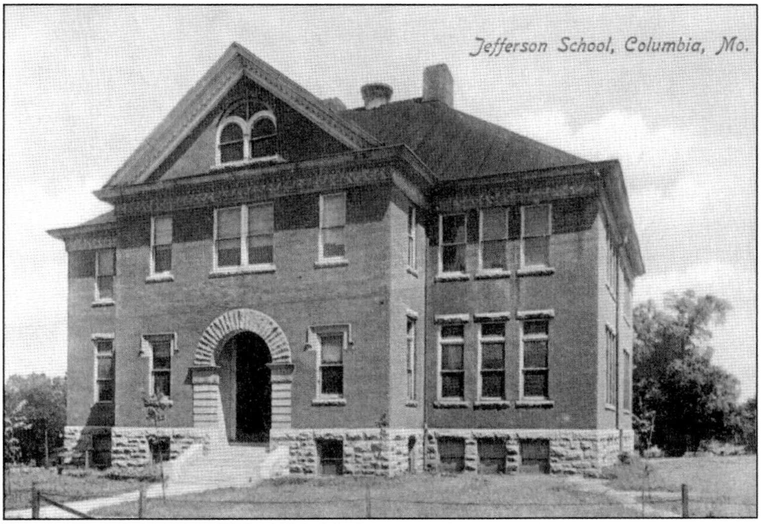

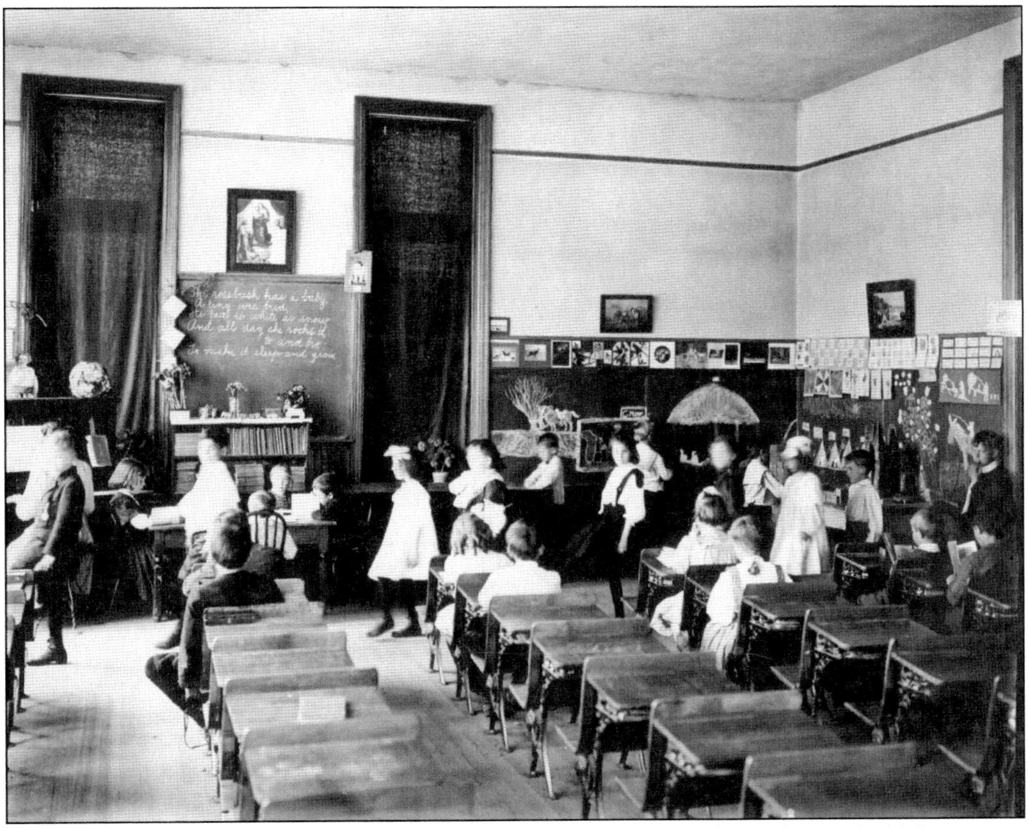

Desk designs and clothing styles may have changed, but much about this early-20th-century elementary school classroom seems familiar. Mrs. Howard Lang Sr. (far left) was the teacher in this classroom at Robert E. Lee School. Her son, Howard B. Lang Jr., was Columbia's mayor from 1953 until 1957. Her cousin was Joy Fewsmith, whose classroom photograph appears at the beginning of this chapter.

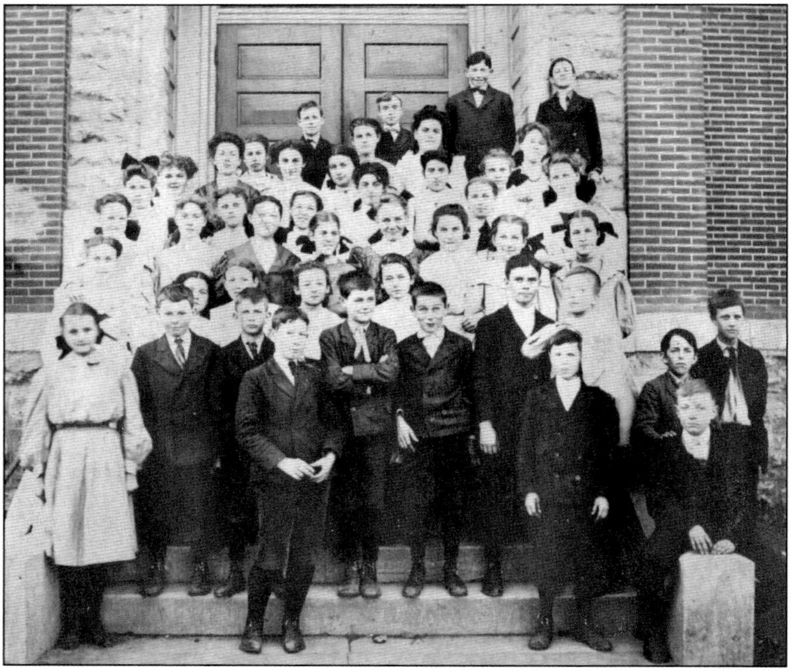

Thomas Hart Benton School opened in a four-room building in 1896. Posing here are the school's seventh-grade students and one class clown. Note the white marks to the left of the building's doors, an indication that chalkboard erasers had recently been cleaned.

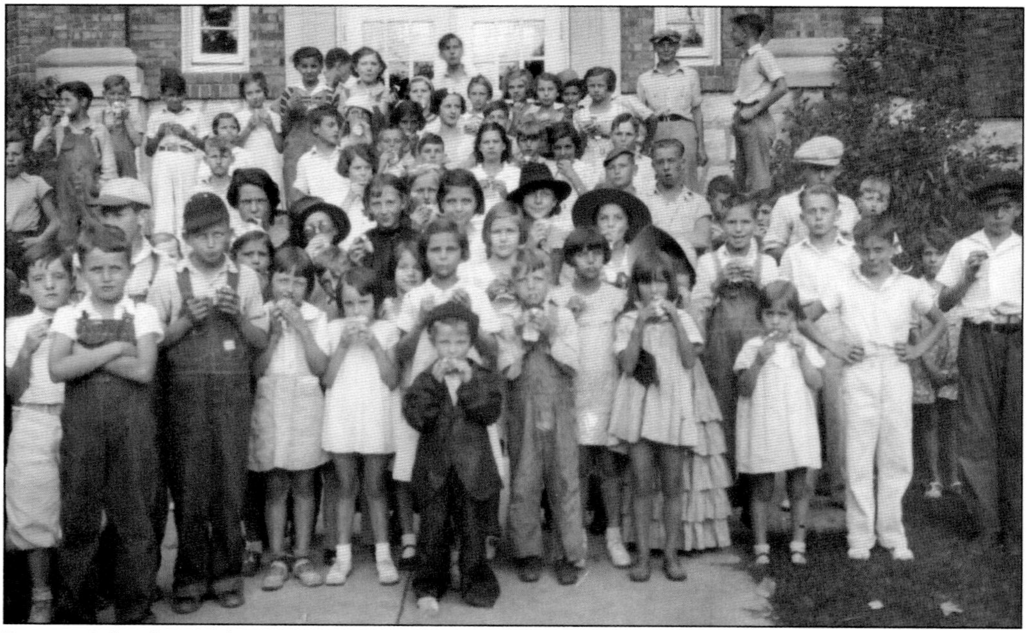

Benton School moved into its current building on Hinkson Avenue in 1927. This 1930s photograph shows students on the school's front steps. Today, the school has approximately 260 students in prekindergarten through fifth grade. Columbia's first "common" school began in the 1830s and operated on a subscription basis. The fee per quarter for reading, writing, grammar, spelling, and arithmetic was $2.50. Geography cost an extra $1.50.

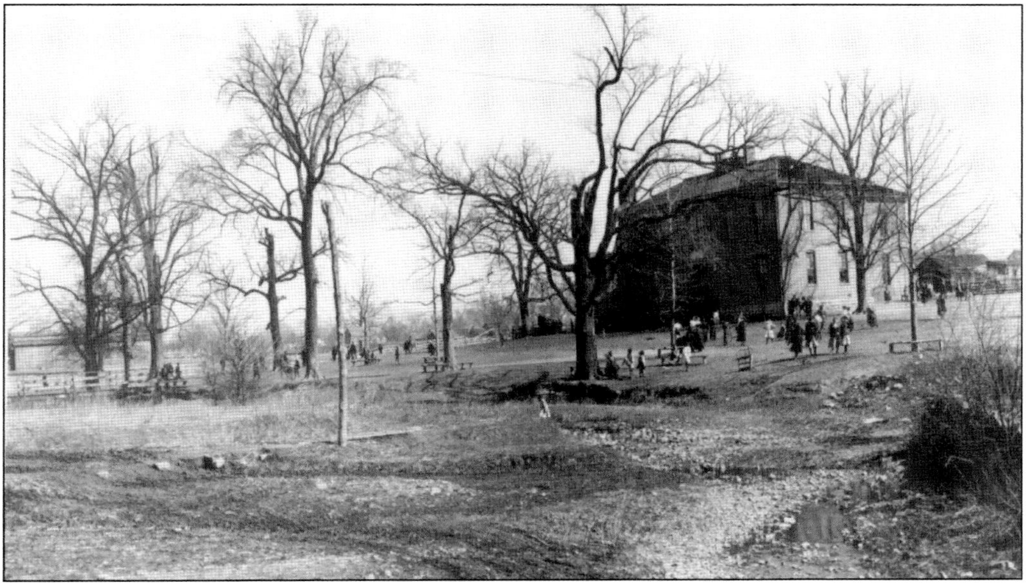

The school that became Frederick Douglass School first opened its doors under the name Cummings Academy. It later was called Excelsior School, then, in 1898, was renamed for the former slave who became an abolitionist speaker and social reformer. This photograph, taken in March 1908, shows children outside the school during recess. A new building was completed in 1917. Today, Douglass is an alternative high school.

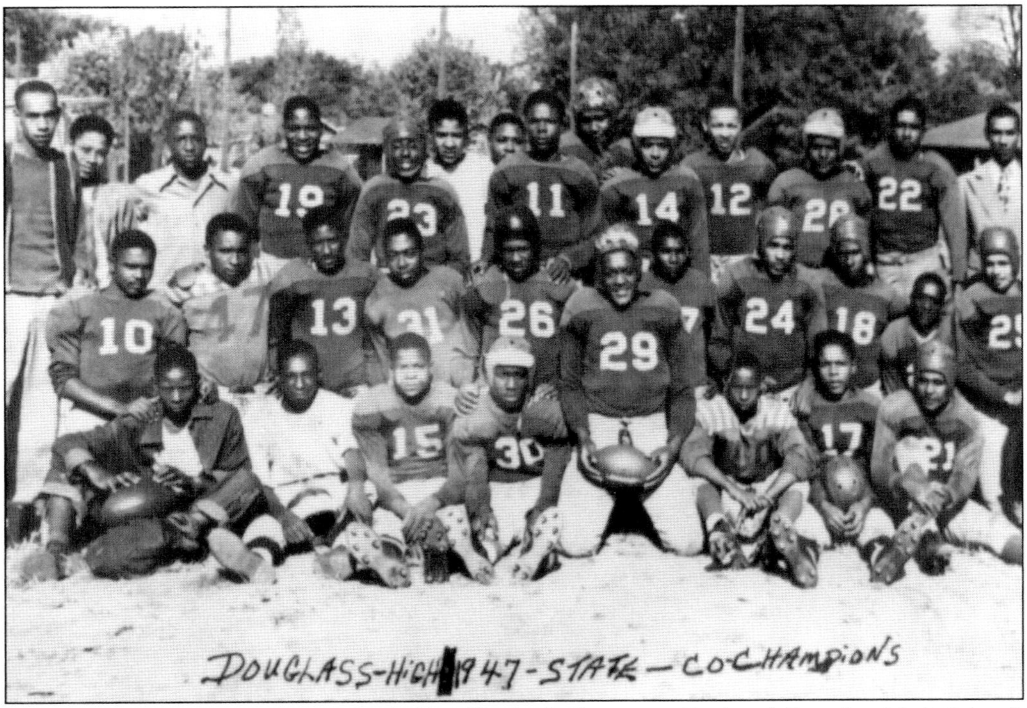

The 1940s were years of winning football and basketball teams at Frederick Douglass High School. Here, the school's championship football team poses in 1947. The school and activities associated with it were important parts of the social and educational fabric of Columbia's African American community. Today, the school is one of Columbia's four public high schools.

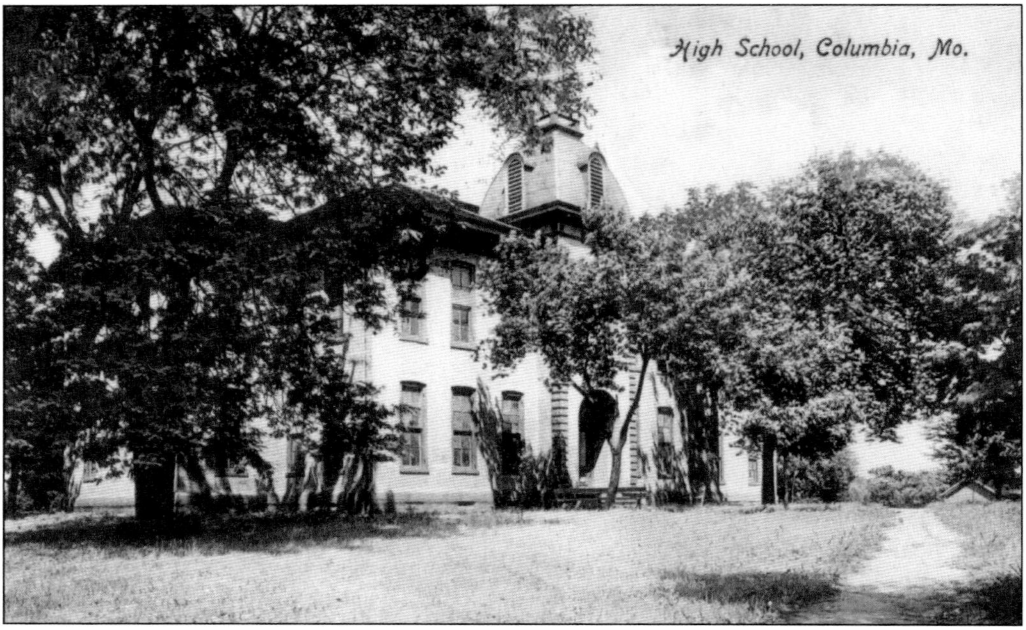

Columbia High School, shown here in 1909, was located at Eighth and Rogers Streets. Columbia's population grew, and programs offered at the school expanded. The original two-year high school program was expanded to four years. By 1912, the old building had been torn down, and a new, three-story school was built on the lot to replace it. The school's first athletic teams were organized in 1905.

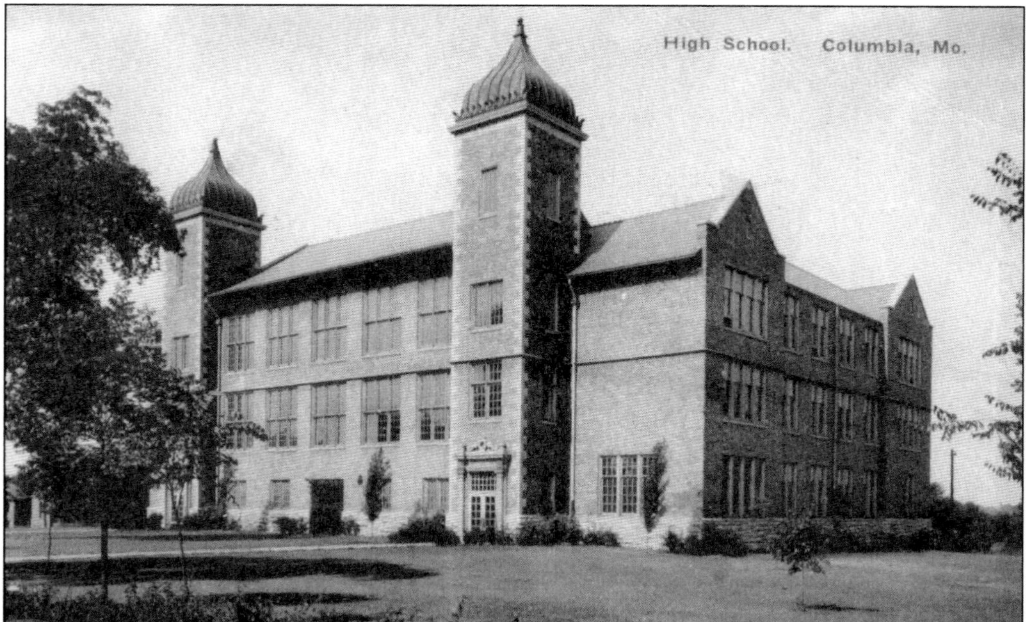

Columbia's population growth continued. In 1927, a larger high school was built on property donated by legislator and educator David Henry Hickman near US Route 40. The school's name changed to Hickman High School, but the school mascot and yearbook remained the same—the Kewpie and *The Cresset*. The old building, seen here in 1912, became Jefferson Junior High School.

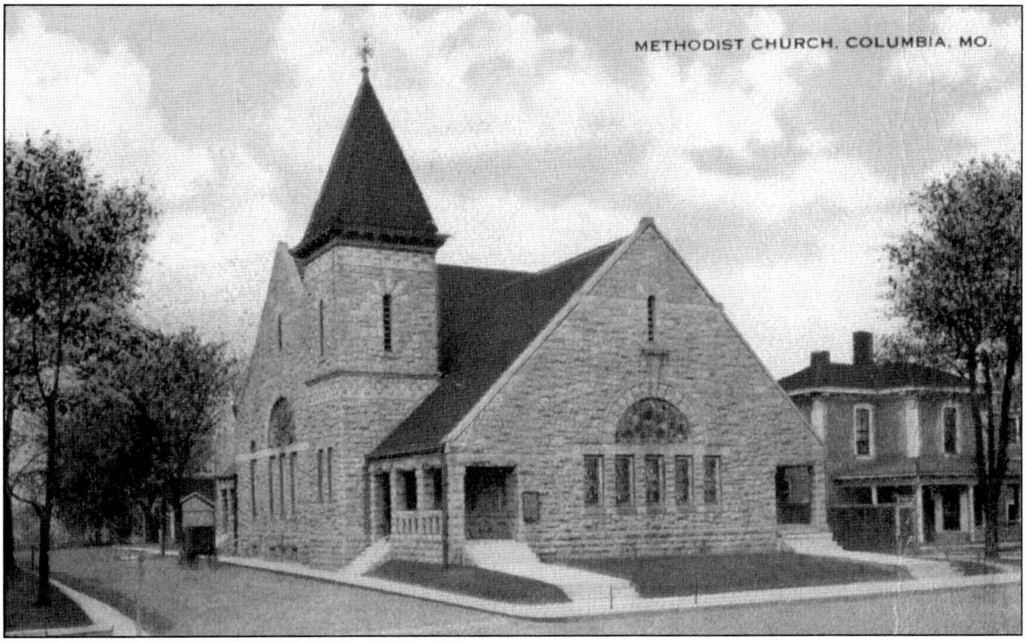

The Methodist denomination arrived in Columbia about 1820 in the form of a Methodist circuit rider. Worshipers met in homes, the courthouse, and outdoors before a shared facility was built with the Baptist congregation in 1837. The Methodists built their own facility on Broadway in 1849 and again in 1852. This 1923 photograph shows the Broadway location. Work began two years later on a building closer to the university campus, completed in 1930.

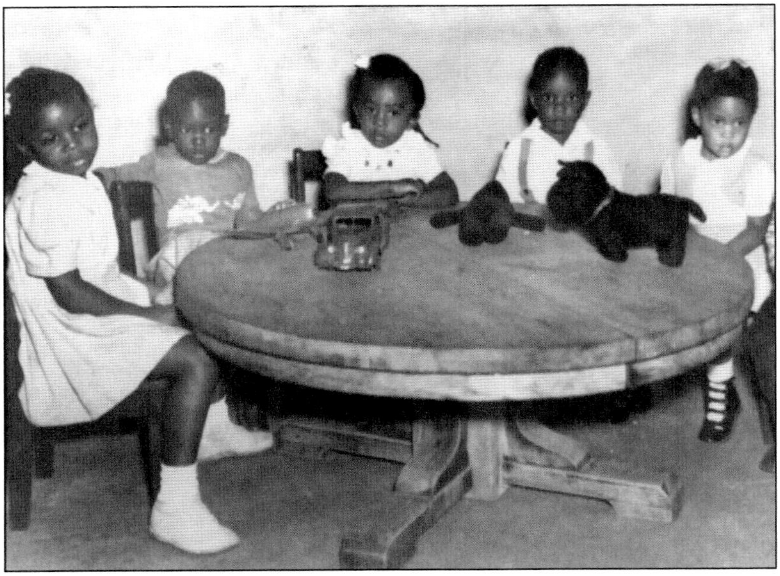

Worship and church-related activities have been important in the lives of generations of Columbia African Americans. This mid-20th-century photograph shows immaculately dressed and groomed kids seated around a small wooden table for a children's worship gathering.

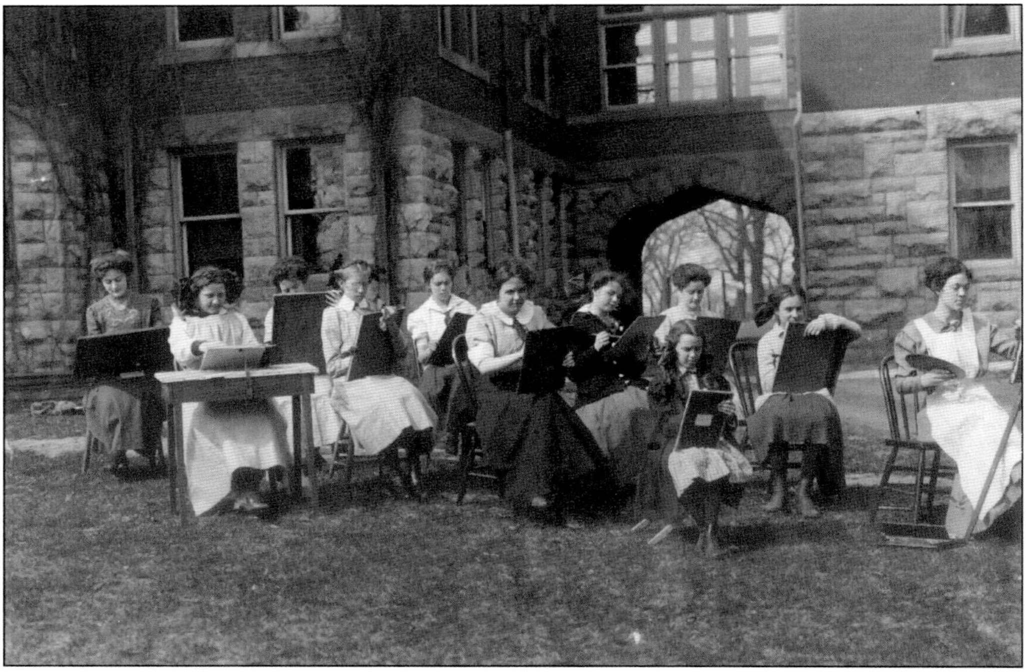

When the Missouri legislature granted a charter to Christian Female College in 1851, it became the first women's college west of the Mississippi River chartered by a state legislature. At that time, the University of Missouri did not admit female students. Christian College remained a female college until 1970, when it became Columbia College, a four-year coeducational institution. Here, students in an art class set up sketchbooks on the campus grounds.

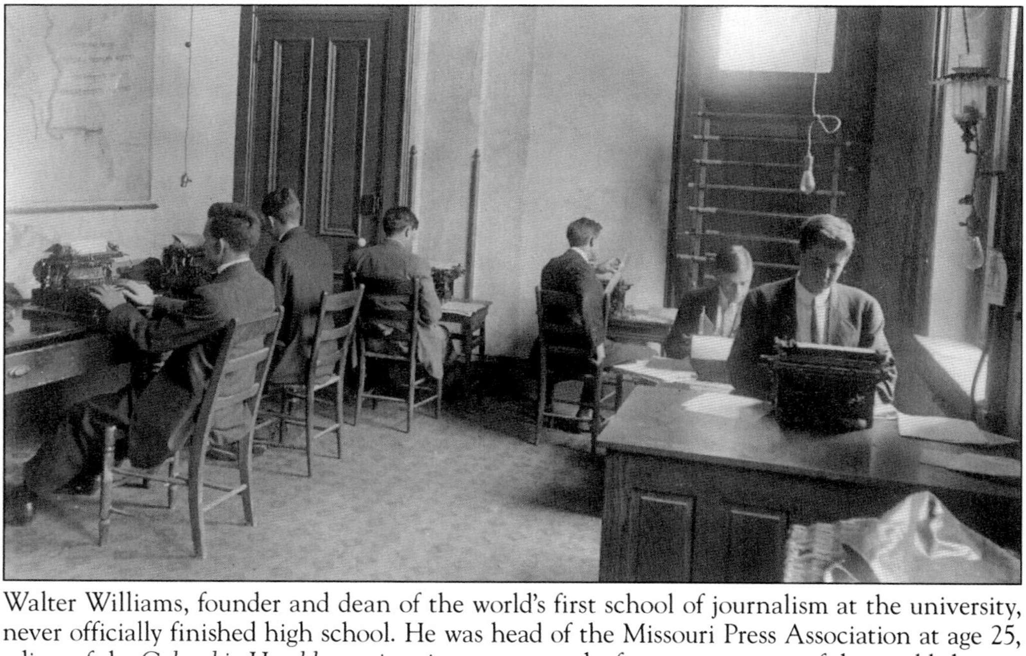

Walter Williams, founder and dean of the world's first school of journalism at the university, never officially finished high school. He was head of the Missouri Press Association at age 25, editor of the *Columbia Herald*, a university curator, and a fervent supporter of the establishment of a school of journalism. His dream became reality in 1908. Here, early journalism students are at work at typewriters.

Eight

Medical Care

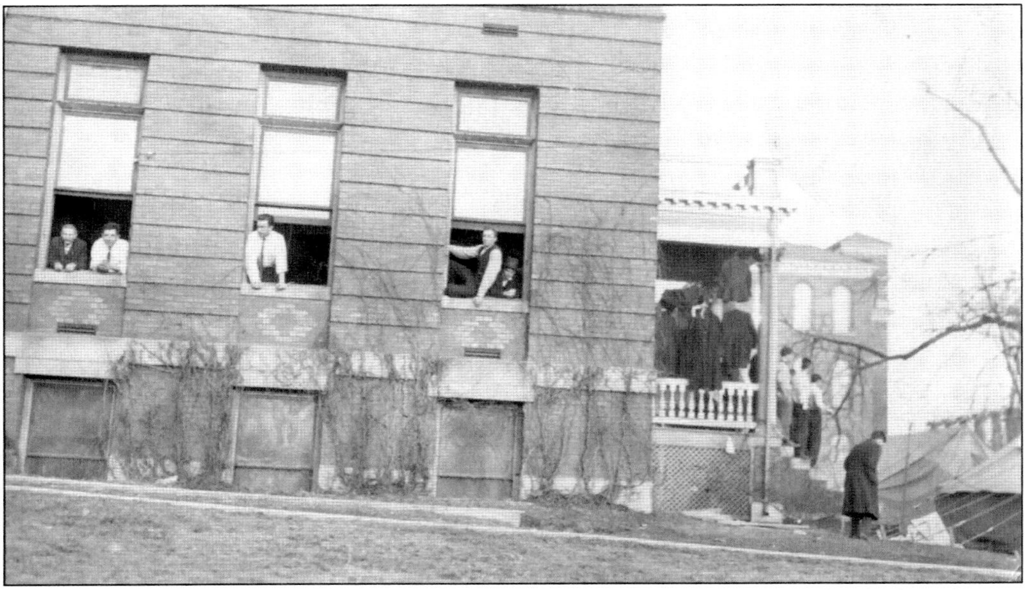

Parker Memorial Hospital opened at the university in 1901 as part of the School of Medicine's program, which was established in 1872. It was Columbia's first hospital. Women also were admitted to the medical program in 1901, and the 20-bed facility soon expanded. A larger facility was completed in 1921. The men shown here are student doctors on break. With windows open and suit coats airing, it is likely a warm day.

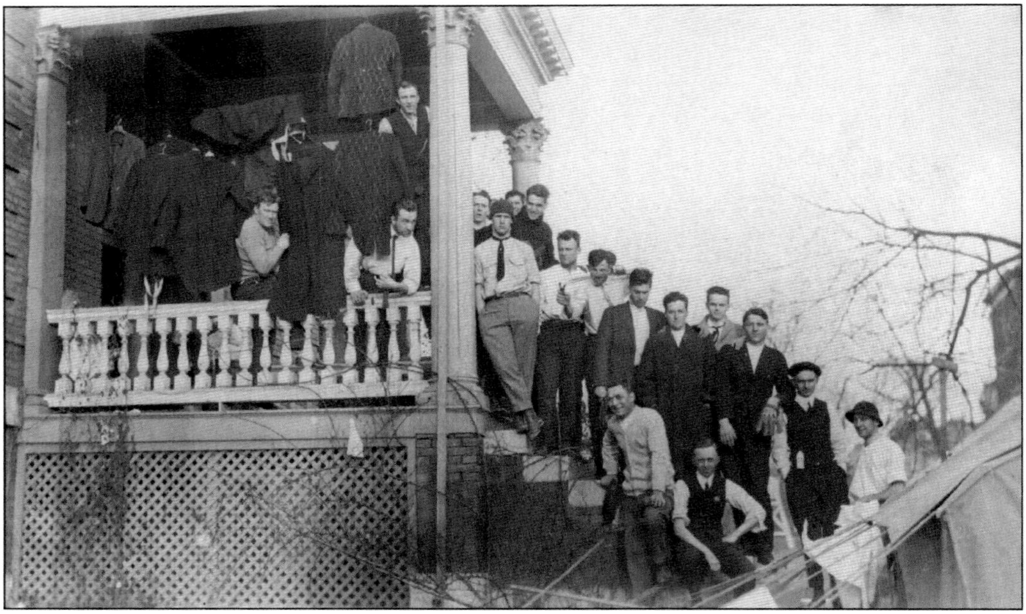

The training these university medical students received in the early 20th century hardly resembles the medical instruction students receive today. The worldwide influenza epidemic during World War I spread throughout the country and the world, including Columbia. Influenza was widespread among students. The university closed for three weeks, and the city and university were quarantined. A shortage of medical facilities was quickly noted and addressed in subsequent years.

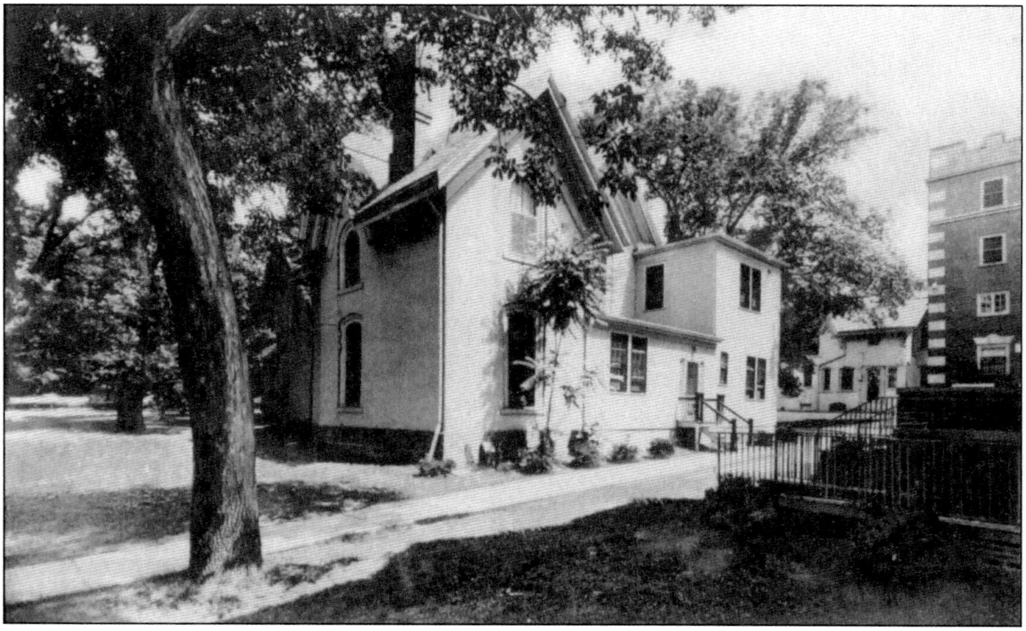

Although small, Stephens College had its own infirmary on campus. When a student was ill and away from home, she sometimes needed medical assistance that her roommates and friends could not provide. The Stephens College infirmary was located in a comfortable, home-like building and was staffed by an experienced nurse. During the influenza epidemic in 1918, Stephens, Christian College, and the university each set up emergency hospitals.

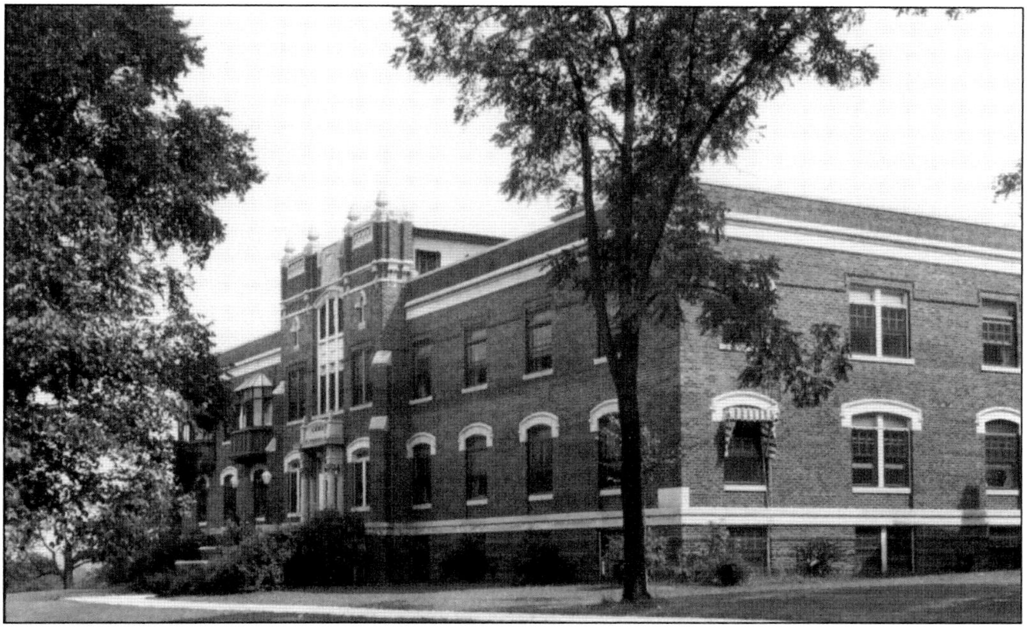

Boone County Hospital opened in December 1921 to serve the medical needs of those living in and around Columbia. Initial plans called for it to have 20 beds, but this was modified to allow for 40 beds. Demand for medical services increased through the years, and the hospital expanded. Today, Boone Hospital Center offers the latest in medical services and procedures. The original building (pictured) is still in use.

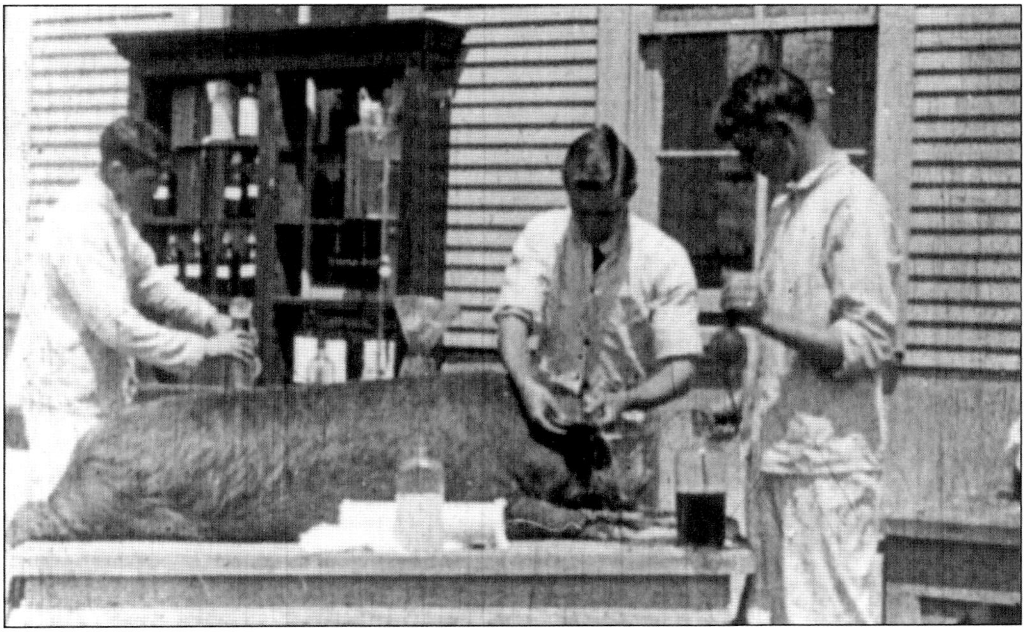

The university first offered a veterinary science class in 1884. The program grew to a veterinary science department, a school of veterinary medicine as part of the agricultural sciences department, and a veterinary medicine school in its own division. Today, it is called the College of Veterinary Medicine. Here, students perform a procedure on a pig in 1907. The examination table and equipment cabinet are outdoors.

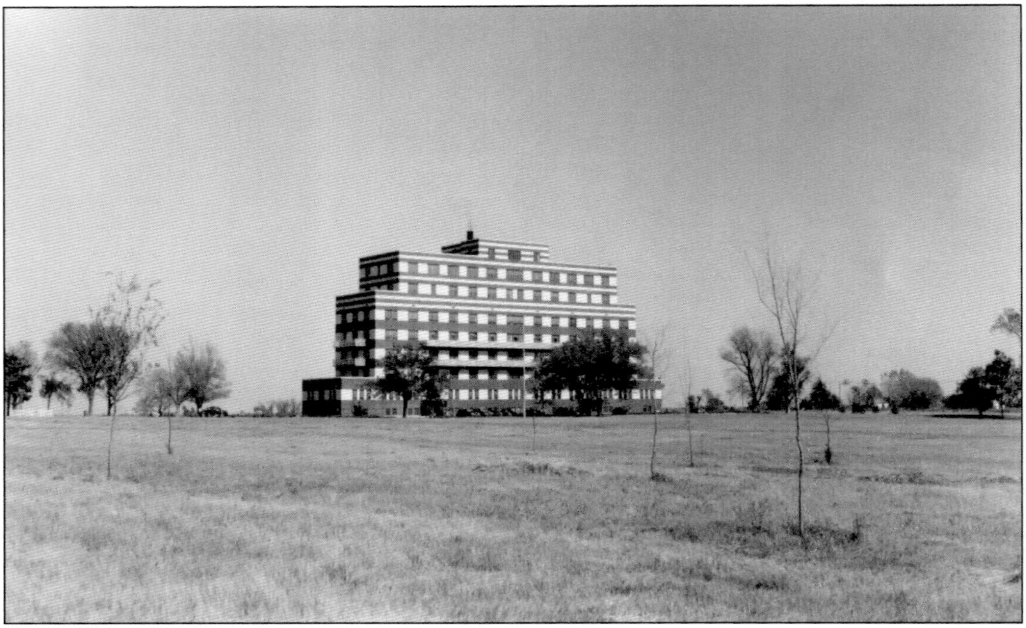

When Ellis Fischel State Cancer Hospital opened its doors in 1940, it became the first cancer hospital west of the Mississippi River and only the third in the country. Dr. Fischel was a proponent of statewide cancer treatment. In 1937, the Missouri State Cancer Commission chose Columbia as the site for the hospital due to its location in the center of Missouri and its accessibility to major highways.

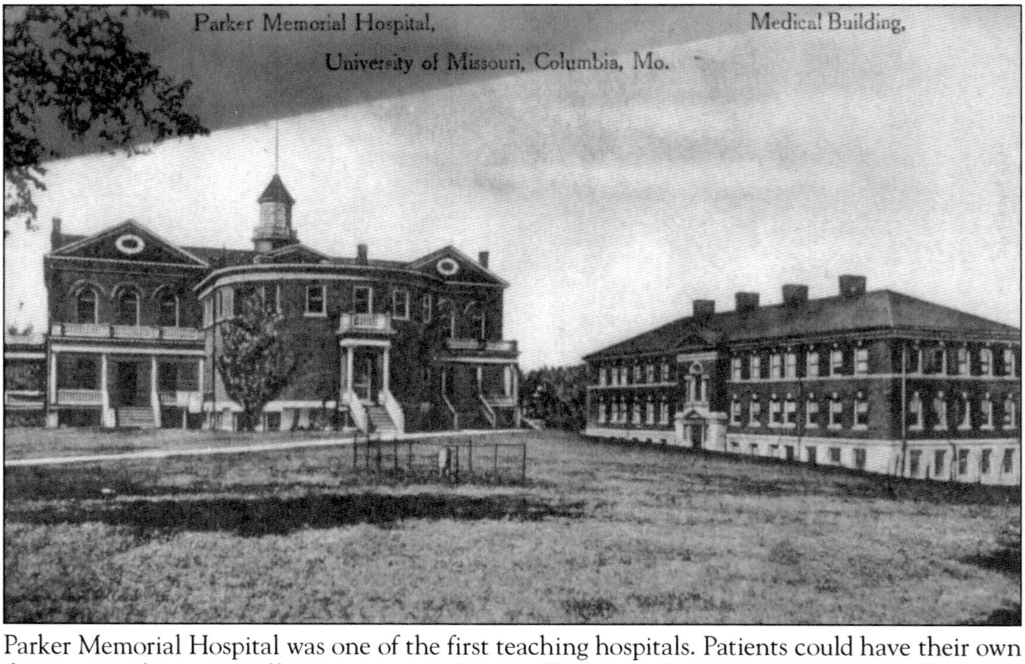

Parker Memorial Hospital was one of the first teaching hospitals. Patients could have their own doctor treat them, even if he was not part of the staff. The nearby Medical Laboratories Building, completed in 1902, housed the university's medical school. It was named for Dr. Andrew Walker McAlester, a former dean of the School of Medicine. Today, Parker Hall houses testing and counseling services. McAlester Hall houses the psychological sciences department.

Nine

Famous People, Notable Sites, and Local Landmarks

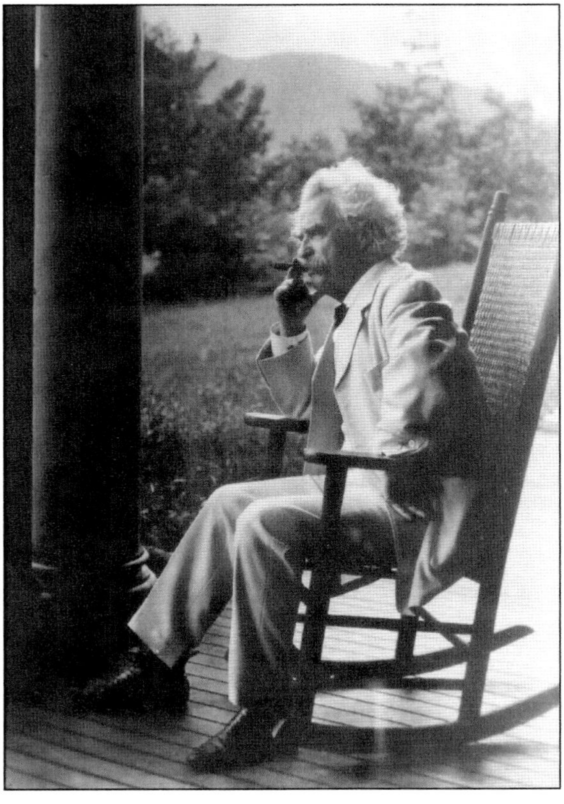

Writer Samuel Langhorne Clemens (Mark Twain) famously chronicled life as a Missouri boy in his stories about Tom Sawyer and Huckleberry Finn. He returned to his home state in June 1902, when the university conferred upon him the honorary degree of Doctor of Laws. Dressed in a cap and gown for the ceremony, he also delivered diplomas to the university's graduating class members.

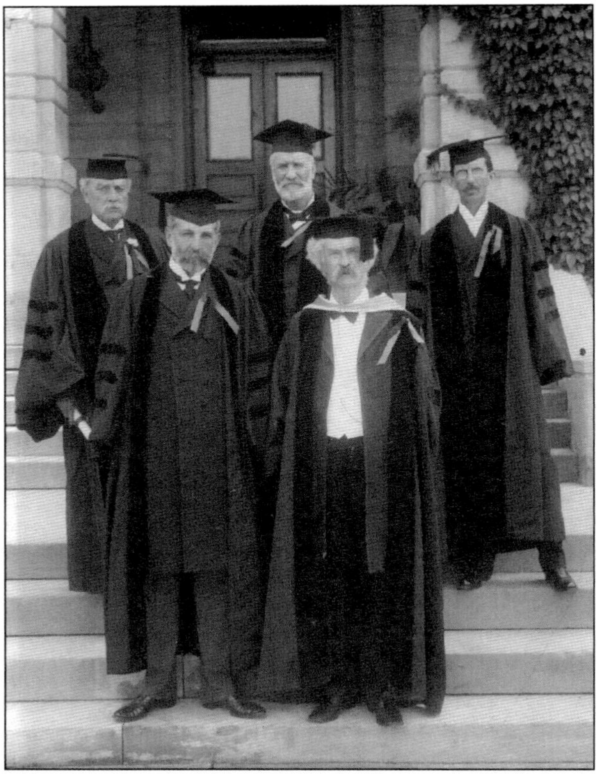

While in Missouri to receive the honorary degree, the highest honor the university could bestow, Mark Twain (first row, right) also visited St. Louis and his hometown, Hannibal. It was his last visit to the area that inspired so much of his writing. While in Columbia, Twain stayed at the home of his friend, Edwin W. Stephens, publisher and editor of the *Columbia Missouri Herald*.

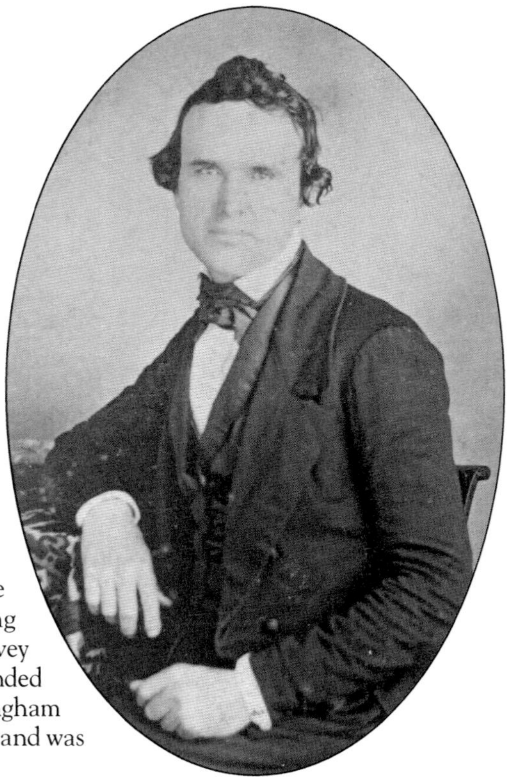

George Caleb Bingham showed artistic ability at a young age. Before photography, people often hired artists to paint portraits, and Bingham became a successful portrait artist. He also held strong opinions about political issues and used art to convey his views. While painting in Columbia, he befriended James Sidney Rollins, father of the university. Bingham became the first professor of art at the university and was appointed to several state positions.

Approximately 250 million years ago, Columbia was covered by water. The water was full of tiny creatures, the remains of which were fossilized and became part of the limestone formations at The Pinnacles. Located 12 miles north of town off Highway 63, The Pinnacles has long been a popular gathering place for local residents. This 1927 photograph shows two dress-clad women at the top of a formation.

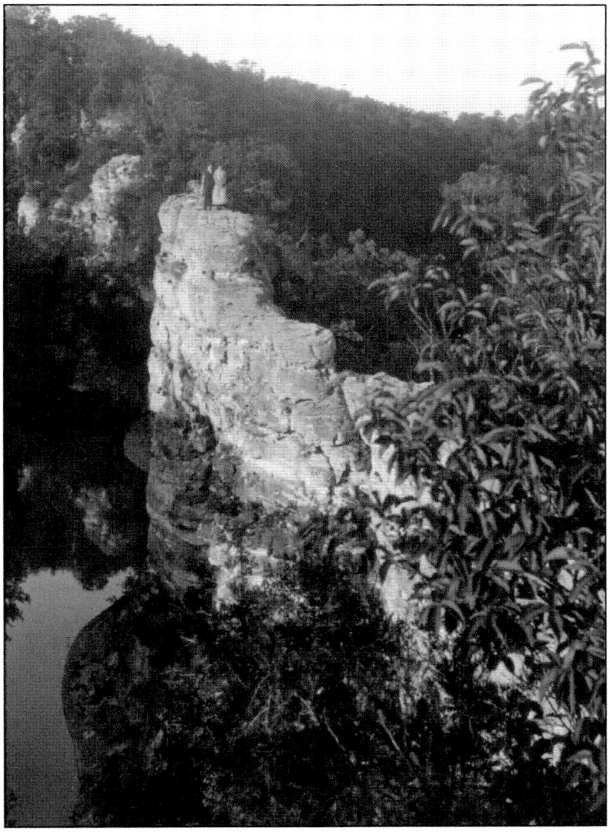

A 100-foot-wide natural rock bridge spans Little Bonne Femme Creek south of Columbia. Early residents built a mill, a distillery, and a store there. Today, the property is called Rock Bridge Memorial State Park and is part of Missouri's park system. Visitors can hike and see various caves, sinkholes, the rock bridge, and an underground stream at the Devil's Icebox. One of the caves is seen here in 1927.

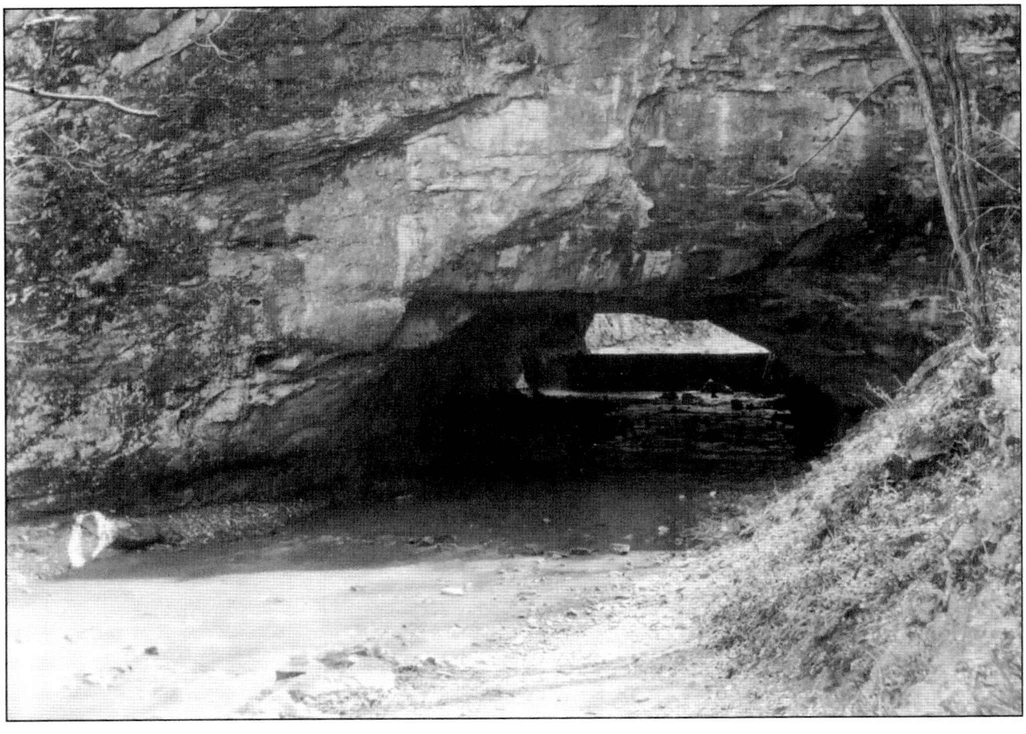

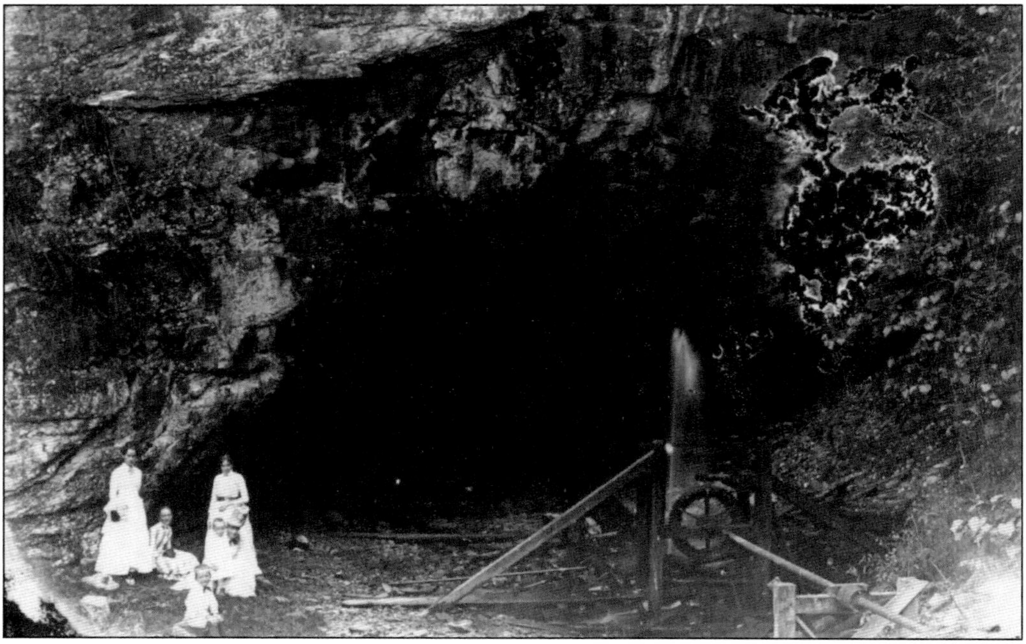

Generations of Columbia residents have enjoyed the tranquil beauty and natural rock formations found south of town. Here, a family poses beside a waterworks operation on Little Bonne Femme Creek and underneath a natural rock bridge in 1900. The area provided a cool respite during the hot and humid days of summer.

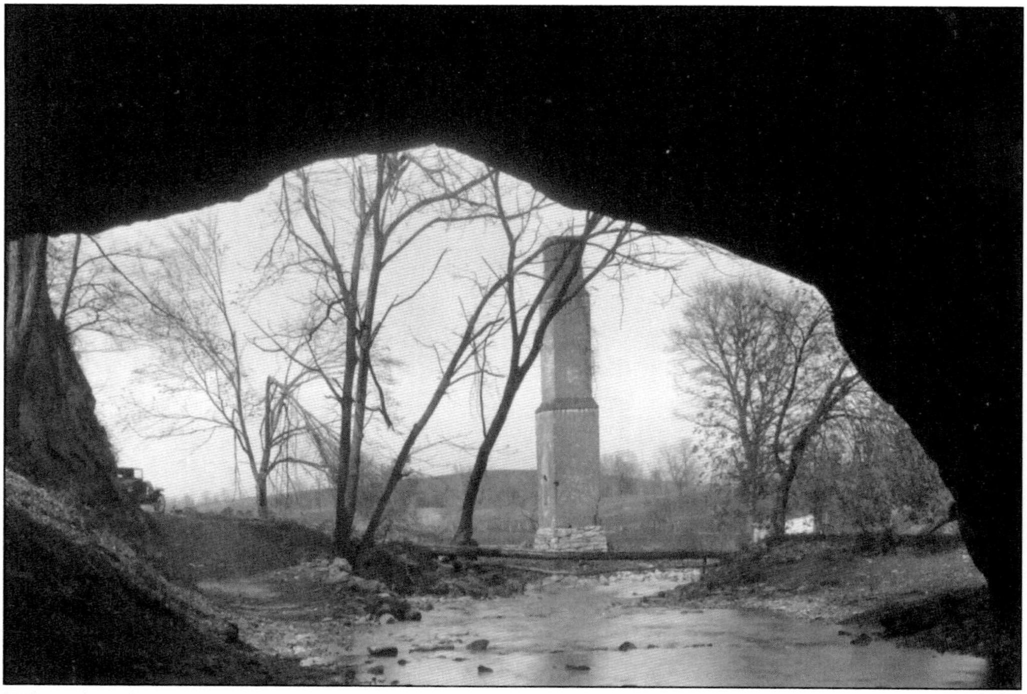

When this photograph was taken in 1927, all that remained of David Martin Emmitt's 1800s distillery was the chimney. An abundant supply of fresh water from Little Bonne Femme Creek made this an ideal location for the distillery, which operated here for many years after the Civil War.

This rock cliff, millions of years old, was called Lover's Leap. It was located on the bank of Hinkson Creek, off the Old Plank Road south of Columbia. It was the scene of a suicide, as reported in the May 24, 1922, edition of the *Columbia Evening Missourian*.

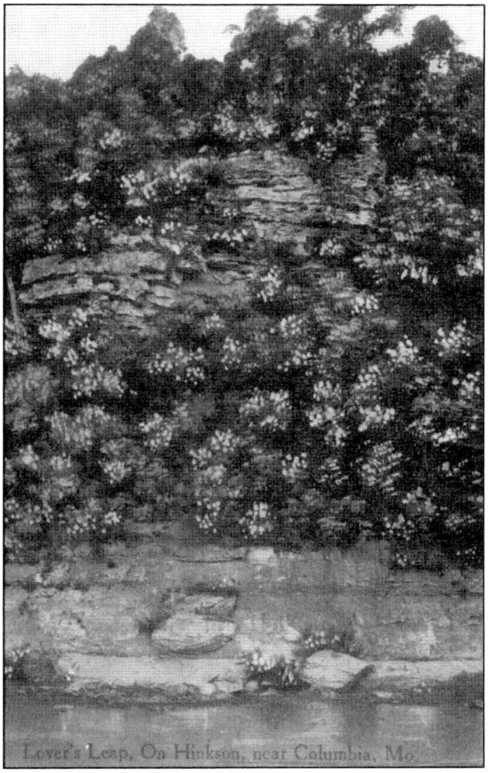

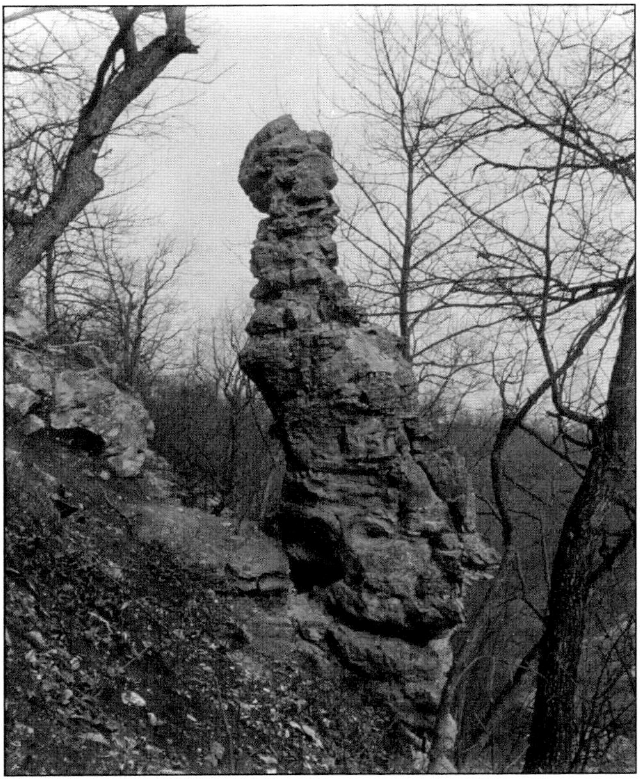

Balance Rock was a unique pinnacle rock formation overlooking Hinkson Creek at what was called the State Farm south of Columbia. It was a favorite gathering spot for students 100 years ago. This formation no longer exists, but other rock formations can be found in Boone County. Today, these are popular places to climb and hike.

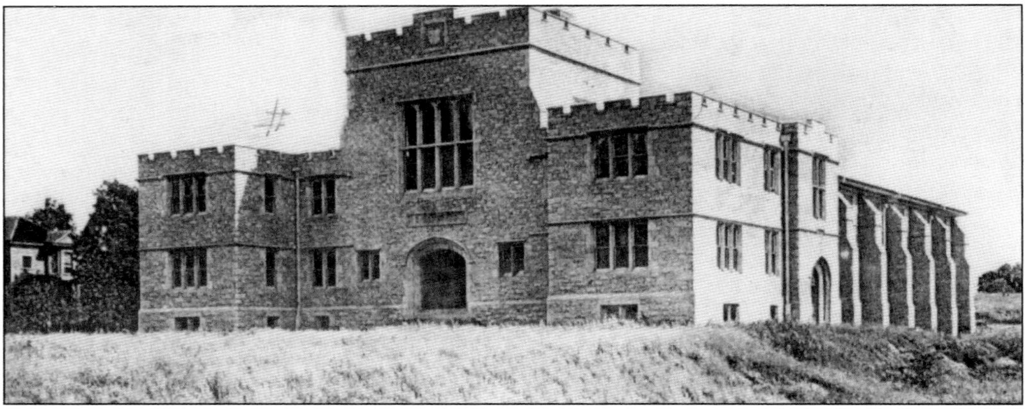

In May 1904, the university announced plans to build a men's gymnasium east of Rollins Field. It would include outdoor as well as indoor facilities and would cost approximately $70,000. The building was completed in 1906 and named for Gideon F. Rothwell, former president of the board of curators. When this photograph was taken in 1907, construction of a women's gymnasium had been discussed, but no definite plans made.

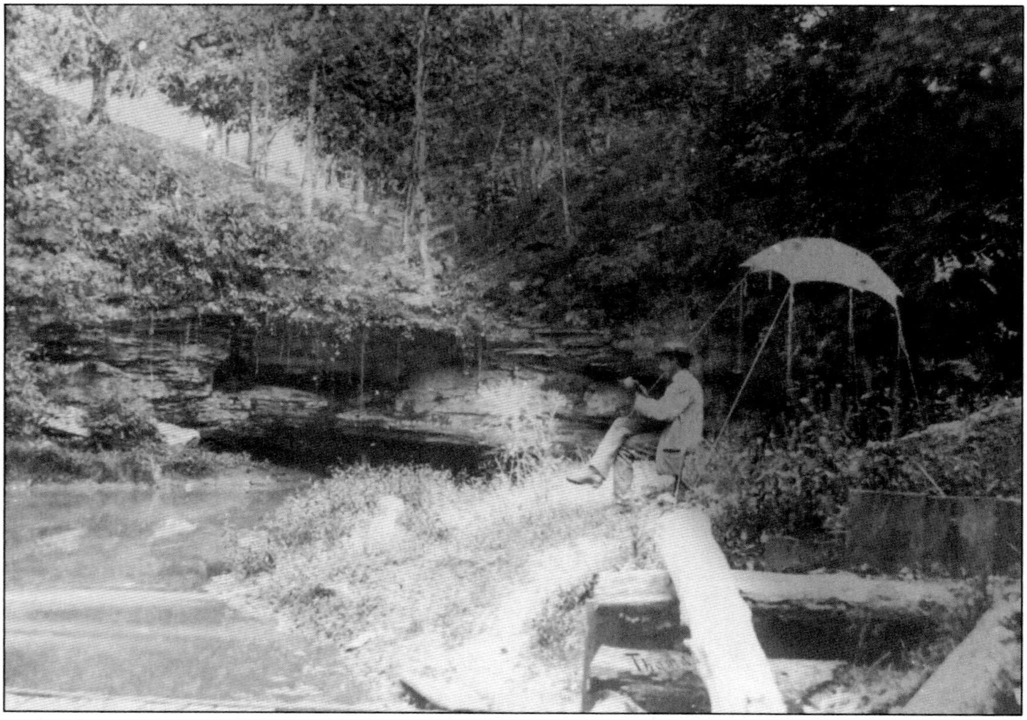

Columbia residents and students have long enjoyed the convenience of a bustling downtown business district along with the close proximity of undeveloped recreation areas. Here, a man sketches while sitting alongside a Columbia stream in 1890.

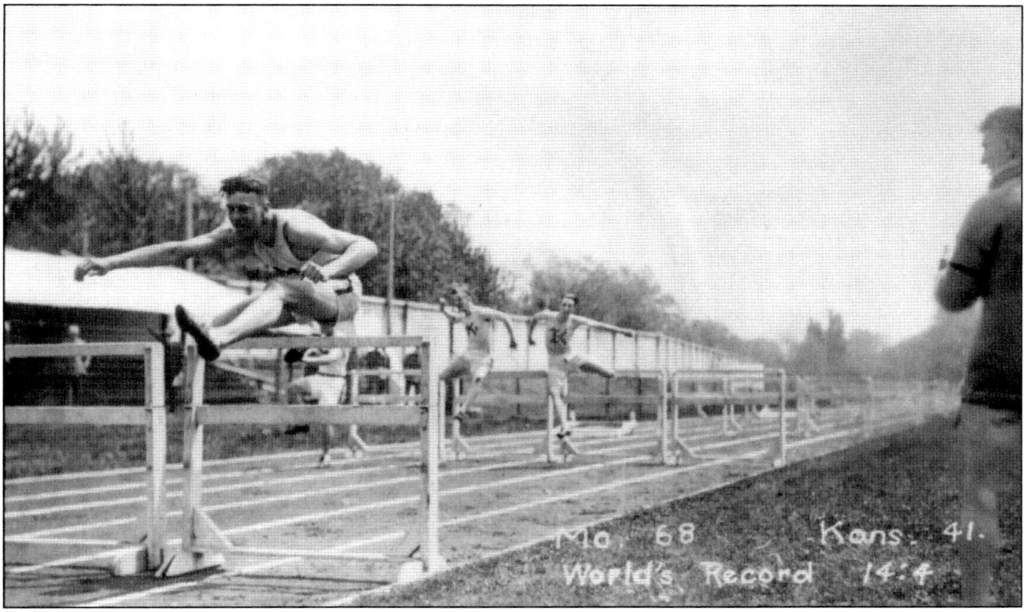

Robert J. Simpson was one of the world's best hurdlers. He lettered at the university in 1915, 1916, and 1917. In 1916, he broke a world record for the 120-yard hurdles, a record he held for four years until his brother-in-law, Earl Thomson, of Canada, broke it. From 1920 to 1926, Simpson was the university's head track coach. He was inducted into the USA Track & Field Hall of Fame in 1974.

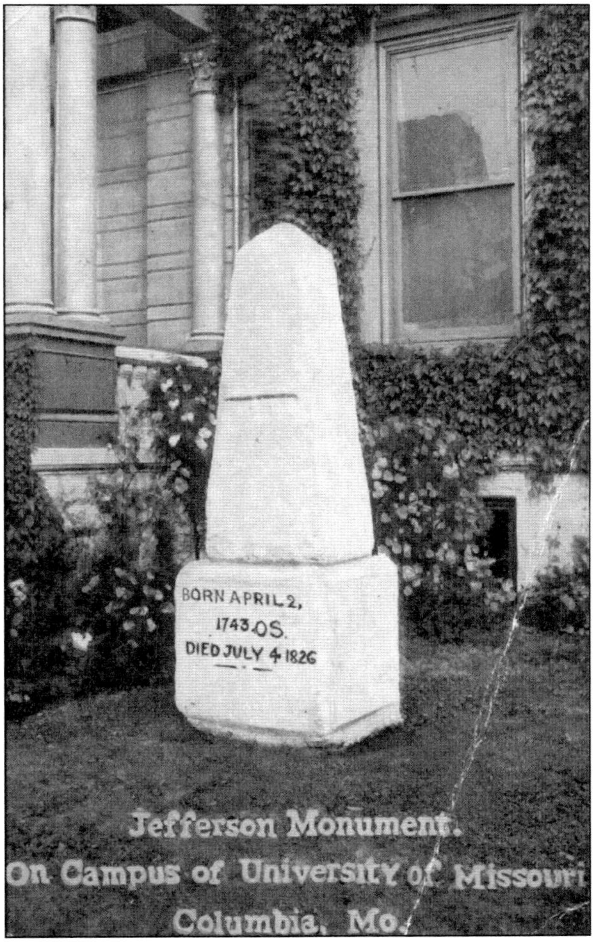

Thomas Jefferson's tombstone has been part of the university's Francis Quadrangle for more than 100 years, but Jefferson is not buried there. The monument for many years marked Jefferson's final resting place at Monticello. When university officials learned that Jefferson's family planned a new monument, they requested the old one. It seemed only fitting that the first land grant university in Jefferson's Louisiana Purchase territory should have such an honor.

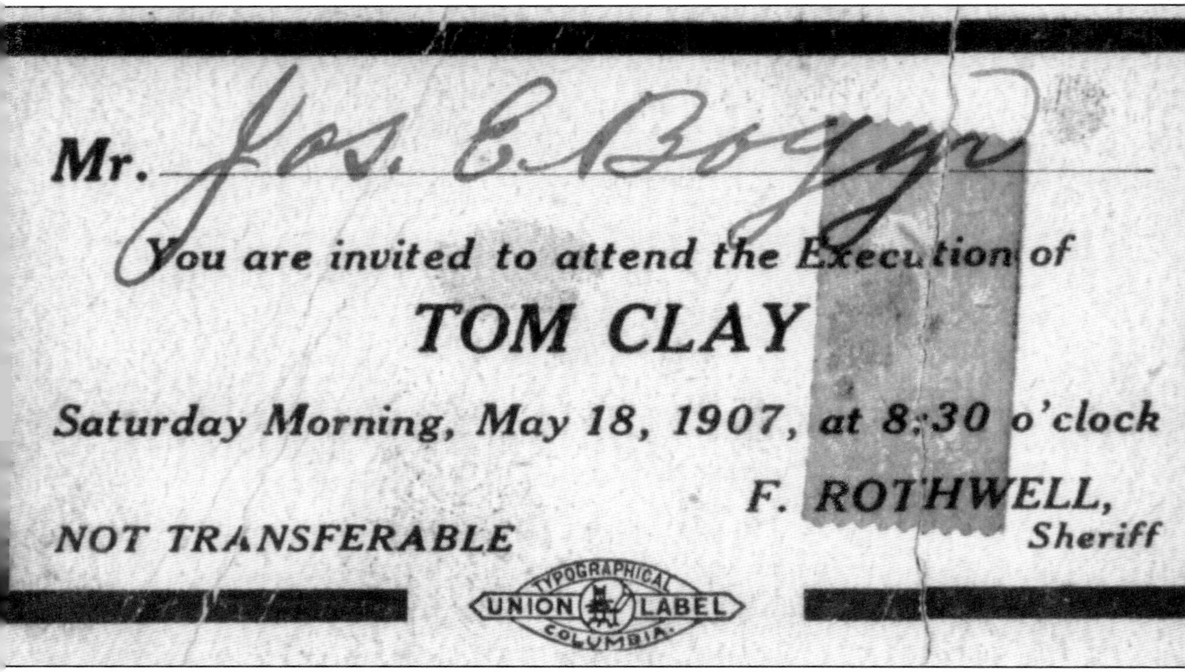

Mr. Jos. E. Boggs

You are invited to attend the Execution of

TOM CLAY

Saturday Morning, May 18, 1907, at 8:30 o'clock

F. ROTHWELL,
Sheriff

NOT TRANSFERABLE

TYPOGRAPHICAL UNION LABEL COLUMBIA

Death by hanging remained a common punishment in the early 20th century. Hangings often drew curious townspeople, and Columbia was no exception. In 1907, Boone County sheriff Fountain Rothwell issued printed invitations to the May 18 execution of Tom Clay, accused of murder. But the hanging did not happen. The execution was rescheduled for June 27. Again, it did not happen. Gov. Joseph W. Folk "granted a respite till July 25."

Ten

Houses and Buildings

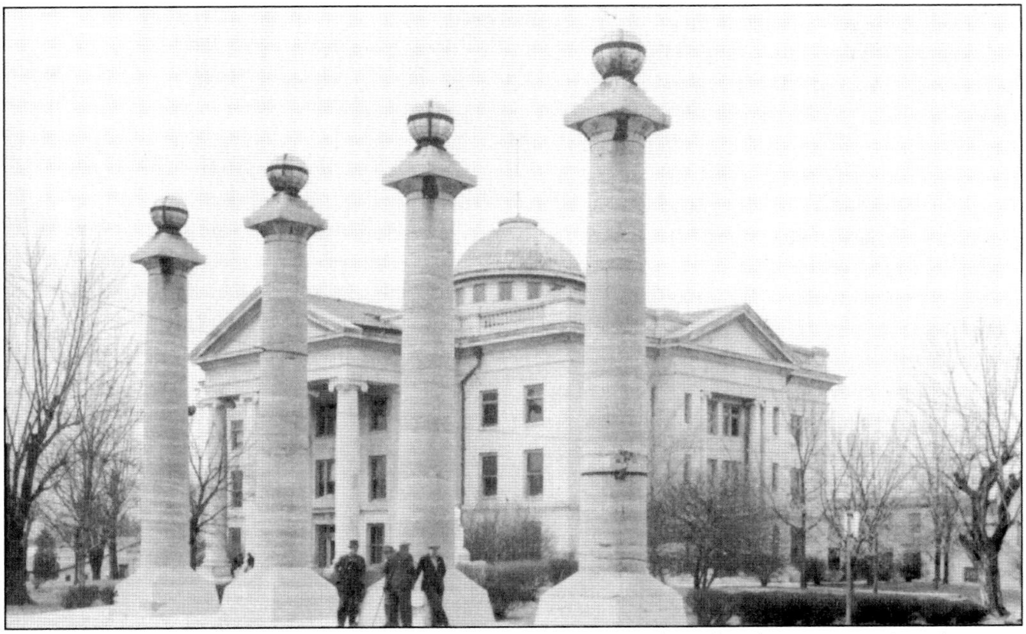

Boone County's first courthouse was built in the 1820s, but lasted only 20 years. Another was completed in 1847 and used until 1909. Its columns sat in perfect alignment along Eighth Street with the university's columns. By the early 20th century, yet another courthouse was needed. Plans were to raze the old building and columns, but public outcry led to preserving the columns. Electric lights were added later.

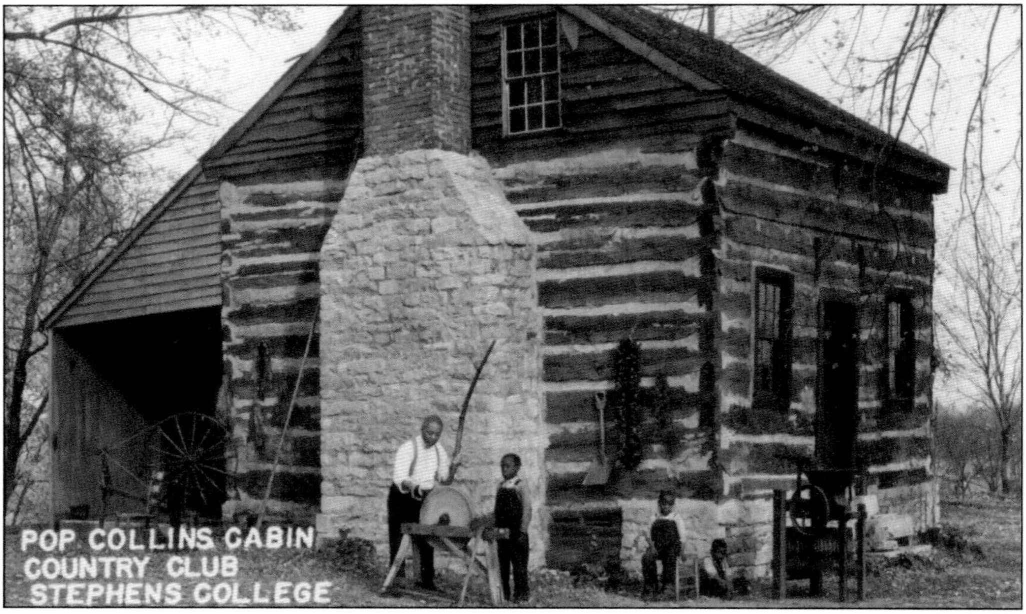

Kentuckian Capt. David Gordon and other land speculators formed the Smithton Land Company, settling on land that became Columbia. Captain Gordon built this cabin near Hinkson Creek in 1818. He and his family lived there for about five years while a larger home was built. The cabin later housed servants. Stephens College administrator Enoch Arthur "Pop" Collins had the cabin restored in 1935. It is a National Register property.

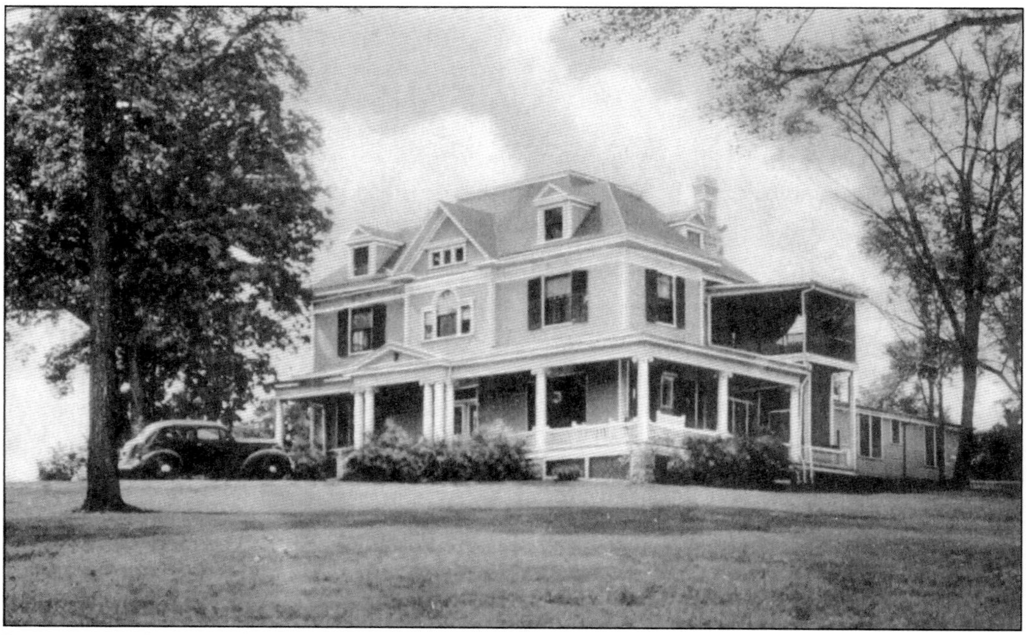

In 1926, Stephens College bought approximately 100 acres of land from the Gordons, a pioneer Columbia family. The college opened a country club with lush grounds featuring a nine-hole golf course, a lake, and picnic shelters. Annual dues in the early days were $50. The City of Columbia took possession of the land in 2001 and opened it to the public as Stephens Lake Park.

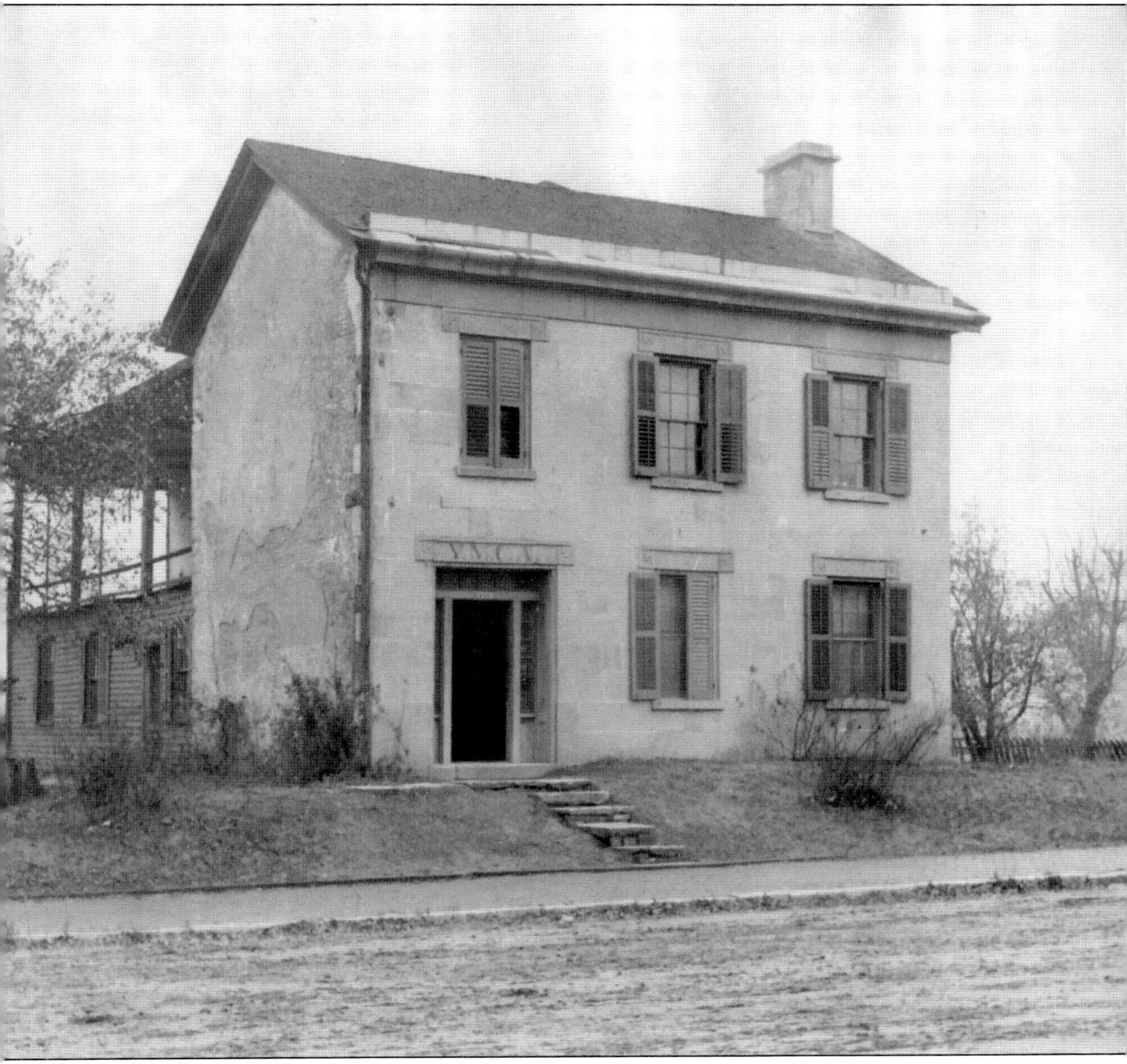

The YMCA affiliated with the university in January 1890. Its objective was to unite Christian men in Christian work. Student members studied various disciplines, meeting on Sundays to hear speeches by professors and businessmen. Bible studies and discussions also were held. This 1901 photograph shows Columbia's first YMCA building. A larger, stone facility was constructed on Elm Street in 1910.

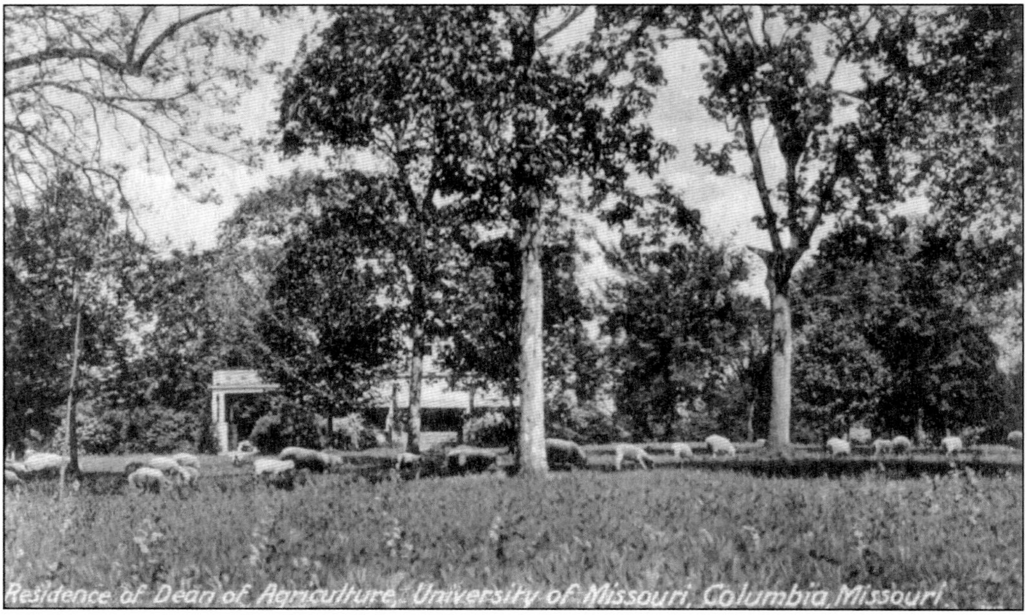

Henry J. Waters was the dean of the College of Agriculture and Mechanic Arts from 1895 to 1909. On November 11, 1897, his residence, Hudson Mansion, and the nearby university dairy burned down. A new home was constructed on College Avenue. Here, sheep graze peacefully in the side yard of Dean Waters's home in 1912.

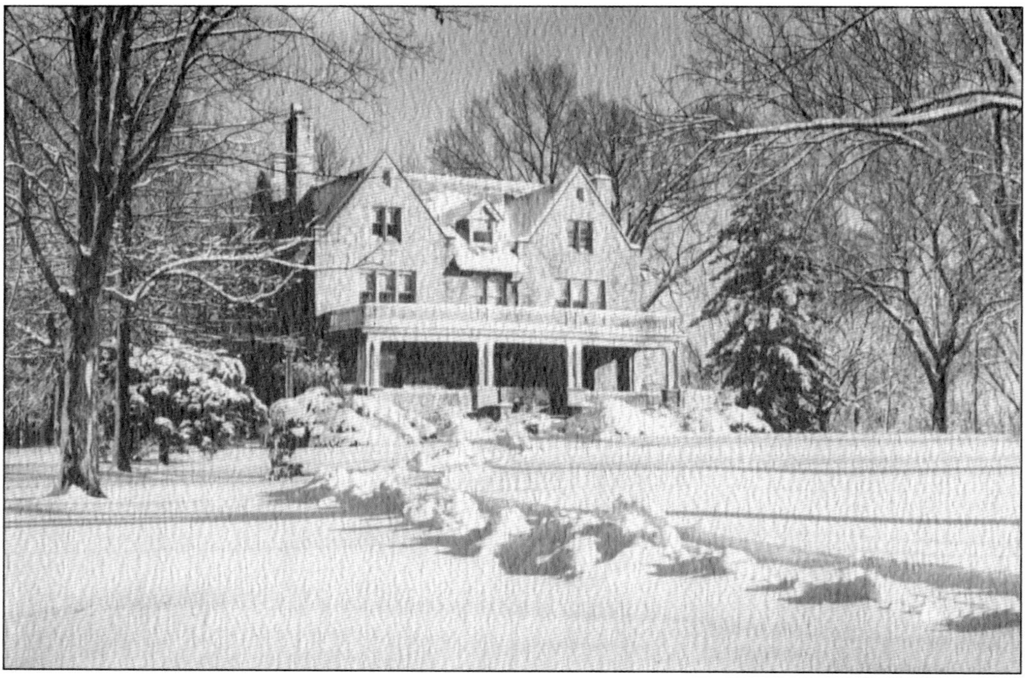

Snow blankets the home of College of Agriculture dean Henry J. Waters, at 812 College Avenue. Waters grew up on a Missouri farm and graduated from the university. He was just 29 years old when he became the college's fourth dean. A member of the state board of agriculture, he was instrumental in constructing white limestone buildings for agriculture programs—the university's white campus.

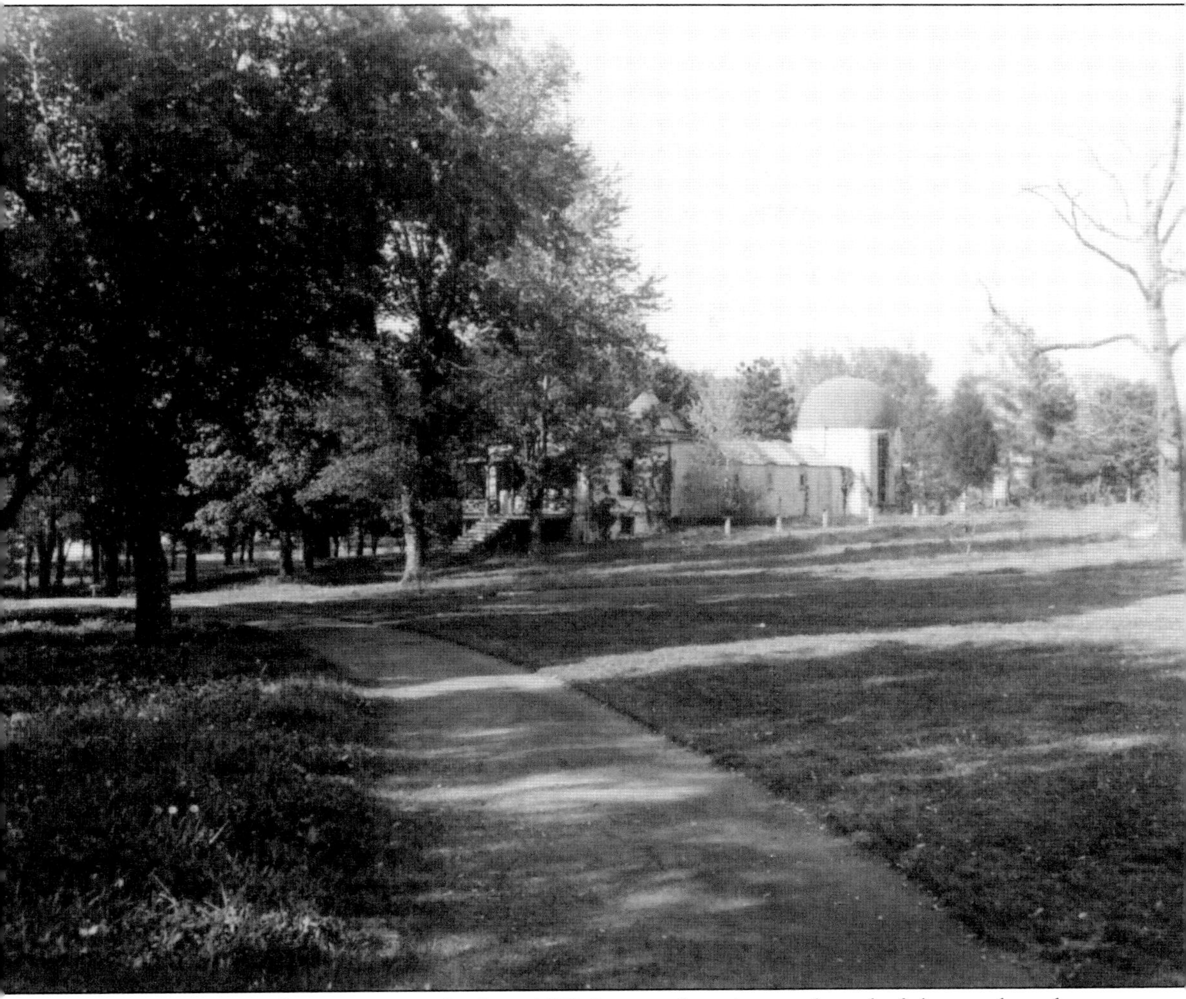

The first university observatory was built in 1853. It moved to the north end of the quadrangle and was expanded in 1880. It became Laws Observatory when Dr. S.S. Laws, former university president, gave money for a telescope and building. The telescope was the first of its size west of the Mississippi River. The observatory, shown here in 1908, was razed in 1919 for the construction of the School of Journalism's Neff Hall.

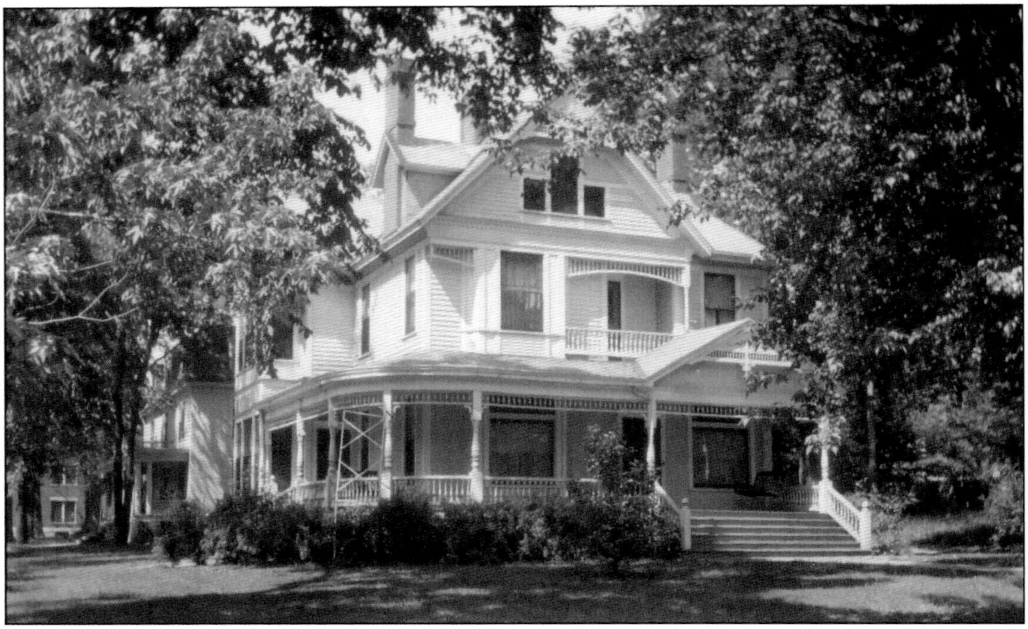

The university has one of the largest Greek life systems in the country. Greek fraternities arrived in 1869, and sororities came later. This 1927 photograph shows the Zeta Tau Alpha women's fraternity house, at 1101 University Avenue. Zeta Tau Alpha membership has increased through the years. The organization has built and occupied two additional houses since this one. The current house is located on Richmond Avenue in Greek Town.

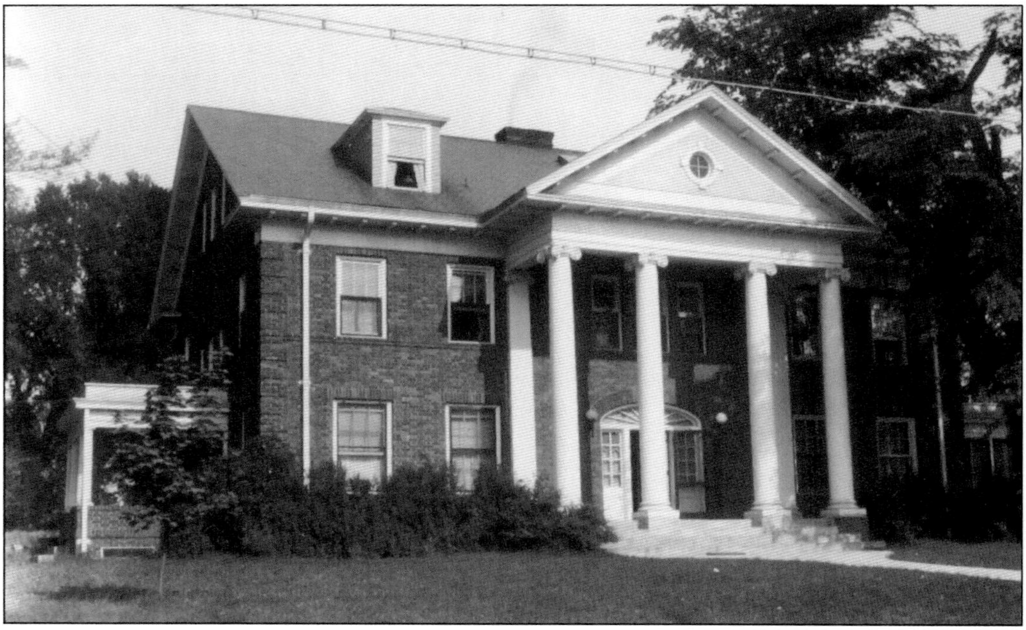

Phi Kappa Psi became the university's first Greek fraternity in 1869. In 1916, Curtis Burnam Rollins sold land on Providence Road to the fraternity. This house, shown in 1927, was built. In the 1950s, Grasslands, the estate across the street built by Curtis's brother George Bingham Rollins in 1878, was for sale. The fraternity purchased it and continues to occupy it. The lawns become parking lots on game days.

Edwin W. Stephens was long regarded as one of Columbia's leading citizens. Born in 1849, he began publishing the *Columbia Missouri Herald* in 1873. He also operated printing and publishing firms in St. Louis and Jefferson City. He was president of the board of curators of both the university and Stephens College, which was named for his father, a Columbia merchant. Stephens's home was the scene of memorable social gatherings.

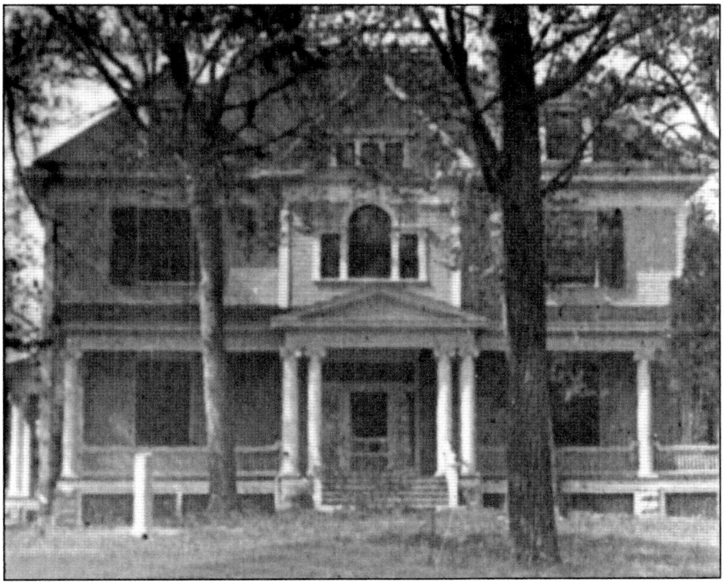

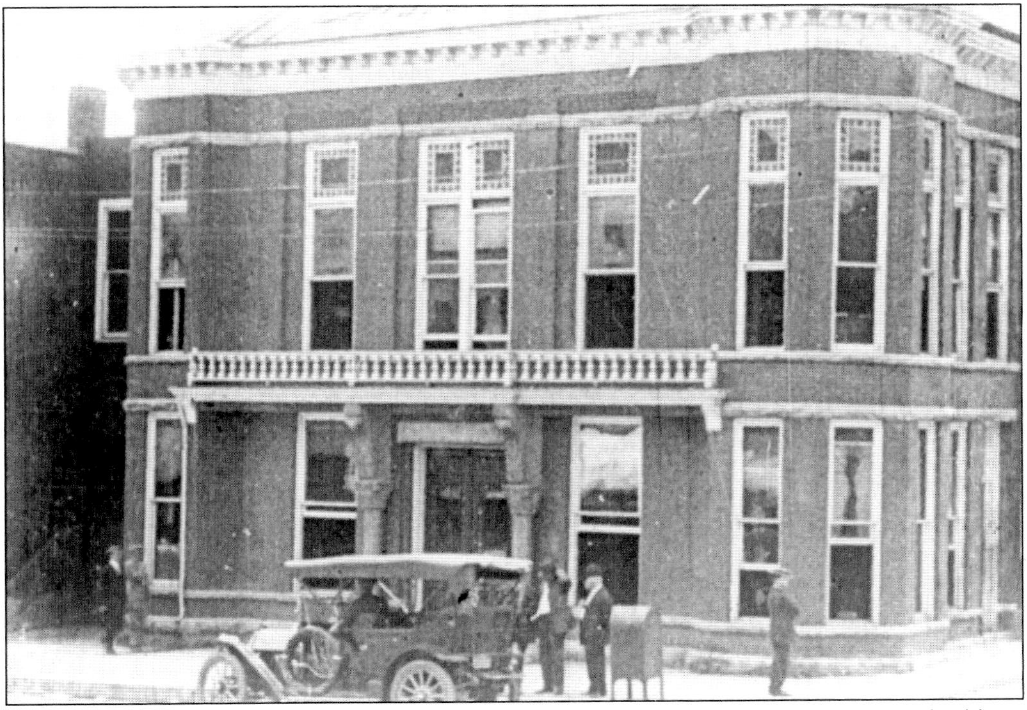

The *Columbia Missouri Herald* was published from 1873 until 1913. The newspaper's building, located in the 1000 block of East Broadway and shown here in 1907, was constructed in 1892. The building is one of the properties included in the Downtown Columbia Historic District and is listed in the National Register of Historic Places. It still retains its long, narrow windows and art glass transoms.

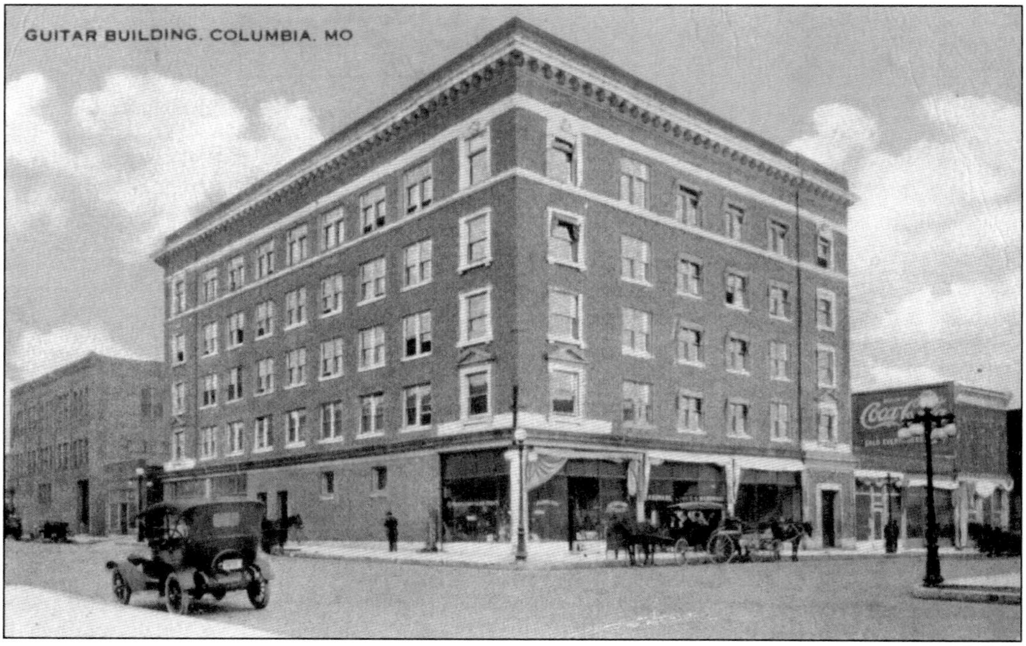

The five-story, Beaux-Arts Guitar Building was considered a skyscraper when built in 1910. The building is located on North Eighth Street, across from the courthouse. Shown here in 1915, it is one of the properties included in the Downtown Columbia Historic District. At the time of the photograph, the first floor was occupied by a hardware store and an ice-cream shop.

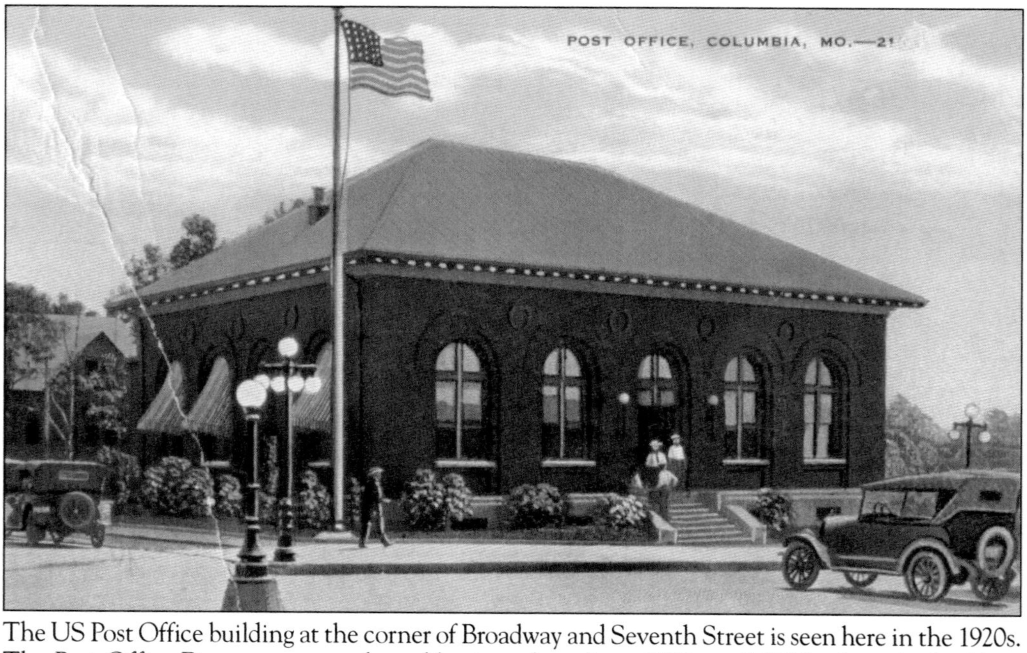

The US Post Office building at the corner of Broadway and Seventh Street is seen here in the 1920s. The Post Office Department conducted business here from 1906 until 1936, when the building was sold to the City of Columbia. It has housed various city services since then, including the public library, the water and light department, and the parks and recreation department. Before railroad connections, mail bags were tossed from stagecoaches.

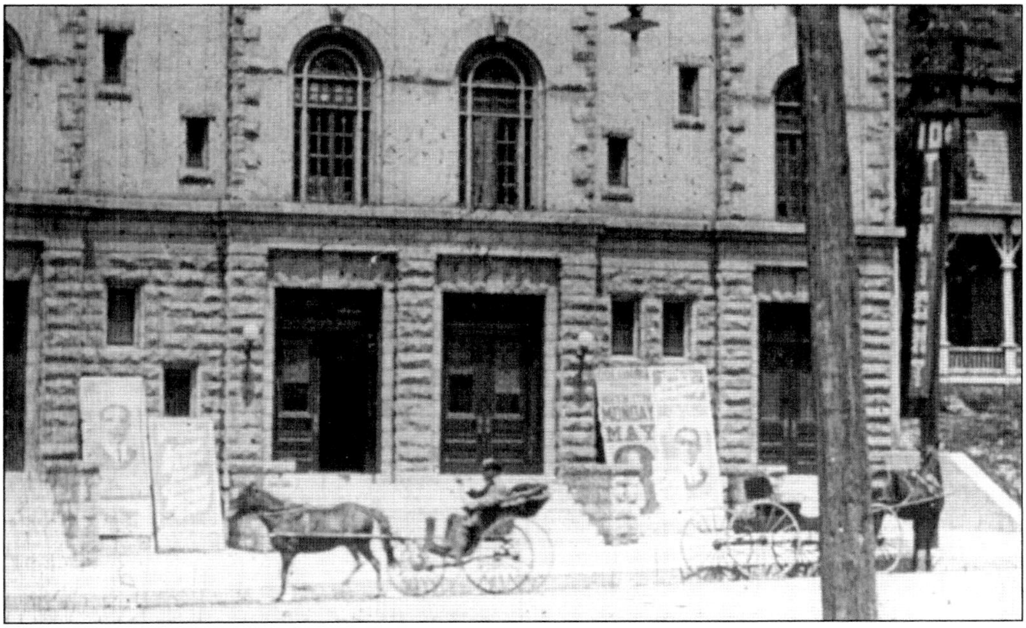

Horses and buggies were still popular modes of transportation in 1907 when this photograph of the limestone Columbia Theater was taken. Located on East Broadway, the Columbia was one of the city's elaborate theaters where locals went for entertainment. It seated 1,047 on three floors. According to the sign, admission was 10¢. The theater's top two floors were razed after the roof collapsed in 1951. Law offices occupy what was once the ground floor.

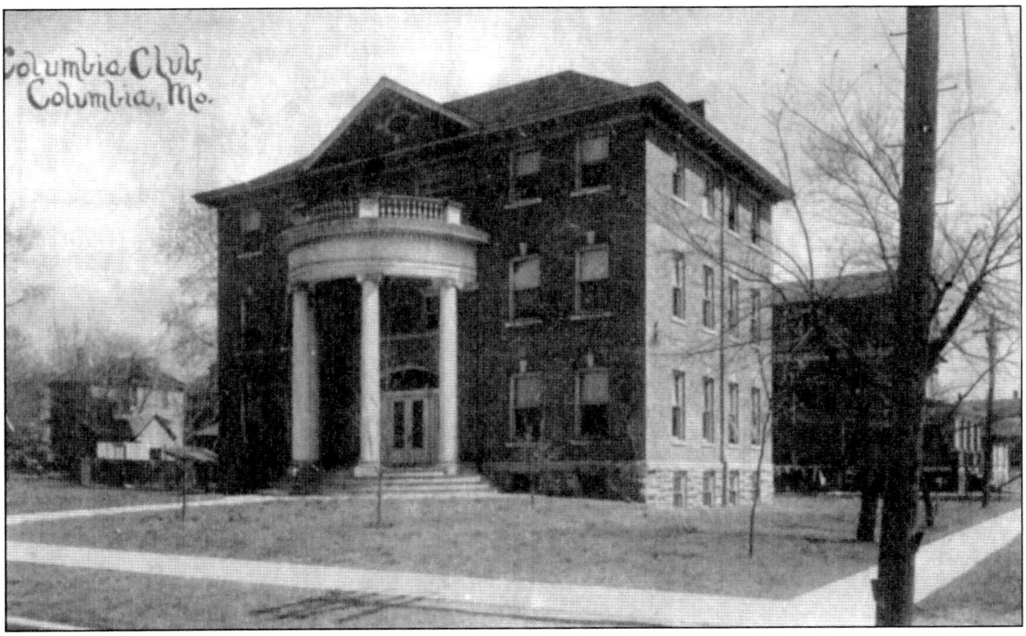

Private men's clubs were popular in the late 19th and early 20th centuries. Men of power, wealth, and education came together to discuss business, current events, and civic affairs. The Columbia Club, shown here in 1908, was established in the mid-1890s for Columbia's well-connected gentlemen. Two decades later, many of these men were part of the Columbia Commercial Club, predecessor of the chamber of commerce. The Commercial Club's motto was "Be a Booster Rooster."

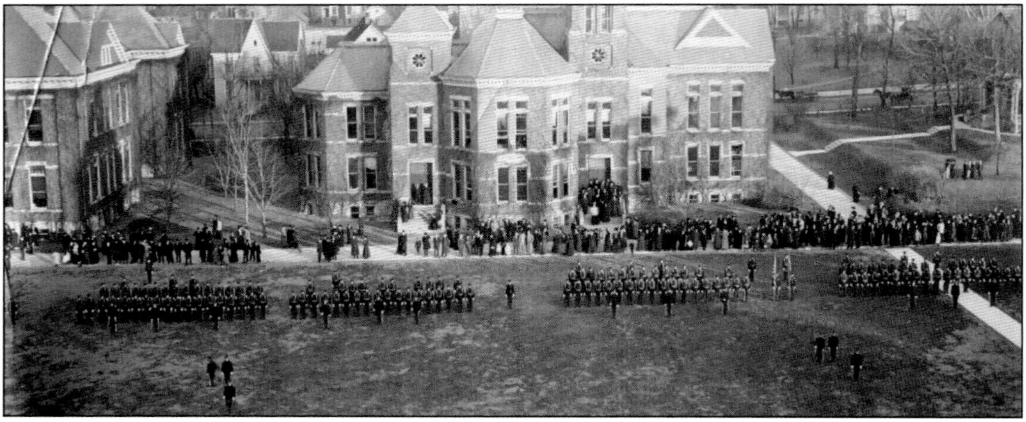

Fulton resident Morris Frederick Bell did not receive formal training in architecture, but he designed many well-known Columbia buildings. He designed most of the buildings on the university's red campus, including Jesse Hall, Pickard Hall, Swallow Hall, the sociology building, and the Engineering East building. He also designed for Stephens College and drew up plans for the E.W. Stephens Publishing Company building, which housed the *Columbia Missouri Herald*. Bell also did work in various other cities throughout Missouri.

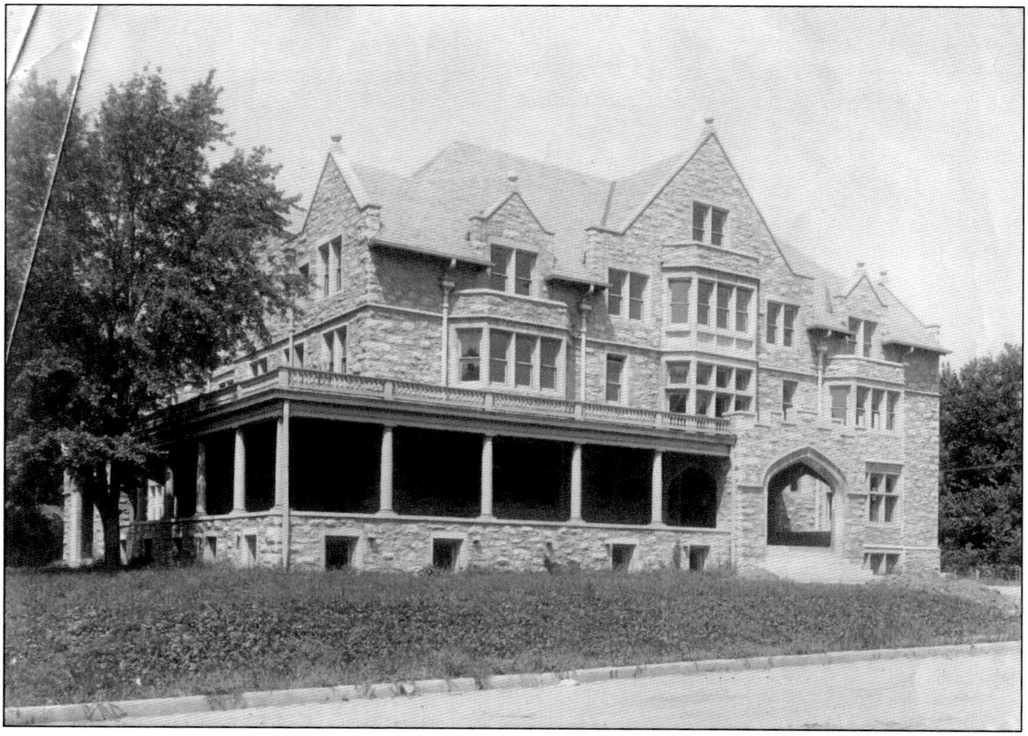

St. Louis architect James P. Jamieson and his companies designed many of the university's white campus buildings in the early decades of the 20th century. The buildings he designed include the Memorial Union, Ellis Library, and Mumford Hall. Jamieson also designed some of the red-brick buildings on Stephens College's south campus, including Hickman Hall, Wood Hall, and Columbia Hall. He also designed the university YMCA building (pictured), a social and religious center located at Eighth and Elm Streets. The site is now occupied by the *Missourian* offices.

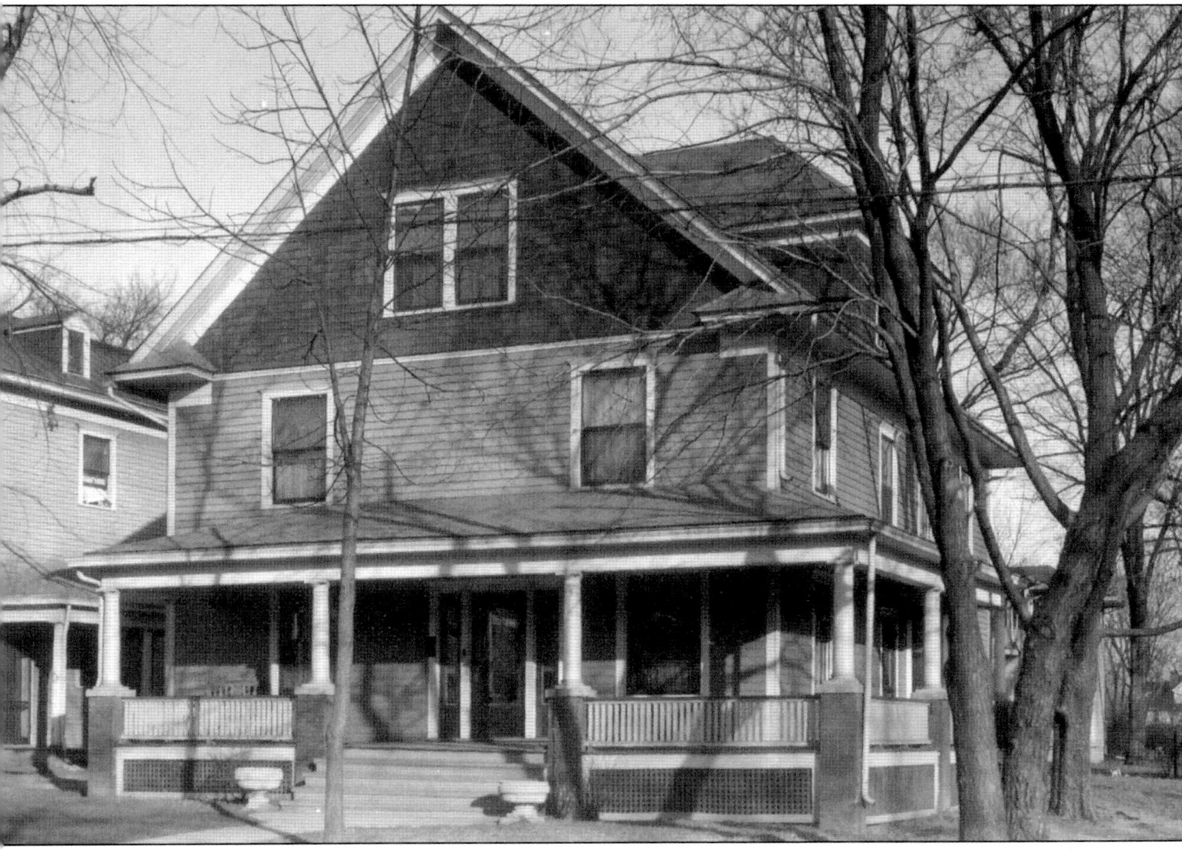

Columbia's residential areas expanded outward from the central Broadway corridor. A variety of architectural styles were used in constructing houses, from Victorian to bungalows to Foursquare. As the popularity of automobiles increased, attention was given to roadways. Some were macadamized with small rocks. Others were paved with bricks manufactured in Columbia. In 1908, the Edwards Brick Company produced 25,000 paving bricks each day and employed 40 men.

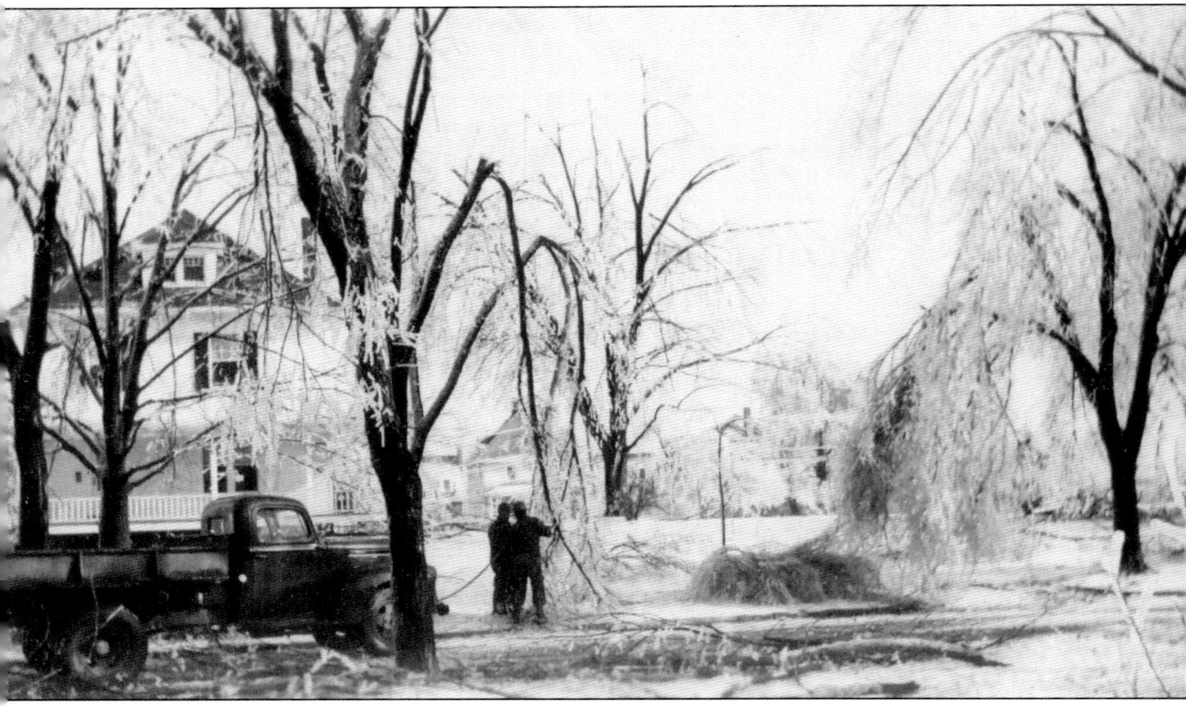

Columbia is a city of weather extremes, from subzero winter wind chills to sizzling 100-plus-degree summers. Although large snowfalls and heavy ice storms happened through the years, the area remained a popular place to build homes and businesses. In 1912, the city had several wood planing mills, a brick factory, 18 miles of paved streets, and 60 miles of "granitoid" sidewalks.

Bibliography

An Illustrated Historical Atlas of Boone County, Missouri. Philadelphia, PA: Edwards Brothers, 1875.

Board of Curators, University of Missouri. *Biennial Report of the Board of Curators, University of Missouri to the General Assembly*. Columbia, MO: January 1, 1907.

Christensen, Laurence O., and Gary R. Kremer. *A History of Missouri, Volume IV, 1875 to 1919*. Columbia, MO: University of Missouri Press, 1997.

Hale, Allean Lemmon. *Petticoat Pioneer—The Story of Christian College (Oldest College for Women West of the Mississippi)*. Saint Paul, MN: North Central Publishing Co., 1951.

Library of Congress, Chronicling America—Historic American Newspapers. *University Missourian, Columbia Evening Missourian*. Washington, DC: Library of Congress, Endowment for the Arts. Retrieved from www.chronicalingamerica.loc.gov

Missouri Historical Review Collection. Columbia, MO: The State Historical Society of Missouri. Retrieved from http://statehistoricalsocietyofmissouri.org. Issues from 1906 to 1950.

————. *Polk's Columbia City Directory*. Kansas City, MO: R.L. Polk and Company, 1940.

————. *R.E. Hackman's Columbia City Directory*. Quincy, IL: R.E. Hackman, 1907, 1909. Retrieved from http://shs.umsystem.edu/research/microfilm/.

Russell, Vicki. *Columbia, Missouri: Images of Our Lives Since 1901*. Columbia, MO: Tribune Publishing Company, 2001.

Stephens, E.W. *History of Boone County: An Illustrated Historical Atlas of Boone County, Missouri*. Philadelphia, PA: Edwards Brothers, 1875.

Switzler, William F. *History of Boone County, Missouri*. Chicago: Western Historical Company, 1882.

————. *The State Historical Society of Missouri Manuscript Collections*, "Christian College Records, 1836–1986;" "Conley-Miller Family Papers, 1792–1967;" "North Todd Gentry, 1837–1947;" "Merritt F. Miller Collection, 1906–1927;" "Boone County, Missouri, Black Archives Collection;" "John C. Crighton, Stephens College;" "Lewis M. Switzler, 1841–1925;" "University of Missouri Subscription List, 1839;" "Morris Frederick Bell, 1849–1929, Architectural Drawings, University of Missouri, Stephens College;" "Columbia Female Academy Papers, 1841–1853." Columbia, MO: various years.

————. *US Department of the Interior, National Park Service, National Register of Historic Places, "Downtown Columbia Historic District, Boone County, Missouri."* Washington, DC: 2006. Retrieved from http://www.dnr.mo.gov

Viles, Jonas. *The University of Missouri: A Centennial History 1839–1939*. Columbia, MO: University of Missouri, 1939.

Williams, Walter. *A History of Northeast Missouri Volume 1*. Chicago: Lewis Publishing Company, 1913.

Index

About The State Historical Society of Missouri

The premier resource for the study of Missouri state and local history, The State Historical Society of Missouri (SHSMO) collects, preserves, and shares the rich history of the state and the Midwest. With research centers in six communities—Cape Girardeau, Columbia, Kansas City, Rolla, St. Louis, and Springfield—the SHSMO's vast holdings include over 3,500 titles of historic newspapers, over six million photographs, more than 9,000 manuscript collections, more than 4,000 maps, and over 4,800 oral histories.

The Research Center–Columbia's art collections feature George Caleb Bingham and Thomas Hart Benton, plus modern works, including more than 18,000 editorial cartoons, including images by Daniel F. Fitzpatrick and Tom Engelhardt. Learn more by visiting shs.umsystem.edu.

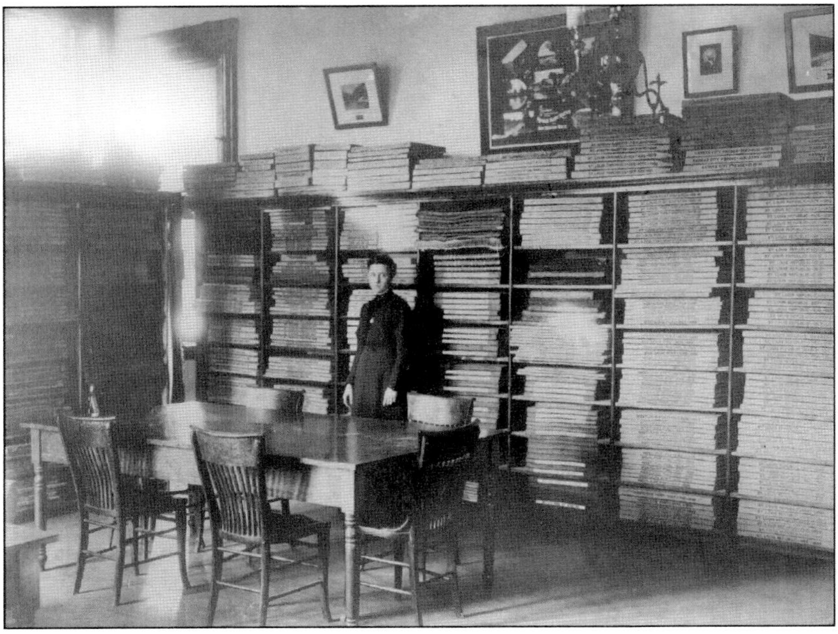

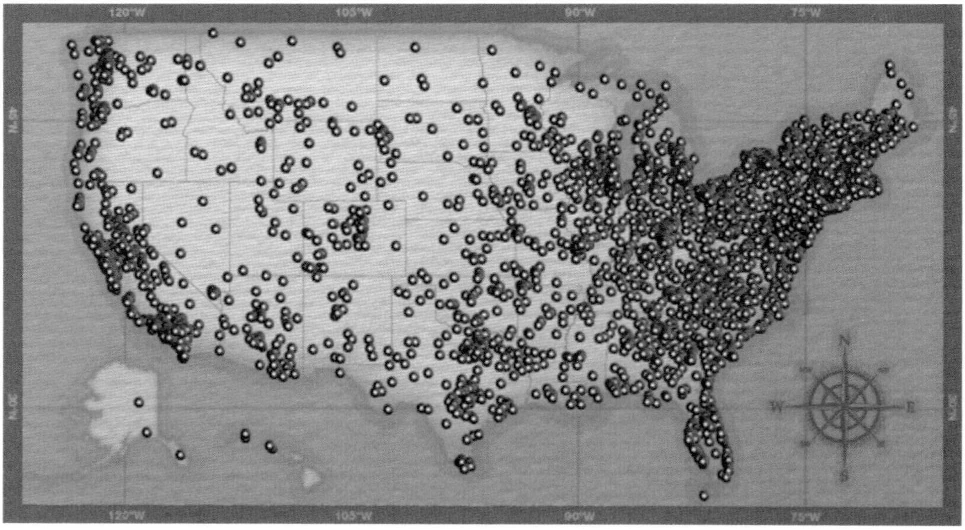